Clark Howard's
CONSUMER SURVIVAL KIT III

By Clark Howard and Mark Meltzer

LONGSTREET
Atlanta, Georgia

FOR LANE, REBECCA, NANCY AND CONNIE, WHO INSPIRE US TO DO OUR BEST

Published by LONGSTREET PRESS, INC.,
a subsidiary of Cox Newspapers,
a subsidiary of Cox Enterprises, Inc.
2140 Newmarket Parkway
Suite 122
Marietta, Georgia 30067

Printed in the United States of America

2nd printing, 1998

Library of Congress Catalog Number: 98-86476

ISBN: 1-56352-506-2

Book and jacket design by Burtch Bennett Hunter

Contents

Preface

A lot of people think I'm the cheapest person they know. I often drive an extra couple of miles to save a few cents on gasoline, buy my lunch at a warehouse club, and catch a ride with a friend to avoid having to pay for parking.

But I don't mind spending money on a bargain. I've flown from my hometown, Atlanta, to San Francisco for just $79 round-trip. I've flown to Portland, Oregon, for just $100. I bought carpet — great carpet — for $3.99 a yard. I once had the owner of a car dealership throw the keys to my new car at me because he was annoyed at how little I paid for it.

I hope you'll find *Consumer Survival Kit III* to be a huge bargain, because the information I've put in it can save you real money every day.

Getting ready to buy a car? Don't do it until you read the Cars chapter. Thinking about buying a house or renting an apartment? You might want to read the Real Estate chapter first.

In this book, you'll find plenty of easy-to-read information to help you spend your money more effectively than ever before, save for your future, and invest well.

If your main interest is in investing, I can't tell you this is the only book you'll ever need. If you look around a bookstore, you'll see hundreds of titles on investing and managing your money. I've taken an entirely different approach, and that's how to manage your entire financial life: making money, saving money, spending money, and especially how to avoid wasting money.

We're often in situations in which a store or company knows more than we do as buyers. What I want to do is even the odds. I want you to know how to make calm, reasonable, and unemotional financial decisions.

I also want to do everything I can to help you avoid being ripped off. There are a lot of crooked people out there who want to take your money, through a variety of schemes. I've seen them all, and I'll tell you how to steer clear of the scams.

As the title implies, this is the third edition of the *Consumer Survival Kit.* It has been revised extensively since the first two editions. I was amazed how much material from the second edition had to be completely rewritten to create this new version.

There are words in this book that weren't even known in 1995, when the last edition was published. Back then, nobody knew about the Internet, and few people used E-mail, or even knew what it was. Cellular telephones were only for the rich, and faxing was cutting-edge technology. But all that has changed.

The growth of the Internet has forced me to completely change a lot of the advice I give. I used to tell someone who was thinking of buying or selling a used car to buy a price guide to see how much the car was worth. Now I tell him to save the $6 and get the information instantly at the Edmund's Web site, www.edmunds.com.

I used to recommend paying $50 to get a quote on low-cost life insurance. Now I tell people to check Quotesmith, at www.quotesmith.com, and get the information in seconds, for free.

One of the most valuable changes I've made to this book is the addition of a list of some of my favorite Web sites. Because the Internet continues to change rapidly, some of the information available at these sites may be located at different sites over the next few years. I'll post updated links to these sites, and to more of my favorites, at my Web site (www.clarkhoward.com).

I started my career as a travel agent, opening a chain of travel agencies that I sold in 1987. Thanks to my travel experience, *Consumer Survival Kit III* is one of the few consumer books that includes advice on travel.

After I sold my travel agencies, I moved into radio, first as host of a travel show, then as host of a wide-ranging consumer show based in Atlanta. If you can't listen to my radio show over the airwaves, you can listen weekday afternoons on the Internet, via my Web site.

Every day on my show, I speak with folks looking for solutions to the consumer problems we all face. Many of my best suggestions are in this book. I hope they help you win more of life's everyday battles.

CLARK HOWARD

Acknowledgments

Putting together a book like this requires a lot of help, and I'm grateful to the many people who were so willing to provide it. A couple of people deserve special thanks: Kim Curley, executive producer of my radio show, and Nancy Meltzer, the wife of my coauthor, Mark Meltzer.

Kim's knowledge and skills were a valuable resource as we researched the many details presented here, and they were vital in making this work as thorough and accurate as possible.

Many of Nancy's ideas became elements of this book, and her input helped make it more complete and readable. She also did a lot of the less glamorous but important work.

More than a dozen people and organizations provided expertise in specific subject areas, particularly those listed below. My thanks to them all.

Joni Alpert

Dan Blake

Deb Elvin

Steven L. Hale

Neal Howard

Jerry Hunt

Gary E. Jackson

Mike Kavanaugh

Daniel H. Kolber

Mac the Mechanic

Elizabeth Manley

Robert G. Martin

Michael Perling

Joe Turner

Jack Sawyer

Real Estate

The cost of housing usually is the largest number in the family budget. Knowing the right way to buy housing can make a big difference in your life, whether your goal is having a great home, accumulating wealth, or both.

In this chapter, I'll tell you how to make smart choices in buying, renting, and selling real estate, so that you can live where you want, or get what you want, out of your housing dollar.

BUYING A NEW HOUSE

Buying a house is a cornerstone of what many people want to accomplish as adults. It is a symbol of much more than simply finding a place to live. But making this major purchase is also a complex process with plenty of potential for costly mistakes.

Because of its symbolism, home ownership is as much an emotional matter as it is a practical one. There was a time when housing values increased so steadily that buying a house was automatically a smart financial decision. That's not true anymore. It's important to decide whether you're buying a house for financial or personal reasons.

If you're buying a house strictly for financial reasons, evaluate each house you're considering just as you would evaluate a purchase of stocks or bonds. It just so happens that the house is a living, breathing investment because it's where you will live.

To buy a house as an investment, it's best to look for one with "people problems," generally a used house that is selling for below the fair market value because of special circumstances such as a divorce, a death, a relocation, or a foreclosure. Houses being sold for those reasons are wise purchases because you are likely to be able to increase their value.

You get a true bargain on a people-problem house only if you've done your homework first. Figure out the condition of the house and, by researching other homes for sale, its normal market price. Often a house with people problems has been neglected for a while, so you may be facing extensive repairs that will negate the bargain price. You can prevent unforeseen expense by making a purchase offer contingent on an inspection of the house. Even if the inspection reveals problems, the purchase might be worthwhile.

More often, people want to buy a house as a place to live. They want something that they like and can afford, and they don't want to make any mistakes. One of the most important guidelines I can offer is to not buy one of the first houses in a subdivision. It's too risky, primarily because the developer could go bust and be unable to complete construction. Early buyers can end up in a home surrounded by scarred and abandoned land. Even worse, these houses could be surrounded by partially built homes. There's also the danger that amenities promised by the developer, such as a pool or tennis courts, might not be built. If the developer fails, those promises disappear.

I think it's wise for new home buyers to find out a little about the builder of a house they're considering. When you buy a car, you look for a model made by a manufacturer with a reputation for quality. But few people think to ask about builders. If you're interested in a house, ask what other homes the builder has constructed. Then ask the owners how they like their houses. Most homeowners will be happy to tell you whether their house was well built or whether the builder did a shabby job.

Make any offer on a home contingent on its passing an inspection. Some people don't bother to inspect a new home, because they figure there shouldn't be anything wrong with it. But an inspector could discover shortcuts in materials used or necessary work that wasn't done. If that happens, the builder could be forced to make repairs. You can locate a certified inspector through the American Society of Home Inspectors.

Also, be sure to include a financing contingency in your purchase offer. The purchase should be contingent not just on your ability to qualify for financing but on your ability to get financing at or below a set interest rate. You might not be approved for financing at 8 percent, but you could be approved at 12 percent, even if you believe you can't afford to buy with a 12 percent mortgage. Including such a contingency in the offer lets you get out of the deal if you can't get financing you can afford.

As part of your loan, you'll be required to purchase a title insurance policy, which protects the lender in the event your ownership of the property is ever challenged. I recommend a very low-cost addition — owner's title insurance. It protects you if anyone ever claims you are not the legal owner of the property. Owner's title insurance can cost as little as $100 if you buy it at the time you buy a house. Ask the closing attorney for a quote. If the quote seems high, see if you can negotiate down the fee.

There was a title case a few years ago in which residents of an entire community almost lost their homes. A woman claimed she was part-owner of a tract of land that later was divided to form a subdivision. She sued the homeowners in the community for a partial share of the land. The woman eventually agreed to a settlement, but the homeowners spent several thousand dollars in legal fees to defend their property rights. Owner's title insurance not only protects you from loss, but it also forces the title company to defend you if your ownership is ever challenged.

There are two kinds of "new" houses to consider. There's the off-the-shelf new house that a builder has recently completed. There's also the new house that is either custom-built from scratch or custom-finished according to the wishes of the buyer. Some buyers like to buy a house while it's under construction, then dress it up with special features such as whirlpool tubs, skylights, or premium-grade carpet. Most of the problems I hear about concern the second group — new homes being custom-finished. Two problems tend to come up: the builder either doesn't keep a promise, or he doesn't complete the job by the specified date.

If you're having a home custom-finished and the job isn't done by your closing date, you have to act to protect yourself. If you go through with the closing, you give up your leverage and run the risk that the job will never be completed. If you decide to close with items unresolved, give a letter outlining these items to the closing attorney and the real estate agent or agents involved in the sale. That will prevent anybody from getting amnesia about these issues later. Get assurance from the real estate agent that he or she will help ensure that the work gets completed.

When you're negotiating a contract for the purchase of a house, especially one that has not been completed, a real estate attorney should review the contract. It's wise to spend some money up front to prevent problems that could be costly and hard to resolve. A real estate attorney also will review the closing documents. You should require in your purchase contract that the closing documents be made available to you at least two days prior to closing for review by your attorney. Real estate closings are incredibly confusing. You have no idea what documents are being put in front of you — the language is so unfamiliar, and the forms are so complex — and it's easy to make an expensive mistake. Both the lender and the seller will have representatives at the closing. That's why you need to have your lawyer check everything.

If you choose to shop for homes with a real estate agent, there's something you need to know. Rules vary by state, but often the agent who takes you around to look for homes actually is not "your" agent, although he or she may be very friendly and helpful. In many cases, the agent represents the home seller. It's similar to the way a salesperson in a department store represents the retailer. The sales agent is required by law to tell the seller anything you say. So if you offer $120,000 for a house but let it slip to the agent that you can afford to pay $130,000, the agent has to disclose that to the seller. The agent also will pass on information about you, such as your income, that may weaken your negotiating status. It's doubtful, too, that a real estate agent will show you any "For Sale By Owner" houses, because an agent receives no commission on such sales.

Most home sales today involve two sales agents. One is the listing agent, who is hired by the seller to market and sell his or her house. The other is the selling agent, the person who shows you different houses for sale. Because agents split commissions, the selling agent may try to get you to buy a house he or she has been directly hired to sell. In that case, the sale involves only one agent.

Real estate agents can represent the seller, the buyer, or both. To find out whom your agent represents, ask her. She is required to tell you. If you're moving from one state to another, the applicable laws are those of the state to which you are moving.

Better yet, you can use an agent who works for you. He or she will prevent home sellers from learning personal facts about you and will allow you to see any home in which you're interested. A buyer's agent will help you decide how much to offer and will negotiate on your behalf. Buyers' agents are paid in the same way as agents who work for the seller. They receive a percentage of the sales price. Consequently, buyers' agents get more if the house sells for a higher price. But buyers' agents tell me it's worth far more to them to negotiate the lowest price possible for a buyer — and get referrals from a satisfied buyer — than to get a nominally higher commission from a higher

TIPS ON BUYING A NEW HOUSE

- If you're buying a house strictly for financial reasons, evaluate each house you're considering as you would stocks or bonds.

- If you are buying a house as an investment, look for one that is selling for below the fair market value, because of special circumstances such as a divorce, a death, a relocation, or a foreclosure.

- Don't buy one of the first houses in a subdivision. The developer may go bust and be unable to complete the development.

- Check out the reputation of a builder by talking with people who live in houses the builder has built.

- Make any offer on a home contingent on its passing an inspection. The purchase also should be contingent on your ability to get financing at or below a set interest rate.

- Get an owner's title insurance policy, which covers you, not the lender, if your ownership is successfully challenged.

- Hire a real estate attorney to review the closing papers and, if you're buying a house still under construction, to draft or review the purchase contract.

- Use a real estate agent who represents your financial interests, not the seller's.

- Before you buy a house, try your commute to work during rush hour.

- Learn about the area surrounding the house, including the potential for new roads or new development.

- Look at a property while it's raining to see how water flows across it. Look for signs of poor drainage and danger of flooding.

- Buy a house that's fundamentally sound, in construction and materials, even if it doesn't have the latest, greatest design features.

CONTACT

American Society of Home Inspectors
85 West Algonquin Road
Suite 360
Arlington Heights, IL 60005
1-800-743-2744
www.ashi.com

sales price. You can find buyers' agents at most real estate companies, or ask friends for referrals.

When you give a real estate agent a price range for houses you would consider, it's a good idea to quote a lower figure than you're willing to spend. If you tell an agent you're looking for a $120,000 house, the agent inevitably will use that figure as a floor, not a ceiling, and will show you houses priced at $120,000, $125,000, and $130,000.

Before you buy a house, try your commute to work during rush hour. When you make a long drive from a house to your workplace on a weekend, you don't get a true idea of the travel time. It's also important to learn about the area surrounding any house you're considering. You should know what potential there is for new roads or new development. Is there a chance your backyard will look out on a new shopping center someday? Are there any vacant lots that might be the site of undesirable government or commercial projects? Make sure your real estate agent discloses whether there are any easements. An easement allows a power company or a city to run a power line or sewer line across your property. I know of someone who found out on the day of closing that there was a sewer easement running right under the house, making it possible that the house could be torn down at any time. That scrapped the whole deal.

Look for other potential problems, such as high-voltage power lines near the property. There's no clear opinion as to whether these are dangerous to human health, but being adjacent to them has become less desirable and therefore has made houses near them harder to sell.

It's also a good idea to look at a property while it's raining, to see how water flows across it. Look for signs of poor drainage and danger of flooding. It helps, if you can, to look in the basement of a home during or just after a rainfall.

Drainage problems are quite common these days and can be very costly. One of my callers bought a $121,000 house in a very nice neighborhood, then discovered that during a rainfall, water cascaded across his patio like a river. He spent $1,300 to install an underground drain, but the system still backed up during heavy rains. A civil engineer told him it would cost another $2,000 to design a plan to solve the problem. State laws provide minimal protection for homeowners in these cases, sometimes requiring the builder or developer to make repairs. The best solution is to examine a new house while it's raining before you buy it.

Over the past few years, a lot of homeowners have had problems with building materials that turned out to be defective, including polybutylene water pipes, artificial stucco, and fake wood siding. People who shop for a house often interpret high quality as being extra features, such as a big whirlpool tub, a great sun room, or a lot of crown molding. But although having those features is nice, it's more important that the house be well made. Most of the problems I've seen occurred because builders cut corners by using cheaper materials, as a way of trying to give people more house for their money. You could face thousands of dollars in repairs if you buy a house with synthetic stucco siding, which in a lot of cases has trapped moisture in the walls and caused them to rot. Polybutylene pipe was easier and cheaper to install but wound up leaking and had to be replaced. Artificial wood siding looked good but didn't last, and homeowners had to spend tens of thousands of dollars to put new exteriors on their homes. Go with time-tested materials. Brick and vinyl siding work. Copper and PVC plumbing work. You want a house that's fundamentally sound, in construction and materials, even if it doesn't have the latest, greatest design features.

If you're moving to a new area of the country, I recommend that you rent before you buy. You might not be sure at first which part of the new city you prefer, and if you change your mind six months or a year later and want to move to another neighborhood or city, you won't face the hefty costs of selling another house.

Congress changed the tax law in 1997, eliminating the need for you to reinvest the proceeds of a home sale into a new home. So there's no pressure to run around a new city with a real estate agent and hurriedly buy a house.

HOME WARRANTIES

A home warranty is not a substitute for choosing a responsible builder or for having a home inspected. But a warranty can provide assistance and is a good selling tool when it's time to move. It's a confidence builder for the buyer.

A home warranty that comes with a new house offers a fair amount of protection in the first two years after purchase and minimal basic protection for 3 to 10 years. Pay close attention to the wording of your warranty. Usually your builder is fully responsible in the first year, and the warranty company is responsible in the second year.

The home warranty company generally will be responsible for problems in the second year only if you've followed its procedures correctly. Let's say you have a plumbing problem in the first year and you've asked the builder to fix it, but you never notified the warranty company. By not notifying the warranty company, you may have waived your rights to get help. So it's important to notify both the builder and the warranty company as soon as a problem develops and at the address and in the manner they require. They may require notice by certified mail, or you may prefer to send it by certified mail so you have proof it was sent. You also gain leverage by contacting the warranty company, as officials there usually tell the builder to fix the problem.

TIPS ON HOME WARRANTIES

• A warranty that comes with a new house offers a fair amount of protection in the first two years and minimal basic protection for 3 to 10 years.

• Pay close attention to how your warranty works. Usually your builder is fully responsible in the first year and the warranty company is responsible in the second year.

• It's important to notify both the builder and the warranty company as soon as a problem develops and at the address and in the manner they require.

• With a used home, a warranty is for one year and is renewable annually for an unlimited period. It covers heating, air conditioning, and the other major systems of the home.

• In many parts of the country, it's important to hire a pest control company to protect against termite infestation.

• The best coverage is a repair guarantee, under which the pest control company is responsible for repairing any damage caused by termites.

CONTACT

National Pest Control Network
Oregon State University
333 Weniger
Corvallis, OR 97331-6502
1-800-858-7378
http://ace.orst.edu/info/nptn

If, during the first year of warranty protection, you notify both the builder and the warranty company and the builder attempts a repair but is unsuccessful, send another letter immediately. Document. Document. Document.

The other kind of warranty is for a used home. I bought a home a few years ago that came with a third-party warranty designed to assure me that the basic systems in the home were working. I never had to claim against the warranty, and I let it expire after one year. For around $400, I could have renewed it each year. This kind of warranty is like an extended warranty on an appliance, which costs too much and rarely pays claims. Mainly what it covers is heating, air conditioning, and the other major systems of the home.

Termites are another concern for buyers in many parts of the country. In some states, the seller is required by law or by the mortgage lender to have the house inspected for possible termite damage. Even if it is not required, ask that an inspection be performed if termites or other wood-destroying insects are a problem in your region.

Within the first 90 days of ownership, you should interview and select a pest control company, so that you can protect the property against any future infestation. Check with the Department of Agriculture, entomology division, or the structural pest control board in your state to find out its policy. Or call the National Pest Control Network to locate the appropriate agency in your area. These agencies often will conduct inspections if you suspect a pest control company has given your house inadequate termite control treatment.

Pest control companies provide two principal types of termite protection policies. Under a retreatment policy, the company simply promises to come back and retreat the property. There's no real risk to the company for its failure to spot termites. Your best bet is a repair guarantee, under which the termite company is responsible for repairing any damage caused by termites. With a repair guarantee, the termite company is your partner in making sure your house is well treated because the company is at financial risk if it doesn't do a good job locating infestations and treating them.

A comprehensive, initial termite treatment, including a repair guarantee, can cost several hundred dollars. And pest control companies often won't provide a repair guarantee unless their company has done the treatment. After that, expect to pay for annual, follow-up inspections, with retreatment if needed. A good way to find a company is to ask a real estate agent.

Owners of some stucco homes have had particular problems with termites. Building codes in most states required that the stucco reach to the ground. But it's been discovered that termites can easily enter a home with synthetic stucco — the kind most people have — if the stucco reaches into the ground. Termite companies may refuse to renew your coverage until you create a six- or eight-inch clearance between the stucco and the ground, or they may require you to pay a much higher annual premium for termite protection. Do yourself a favor and pay for the renovations needed to create the clearance.

BUYING A USED HOUSE

Just as with a used car, you often get a better value buying a used house. That's because part of the cost of a new house is the cost of construction. As construction costs increase, new houses become more expensive.

An important advantage of a used home — and I prefer the term "used" to "resale" or "existing" — is that because it is located in an established neighborhood, the house has found its true value in the marketplace. With new construction, particularly in a new neighborhood or a new subdivision, you never have a solid feel for a house's value.

Of course, buying a used house means taking on an added risk of breakdowns and repair costs.

TIPS ON BUYING A USED HOUSE

- You often get a better value buying a used home, because rising construction costs make new houses more expensive.

- A used home often is located in an established neighborhood and has found its true value in the marketplace. With new construction, particularly in a new subdivision, you never have a solid feel for a house's value.

- Buying a used house means taking on the risk of breakdowns and repair costs. Just make sure the purchase is contingent on an inspection, and don't buy a house with major structural problems.

- When you buy a used house, it's important to put at least $50 a month into a repair fund. You never know what can break.

- If you buy wisely, you can get a good home in an attractive neighborhood and not be overrun by the myriad problems of a booming new area. With a new house, crowded schools, poor drainage, and the abundance of new construction can make resale difficult.

I've bought a house built during the Depression and one built just after World War II, and in both cases I bought trouble. But there are two different concerns here. It's a bad idea to buy a house that has major structural problems, with the roof or foundation, for example. But there's nothing wrong with buying a house that has irritations.

I once bought a house from a seller who had already moved to another state. The house had been built in 1937 and needed so many repairs that my late father referred to it as "the Howard Hovel." He couldn't imagine his son living in such squalor. It smelled terrible and had the worst paint job I have ever seen — deep, dark reds, ugly greens, and rooms with absolutely bizarre color trims. The floor in the bathroom was sinking. The front steps were all beat up. The driveway had completely collapsed, was overgrown with weeds, and was not usable, except by a four-wheel-drive

vehicle. Nobody was going to go anywhere near this thing.

I had an inspector come out and carefully go over this place, and he found no structural problems. So I brought in contractors and got estimates of the cost to bring the place up to speed. It cost $17,000, but the house was so cheap that, even with repairs included, I still bought it for less than its market value. The key with this sort of work is to avoid moving walls or expanding rooms, or you could end up paying $17,000 just to renovate a bathroom. It's far cheaper to accept the layout the way it is and change cosmetic weaknesses.

I turned "the Howard Hovel" into a fine house and a good buy with renovations that were mostly cosmetic. I ripped out all the carpet, which completely eliminated the foul odor, and had the hardwood floors underneath stripped and restained. A good paint job and some attractive wallpaper took care of all those weird colors, and some new sheet rock made peeling ceilings look great. I had a great time showing people the house and then bringing out my before-and-after pictures.

In fact, because the house came with a vacant lot next door, it turned out to be the most profitable real estate transaction I've ever made. The lot was considered worthless by everyone because a giant storm sewer ran through the middle of it. A few years after I bought the house, I hired an engineering company to determine if it would be possible to move the storm sewer and build a new house on the lot. It was. I relocated the storm system for $8,800 and ended up with a lot that was worth more than $100,000. It just never occurred to anybody that you could do that.

Look for hidden values and undervalued property. This house turned out to be a grand-slam home run because I got both in the same purchase. Just be careful not to fall in love with a house you're considering. To get the best deal in any negotiation, you have to be willing to walk away.

Use good judgment to pick a used house. If you see potential, a place that can look good with some cosmetic changes, it may be a house that will work. But if you will have to pay for expensive renovations to be happy, it's not a good purchase.

It is critical when looking at used houses to make a purchase offer contingent on an inspection. That's the only way to get a good feel for possible repair expenses.

And, as I discuss in the section on new homes, be wary of homes constructed with building materials that have turned out to be defective, including polybutylene water pipes, artificial stucco, and fake wood siding. If you choose a home built with these materials, factor in the potentially high additional costs that could result from making repairs.

One unexpected expense that can pop up when you're buying a used home is the cost of removing a dead tree. It's not something you think about when you're looking at a house, but the cost of removing a tree, or several trees, can be substantial. To protect yourself, ask the seller if there are any dead trees on the property. If there are, ask him to remove the trees as a condition of the sale. Also, look for problem trees yourself. A dead, leafless tree can be pretty easy to spot in spring or summer but may blend into the background in fall or winter.

When you buy a used house, it's important to put at least $50 a month into a repair fund. In an older home, you never know what can break — pipes, the heating and air-conditioning system, or an appliance.

As you probably can tell, my bias is toward buying used houses in established neighborhoods. If you buy wisely, you can get a good home in an attractive area and not be overrun by the myriad problems of a booming new subdivision.

If you buy a new house in a new subdivision in a growing section of town, many factors will be beyond your control. There is no way to know if the other houses in the subdivision are going to be of the quality and character of your home. The houses developed on the next street over could be a third less expensive than yours, which ultimately reduces your home's value.

I get lots of complaints from owners of new houses about drainage problems. In the typical case, there's no problem for the first year or two of ownership. But that changes after more houses are built and more trees are cut down. Suddenly, every time it rains, the yard is flooded.

Another advantage of an established neighborhood is that you know the schools aren't overcrowded. You don't have to worry about so many new homes being built that your children will have to attend classes in a portable trailer. An abundance of new construction can also cause your house to lose value. Let's say you buy a new house in a new subdivision and two years later you're forced to relocate. Because the subdivision is growing, there are brand-new houses all around your house. That's trouble, because buyers usually prefer a brand-new house to a house that's two years old.

I also prefer the sense of character in an older neighborhood with lots of big trees. Often when you go into a new neighborhood, the only trees you'll see are stick trees. Because of the methods of construction, there may be just a few small trees left between houses.

One advantage to buying a new house is that most tend to have large and attractive bathrooms and kitchens, which people have come to desire over the years. That's a sacrifice I've made by buying older houses.

REMODELING

With the huge bloc of baby boomers in their forties and fifties, America is in a remodeling boom. A lot of homeowners would rather add onto or fix up a house than move into a more expensive house in a new neighborhood.

You have to be very, very careful picking somebody to remodel your home. Do not hire people who drop fliers off in your mailbox, or who ring your doorbell and tell you your roof or gutters need fixing. Phony remodeling is one of the oldest scams around. Typically, the con artists prey on older people, and almost always they take the homeowner's money and disappear.

Your house is the most valuable investment you have. Do some legwork first, before you hire someone. Believe me, that will be far easier than dealing with the problems you'll have if you hire an incompetent or crooked contractor. For a minor

renovation job, take recommendations for a remodeler from friends and neighbors.

For a major renovation job, which I consider anything that will cost you more than $5,000, you need to be much more scientific about the hiring process. Get recommendations from the National Association of the Remodeling Industry or the Remodelors Council of the National Association of Home Builders.

After you've had a few remodelers come out to your home and have narrowed the field, it's time to start checking references. Ask for a list of the last 10 homes they've worked on, descriptions of what they did, the dates they started those jobs, the dates the jobs were completed, and how to contact each owner. The dates are important because it will allow you to see gaps in their work history. Perhaps the contractor couldn't find any work for several months or blew a job and got sued. You'll also get a feel for how many jobs a contractor takes on at one time.

Ask each contractor what kind of insurance he carries. For example, does he carry workers' compensation insurance and have his own liability insurance policy? Some experts might tell you not to hire anybody who doesn't have proper insurance. That's the book answer. But you're going to have some difficulty finding people who have kept their insurance current. If you pick someone who has no insurance, make sure you have enough liability coverage in your homeowner's policy in case the contractor or an employee gets hurt on your property. Be prepared to be sued if any worker gets hurt in or around your house.

Once you decide which contractor will do the work, the next task is drawing up a contract. Most contractors will present you with a standard builder's supply house contract. Don't sign this under any circumstances. Instead, consider using a contract from the American Institute of

TIPS ON REMODELING

- Be very, very careful picking somebody to remodel your home. Do not hire people who drop fliers off in your mailbox or who ring your doorbell and tell you your roof or gutters need fixing.

- For a minor renovation job, take recommendations for a remodeler from friends and neighbors. For a major job, anything costing more than $5,000, get recommendations from the National Association of Professional Remodeling Contractors or the Remodelors Council of the National Association of Home Builders.

- Ask candidates for your remodeling job for a list of the last 10 homes they've worked on, descriptions of what they did, the dates they started those jobs, the dates the jobs were completed, and how to contact each owner.

- Ask each contractor what kind of insurance he carries. Protect yourself by hiring people who have a current certificate of insurance or by making sure you have enough liability coverage in your homeowner's policy in case someone who's uninsured is hurt on your property.

- Don't sign a standard builder's supply house contract for a remodeling job. Instead, consider using a contract from the American Institute of Architects (AIA) or from the American Homeowners Foundation.

- Get subcontractors to waive their right to place a lien on your home if they aren't paid by the contractor.

- Never agree to any contract that calls for a large payment up front. Devise a reasonable timeline and pay schedule with the contractor under which the contractor is paid as work is completed. In the contract, include penalties against the contractor for failing to complete the job on time.

CONTACT

The Remodelors Council of the National
  Association of Home Builders
1201 15th Street NW
Washington, DC 20005
1-800-368-5242, ext. 216
www.nahb.com

American Institute of Architects
AIA Orders
2 Winter Sports Lane
P.O. Box 60
Williston, VT   05495
1-800-365-2724
www.aia.org
(For a remodeling contract, ask for the standard form of agreement between owner and contractor: A101, A111 or A201.)

American Homeowners Foundation
6776 Little Falls Road
Arlington, VA 22213
703-536-7776

National Association of the Remodeling Industry
4301 North Fairfax Drive
Suite 310
Arlington, VA   22203-1627
1-800-440-NARI (for a list of professional contractors in your area)
1-800-966-7601 (other calls)
www.nari.org

Architects (AIA) or from the American Homeowners Foundation. The AIA has dozens of sample contracts that have stood the test of time.

The American Homeowners Foundation has a fill-in-the-blanks prototype contract that's very user-friendly. If the renovation is going to cost more than $10,000, have the contract reviewed by a lawyer before signing it.

In most states, you'll need to obtain lien releases from your contractor as part of the renovation process. A lien release or waiver is a document the contractor can give you that you will ask materials suppliers and subcontractors who work on your site to sign. In most states, subcontractors and suppliers can place a lien on your home if the contractor doesn't pay them, even if you've paid the contractor in full. So you could be forced to pay twice. It's like buying a television set at an appliance store and then months later being asked to pay the television manufacturer for the TV, because the store didn't pay the company.

With a lien waiver, subcontractors and suppliers give up their right to come after you for payment. If you're buying a house or refinancing one, you can ask the general contractor to sign an affidavit swearing he has paid the subcontractors. But you should also get lien waivers from the subcontractors.

I have heard so many sad stories about people who have been financially ruined because they didn't get lien waivers from electricians, plumbers, and other subcontractors. And as more people remodel their homes to provide space for aging parents or teenagers, more people will be taken.

I had a neighbor who put an addition on his home and did a major renovation of his kitchen, and wound up losing an additional $70,000 because the contractor didn't pay his subcontractors. He asked me what to do and I had to tell him it was too late, because the contractor had skipped town with his money.

Never agree to any remodeling contract that calls for a large payment up front. If the contractor is short of cash and says he or she needs money to buy materials for the job, you should buy the materials. Go with the contractor to make the purchases. I've heard sad story after sad story from individuals who gave a contractor a large sum up front and never saw the contractor again.

Devise a reasonable timeline and pay schedule with the contractor under which the contractor is paid as work is completed. Don't front-load the money to the point that the contractor has most of the money while just a portion of the work has been completed. My feeling is that you shouldn't pay anything up front. For a small job, you might pay half halfway through the job, 40 percent at completion, and the final 10 percent once you're satisfied everything has been done correctly and nothing further must be done. For bigger jobs, pay 10 percent of the cost after each 10 percent of the job is done, but hold back 10 percent at the end to protect against problems. You and the contractor should decide in advance how to determine when each 10 percent level is met.

All this may sound petty, but if you're having remodeling work done, it matters. If you set the schedule for payment ahead of time, you keep problems from occurring while the work is going on. You don't want to be in a financial dispute with your contractor in the middle of the project, no matter who thinks the other is being unfair. That doesn't create a spirit of cooperation and communication.

It's possible you could suffer if the job isn't completed on time. For example, if you're renting a place while your house is undergoing renovation, you will have to pay extra rent if the job takes too long. If that's the case, the contract should include penalties if the contractor fails to complete the job on time. If you have to pay an additional $250 a week to live in another house or apartment, the contractor should be penalized at least $250 a week.

Besides losing your money by foolishly paying up front, you could end up getting incompetent work. If you've been damaged in this way, you have a tough road to walk. You're going to have to bring someone else in to finish or redo the job, and often it will cost more to redo it than it would have cost to do it correctly the first time. Then you have to go to court to try to get your money back from the contractor who botched the job. If the contractor has no assets, there's nothing to go after. If you can't prove your case or if you win but can't collect, you don't get anything back. It's tough.

Then there's the distress you endure. When a home renovation gets messed up, people take it very personally and it upsets them and disrupts their lives. There's so much excitement about adding a room or fixing up a kitchen, and when things don't go right, there's an emotional crash.

One more caution about remodeling. Be very wary of contractors who not only brag about their workmanship but also say they can arrange for financing. Home-improvement loans or second mortgage loans arranged by a contractor tend to be extremely costly, and interest rates are usually far above market rates. If you need to borrow money to renovate, repair, or add to your home, go to your bank or credit union and stay away from contractor-supplied referrals.

SELLING YOUR HOUSE

While many parts of the country have seen large increases in real estate values in recent years, other regions have seen values stay the same or decline.

People in areas where values have not increased are in a difficult fix when they try to sell their home, because their house, minus the real estate commission, might actually be worth less than what they paid for it. That's led to a mass of people posting signs saying "For Sale By Owner" (FSBO). They try to market and sell their homes themselves, to avoid the commission, so they can sell without losing any money. The Internet has also given people the ability to put ads for homes online.

But an FSBO is not a panacea. Many people find it very hard to sell their home themeselves, primarily because they have no training or experience in selling. They may not price the house correctly and may be offended when buyers criticize the house. Owners who sell their own houses also have to be incredibly patient, because they have to deal with unqualified buyers and with people who make appointments to see the house but don't show up.

When you sell your own home, always specify on the sign that brokers or agents are welcome. That way you will protect yourself from "steering," in which agents avoid your street and don't show buyers your home because you're not paying commission. If you indicate that brokers or agents are welcome, you're agreeing to split the commission with a selling agent who brings you a buyer. Generally you should offer 3.5 percent. Don't get greedy. If that 3.5 percent brings you a willing buyer at a reasonable price, that's a smart decision on your part. You've still saved 3.5 percent.

The hardest part of selling your house yourself is negotiating the selling price. There's a tendency among people who don't do this often to play their cards badly and let the buyer know too much. You may end up costing yourself more money than if you'd had an experienced hand at the wheel helping with the negotiating. If you want to try a by-owner sale anyway, set a reasonable time limit. If you were going to give a real estate agent a three-month listing on a home, give yourself three months to try to

TIPS ON SELLING YOUR HOUSE

• Many people try but find it very hard to sell their own homes. They may not price the house correctly and may be offended when buyers criticize the house.

• When you sell your own home, always specify on the sign that brokers or agents are welcome. That way you will protect yourself from "steering," in which agents avoid your street and don't show buyers your home because you're not paying a commission.

• Interview a number of real estate agents before you hire one to sell your home. It's good to deal with someone who sells a lot of houses in your neighborhood.

• When you interview an agent, ask for a detailed, written sales plan of how he or she would market your home. Limit the listing time with that agent to three months or negotiate a fee you can pay to get out of the listing after that time.

• Consider every offer for your house, and always make a counter offer.

• Prepare your house for sale. It should be clean, bright, uncluttered, and uncrowded.

sell it. If you find you're miserable doing it, then stop and hire an agent.

Be aware that when you are trying to sell your house FSBO, you will be approached by a lot of agents trying to get the listing. Some agents will be greedy and try anything to get you to give them the listing. Others will be helpful, giving you advice and information, with the thought that later, if you're not successful in selling the house yourself, you'll select them to be the listing agent for your property. I call that enlightened

self-interest; it is in both parties' best interest.

Interview a number of real estate agents before you hire one to sell your home. Ride around the neighborhood first and see which names keep popping up on lawn signs. When you see the same agent's name several times in your area, you know that agent is "farming" your area. You want to deal with a farmer. Farmers know the agents who traffic that area, they know the true value of your home, and, if they have multiple listings, they probably have good strategies for selling homes in your area. If you still know how to get in touch with former neighbors, call them and ask their experiences with the listing agents they had on their homes.

When you interview an agent, ask for a written sales plan of how he or she would market your home, with specifics. Limit the listing time with that agent to three months. Agents will always present you with a six-month contract, but my attitude is that this gives them all the rights and privileges and you all the responsibilities. If an agent balks at doing a three-month listing because of the expenses he or she has, then reach an agreement that you can back out of the listing after 90 days in return for paying the agent a fee. If you're miserable with an agent, paying the fee is worth it.

By law, real estate commissions are negotiable. However, in many real estate markets, there is de facto price setting so that, by tradition or design, commissions in that area are set. It may be known as a 7 percent, a 6 percent, or a 5 percent market. You can try to negotiate a commission, but you'll probably have to live with the de facto fixed commission in that market.

Give serious consideration to any offer for your house, and never be insulted by it. Always make a counter offer. So often when I've sought to purchase a house, agents have told me the seller would be insulted by my offer. I've always told them to pass along my offer anyway. You're in a negotiating situation and, as the potential buyer, you should not make a ridiculously low offer. However, you shouldn't make an offer that's too high either; then you narrow the range within which you and the seller can negotiate. Make a reasonable offer but one that is a little on the low side.

As the seller, you must first price your house reasonably, not high above the market price, and be willing to enter into a good give and take with a potential buyer. Let's say you have a house listed at $135,000 and a potential buyer offers $110,000. You know in your heart and mind that your house is worth more than that and the low offer makes you angry. Put aside your anger and come back with a counter offer with which you'll be happy. If you and the buyer can't reach an agreement, fine. At least go through the process of offer, counter offer, counter. The first buyer is very important. It may sound trite, but it's generally true that the first offer you receive on a house will be the best offer. I've bought two houses in which the sellers accepted less than they rejected earlier.

If you think your house is worth $139,000, you should probably price it at $146,000, or about 5 percent above what you'd like to get. But if you list it at $160,000, you may be so high that you won't get any offers at all.

A real estate agent will help you price your house by checking the selling prices of other homes in your neighborhood. You should also check the Internet sites of real estate companies in your area for homes of similar style and location to yours. Remember that real estate agents face constant battles to get listings for homes. Sometimes we make the mistake of choosing one agent over another because one gives us a higher estimate of the selling price. That's speculation. More important is the person's plan for selling your house.

When you're asked about your house, tell the truth. If you're asked about the condition of your roof and you don't know what it is, don't say it's in great shape. Say you don't know. If you're asked about the air conditioning and you had to have it fixed last summer, say so. Don't lie. Generally you'll be asked to fill out a seller's disclosure statement. These forms are required by law in only a few states, so it's your choice. But I recommend that you fill one out. I think disclosing the condition of the house creates a sense of trust that helps make the sale. You won't be able to deceive most buyers anyway, since most will have a house inspection, which may disclose problems you've tried to hide. You're better off being honest and telling potential buyers about problems up front. If the buyer finds out about a defect just before closing, it could kill the sale or force you to lower the price or pay for repairs.

If you were selling your car, you would probably clean and wax it, vacuum the interior, and fix any minor flaws, like a broken tail light. The same holds true for your house. You want it to be clean, bright, uncluttered, and uncrowded. Areas around the home need to be well lit. If you furnish your house to the max, get rid of some of the furniture. Closets need to be clean. If you have both winter and summer wardrobes in your closets and they're stuffed, take out the opposite-season clothes and store them. People are buying a fantasy; they don't want it ruined by a crowded closet. They're also looking to see if their furniture and possessions will fit, so you need to make the house seem like it's at less than capacity when people walk in.

Some sellers are having their own inspections done to check out their houses before they sell them. If you don't want to go that far, go through the house yourself and make sure things work. Check the heating and air-conditioning system, and fix minor problems such as loose doorknobs or railings. Clean, paint, patch, or replace anything that isn't up to speed, paying special attention to the kitchen and bathrooms.

Buyers also want a house to seem fresh and inviting. Having fresh flowers in the house and decorating the front walkway are good ideas. Some agents recommend putting a saucepan on the stove with cinnamon or potpourri in it to give a fresh scent to the air. Sometimes little touches can give people the feeling of warmth they want their home to have.

MOVING

Whether you're buying a house or renting an apartment, changing residences means packing up your possessions and moving.

For some people, moving means renting a truck, getting some friends together to help, and ordering a few pizzas and some beer as a reward. But as we get older and acquire more furniture, books, and other items, and as our backs get weaker, we're more likely to turn to professional help for a big move.

Unfortunately, there's no reliable way to tell which movers will do the job well and charge a fair price, and the chances of overpaying or having your belongings damaged or delivered late are too great.

In all the years I've been doing a radio program, the problems my staff and I have had trying to resolve problems with movers have ranked among the most difficult. I'll talk to a caller who has done everything one should do to solve a problem — she's called, written, sent follow-ups, sent certified mail — and the movers don't seem to care. Not every mover, but many. In one situation, a major moving company hung up on my producer for no other reason than she was inquiring on behalf of one of our callers.

The most important way to protect yourself when you shop for a mover is to get a binding estimate of what it will cost you. If you don't, the move could cost you hundreds, or thousands, of dollars. Let's say you call three movers and you get estimates of $995, $1,300, and $1,600, but none of the estimates is binding. You choose the mover who gave you the $995 quote. When it completes the move, the crew leader hands you a bill for $4,000. Under the law, the company can charge you anything it wants and you're required to pay. If you had a binding estimate of $995, that's all you'd owe. Unfortunately, some states prohibit binding estimates.

It's a good idea to buy insurance from the mover. Choose replacement coverage, which pays to replace an item that is broken in the move. *Consumer Reports* once found that 46 percent of the people who move incur damage, and 11 percent have more than $1,000 worth. It's a real concern.

When the mover drops off your furniture at your new residence, do not sign the release form until you've examined your furniture piece by piece. Use a flashlight if your house isn't well lit yet. Sit in each chair and bounce on your sofa to make sure all the legs are still solid. I know this sounds silly and I know it sounds like the last thing you want to do on the day you're moving to a new place, but actually it gets your adrenaline flowing to bounce on your furniture, so do it. Check the exterior of cartons for signs of damage, and open boxes marked fragile. It's much easier to document a claim while the moving people are still there, before you sign that you received your possessions in satisfactory condition. You can ask for a damage claim form or make a note on the acceptance that some merchandise was damaged.

Many people prefer to do their own packing when they move. And as a *Consumer Reports* survey

TIPS ON MOVING

- Get a binding estimate specifying the cost of your move in advance.

- In your contract, require the mover to pay a penalty if it doesn't deliver your belongings on or before a specific date.

- Buy replacement value insurance on your possessions, in case something breaks during the move.

- Before you choose a moving company, get a clear understanding from that mover what happens if something is broken that you've packed yourself.

- When the mover drops off your furniture at your new residence, do not sign the release form until you've examined your furniture piece by piece.

- The best way to protect crystal, china, and any other extremely valuable and delicate possessions is to move them yourself in your own car.

- If you want to risk hurting your back and move your items yourself, be careful about what packing materials you buy. You'll generally do better renting a truck from a rental company and buying your boxes and other materials somewhere else.

- To save money on the truck rental, move during mid-month or during the week.

INTERNET

www.homefair.com
(To get information on your new city, including salaries and schools.
You can also create a checklist of things to do before moving day.)

once showed, you're less likely to have items damaged when you pack them yourself. But before you choose a moving company, get a clear understanding from that mover of what happens if something is broken that you've packed yourself. Most movers will accept and insure the delivery of boxes you pack yourself, but make sure you do it right. If something breaks, you'll have to show it to the company, along with the packing materials, to prove you did a good job.

The best way to protect crystal, china, and any other extremely valuable and delicate items is to move them yourself in your own car, if you're driving to your new residence. You're going to handle those items more carefully than a mover will.

There's also a risk when you move that your stuff will arrive late, possibly very late. I talked to a woman who moved from the East Coast to California, and her possessions didn't arrive for three months. It probably would have taken longer than three months if my staff hadn't intervened.

The way to protect yourself is to require the mover — in the contract — to pay a penalty if it doesn't deliver your belongings on or before a specific date. The penalty should relate directly to the costs you will incur if the mover is late. So if you will have to spend $75 a day to stay in a hotel waiting for your bed to arrive, the mover should have to pay that amount for each day it's late.

Unless you add a specific penalty for late delivery to the contract, all you have to rely on is the mover's estimate of when it will deliver your belongings. If it doesn't get around to making the delivery for two, three, or four months, you're out of luck.

If you want to risk your back and move your household yourself, be careful about what you buy for the move. One of the big profit centers for truck rental companies is renting and selling moving accessories. You pay a convenience charge when you buy or rent those items from the truck rental company. You'll generally do better renting the truck from the rental company and buying your packing materials somewhere else. Some people like to get moving boxes for free from supermarkets or discount stores. If you want to do that, be sure to get there before the boxes are crushed for recycling.

Try to get a written confirmation ahead of time of the price per day for the rental truck, the cost per mile if there is one, and any additional charges that may apply. On the day you rent the truck, examine the contract carefully to make sure the prices and information match up with those on your written confirmation. Although I've heard allegations about truck rental companies that suddenly change the rates when the customer shows up — because it's moving day and the customer doesn't have other options — I don't believe that's the normal method of operation. I think that more often it's a matter of misunderstanding or a simple mistake on the part of the rental company. That's why protecting yourself with a written confirmation is important.

You can save some money by moving during the middle of a month or mid-week, rather than at the end of the month or on a weekend. Moving companies now use software that enables them to price their trucks based on demand. So trucks will cost more on the last day of the month and on the weekends, when people traditionally move, and much less on weekdays and at other times during the month. You might pay $80 a day for the last weekend of the month but just $45 for a mid-month, mid-week day. This holds true for all sizes of trucks at most rental companies. If your schedule allows, consider moving at off-peak times to get the best deal possible.

Major movers also will negotiate with you on price. My brother-in-law got a quote of $4,400 for an interstate move but got the price knocked down when he said his company would pay no more than $3,000. At first, the moving company representative said he couldn't do it for $3,000. But then he called back and agreed on the $3,000 price.

If you're moving to a new city, you can get some great help on the Internet at the Web site www.homefair.com. It has information on schools and the cost of living in most cities. And if you enter the date of your move, it will create a dated checklist of things you should do several weeks before moving day.

HOME SECURITY SYSTEMS

Many people buy a home security system after their home has been broken into or they've seen a crime story on the news. So they're not in the best state of mind to buy a burglar alarm, making them easy prey for aggressive salespeople.

Regardless of the reason you want a burglar alarm, it's important to divorce yourself emotionally from the decision so you can shop wisely. The first thing to do is make a drawing of your home, or a checklist, and figure out how many doors and windows you need to protect.

Next, call your insurance agent and ask what discounts are available on your homeowner's insurance and what requirements a security system must meet for you to qualify. Generally, you'll have to get a system that's monitored by an outside service, not just a noisemaker alarm intended to frighten a burglar into fleeing. There may be other requirements as well.

Always get smoke and fire monitoring as part of the system. People get home security systems because they are afraid of intruders, but the possibility of a fire is much greater. Usually it costs just a little more to get fire protection.

After you complete your checklist and talk to your insurance agent, call burglar alarm companies for tentative quotes. Don't consider any company that won't give you a quote on the telephone and wants to send a salesperson to your home to give you an estimate. That's a strategy they use to close a deal. They know if the salesperson is in your home, the odds are greater that you'll agree to buy an alarm from their company, regardless of whether it's the best buy. First get at least six quotes and then decide who may come to your house.

Many companies offer supposedly fantastic lease deals, but I don't advise you to lease a burglar alarm. If you need the security of an alarm system, you're going to want it for the long term, not for the length of a short lease. A burglar alarm can also be a confidence builder for a buyer when it's time to sell your house.

The next trap to watch out for is the monthly monitoring cost. Some companies will quote very low prices on the equipment and its installation and then have extremely high monthly monitoring fees. Paying $17.95 a month for monitoring instead of $22.95 may not seem like much,

but it will save you $120 over two years. That's why it's very important to find a good price for monitoring and often less important how much you pay for the system itself. For a truer comparison of quotes, figure the total cost of the system and monitoring for two or three years.

It's become common for companies to try to get you to sign a five-year deal for monitoring service. They may low-ball on the initial cost of the system, then make it up with an incredibly expensive, long-term monitoring deal. Don't sign any contract for monitoring that's longer than one year. Or make sure you have an escape clause that will allow you to terminate the agreement. Forget the cost. If a company's doing a lousy job, you're handcuffed to it and that may put your life in danger. A security company should prove itself to you month after month, and you should want to remain with it because it's good, not because it has forced you to.

The company I use guarantees a monthly monitoring charge of $16 as long as I maintain the service. And the owner has made a lot of money by providing good service at a very fair price.

Sometimes the price quote you get over the phone disappears when a salesperson comes to your house. If that happens, don't give in. Try the next bidder, or call around for more quotes. I've seen some terrible abuses in the sale of home security systems, mostly from companies trying to justify unusually high prices by claiming their systems are far superior to others. Some of my callers have paid as much as $4,000 for security systems that should have cost well below $1,000. By getting multiple quotes and comparison shopping, you'll get an accurate reading of what is a fair price.

Technology changes. The burglar alarm systems I bought 10 years ago are much less sophisticated than the one I put in a year ago. But I

TIPS ON HOME SECURITY SYSTEMS

• Even if you've recently had a break-in, try to stay calm when you buy a burglar alarm so you can shop wisely.

• The first thing to do is make a drawing of your home, or a checklist, and figure out how many doors and windows you need to protect.

• Call your insurance agent and ask what discounts are available on your homeowner's insurance and what requirements a security system must meet for you to qualify.

• Always get monitoring for smoke and fire as part of the system.

• After you complete your checklist and talk to your agent, call burglar alarm companies for tentative quotes. Don't consider any company that won't give you a quote over the telephone. I also advise you not to lease a burglar alarm.

• Watch out for the monthly monitoring cost. Some companies will quote very low prices on the equipment and its installation and then have extremely high monthly monitoring fees.

• Don't sign a monitoring contract for more than one year.

don't buy state-of-the-art technology. I buy current technology. That's a very important distinction. The latest, greatest gadget may be unproven and is usually overpriced. With current technology, competition has reduced the price and time has allowed the system to prove its reliability.

There's no specific technology you need to buy. You'll want monitoring, smoke and fire detection, some form of perimeter security to protect the entrances to your house, and some form of motion sensor. Actually, the motion sensor is usually a heat-sensing device so the alarm isn't set off by some object falling in your home. If you have a dog, the motion sensor can be set to register movement a few feet above the ground, allowing your pet to roam around. Cats are a bigger problem, because they like to climb and jump. If you have a cat, you can keep it in one room while you're out, or use an alarm that's triggered when someone breaks a window to get inside.

One drawback of home security systems is false alarms. If you have a lot of them, you may be fined by your police department, because it's costing police departments a fortune to respond to false alarms. That's a choice you'll have to make in deciding whether you want a security system. I've been close to being fined and had to decide to risk the fine or discontinue monitoring and go with a noisemaker alarm.

REFINANCING

When mortgage interest rates fall, homeowners start to think about refinancing. Very simply, refinancing means taking out a new mortgage with a lower interest rate to pay off your existing mortgage. Through refinancing, homeowners can often cut their monthly payments, shorten their loan terms, or combine a home equity loan and a mortgage into one lower payment.

Because it can be expensive to refinance, you can wind up paying more than you'll save. Let's say it would cost $3,000 to refinance and you plan to sell your house in three years. That means you'd have to lower your monthly payments by at least $84 to make refinancing worthwhile. Just figure the savings per month at the lower interest rate, multiply by the number of months you expect to stay in the house, and compare the savings to the cost of refinancing.

On the other hand, the savings from refinancing can be substantial. The monthly payment on a $120,000 loan at 9.0 percent interest is $966, while the same loan at 7.5 percent costs $839 a month. Experts long recommended that you refinance if current mortgage rates are 2 percentage points lower than your mortgage rate and you plan to stay in the house awhile. So if you have a 9 percent mortgage rate and the current rate is 7 percent, you would be wise to refinance.

An innovation in refinancing has changed the rules completely. If you're not sure you're going to be in your house long enough to recoup the costs of refinancing, you can choose a low- or no-cost refinance and start saving money right away. With a typical no-cost refinance, you'll get an interest rate 5/8 of a point higher than the market rate for a traditional refinance. So if the market rate for a 30-year loan is 7.0 percent, the rate for a no-cost refinance will be 7 5/8 percent. If you have an 8.25 percent or 8.5 percent mortgage, it's a no-brainer. You'll save from the first monthly check you write.

You can figure your savings at a number of sites on the Internet, including www.irwinmortgage.com and www.quicken.com.

You can also get a lower mortgage rate if you use the Internet to shop for your loan. One good Web site is www.countrywide.com, which provides a discount on loan fees for filling out a mortgage application online. Most big-city newspapers list mortgage rates in the Sunday paper, but don't use these for comparison shopping. You can't figure out who has the best deal, because each lender lists a different combination of fees and points. The best way to compare is to get quotes that list zero discount points and loan origination fees (0/0), also called "at-par" quotes.

Refinancing in the traditional manner can be worthwhile if you plan on staying in your house for a long time, or if the new mortgage has a shorter loan term. Let's say you have a 30-year mortgage at 9.0 percent and you can go to a 15-year mortgage at 7.5 percent. That 1.5-point difference may be enough to justify the cost of a refinance if you plan on staying in the home for several years.

If you're sure you're going to be in a house for a number of years, you can get a lower loan rate by taking a loan with a discount point or two. A discount point is a fee equal to 1 percent of the loan amount. If you borrow $100,000 with two discount points, you'll pay a $2,000 fee at closing. If the lower loan rate allows you to make back that $2,000 fee in 36 months or less, that strategy is worth considering.

Before you decide to refinance, think about how long you want to remain in the house and the length of loan you want. If you have a 30-year mortgage with 26 years left, you do yourself a disservice refinancing into a new 30-year mortgage, because you're adding four years to the amount of time you'll be in debt. Approximately half of all people who refinance choose a shorter term for their new loan, and that's a smart decision.

Refinancing may make sense even if you don't plan to stay in a house very long. If you have a fixed-rate mortgage that has a moderate or high interest rate, it could be worthwhile to refinance if you can cut your monthly payments sharply by refinancing into an adjustable rate mortgage.

Be careful with an adjustable rate mortgage (ARM). Studies have shown that ARMs almost always are a better deal than fixed-rate mortgages, but with ARMs, you trade peace of mind for savings. I've purchased homes in recent years knowing intellectually I would have been better off with an ARM, but I couldn't jump the psychological hurdle. I went for the sure thing and picked a fixed-rate mortgage, which was the lowest it had been in

TIPS ON REFINANCING

- Refinancing means taking out a new mortgage with a lower interest rate to pay off your existing mortgage.

- With the advent of low- and no-cost refinancing, it's no longer as important to stay in the house long enough to pay back the refinancing costs.

- If you are doing a traditional refinance, insist on a good-faith estimate of the costs up front, before you give the lender a penny.

- Before you refinance, check your credit report for anything that could foul up the process. You don't want to lay out the money if a credit problem is going to keep you from refinancing.

CONTACT

Mortgage Bankers Association of America
1125 15th Street
Washington, DC 20005
202-861-6500
www.mbaa.org

INTERNET

www.irwinmortgage.com (Irwin Mortgage: mortgage information and calculator)
www.hsh.com (Mortgage information)
www.quicken.com/mortgage/ (Quicken mortgage information)
www.countrywide.com (Countrywide Mortgage: online mortgage application)

decades. But the sure thing and that peace of mind cost me money.

The danger with an ARM is that the interest rate can rise, often by as much as six points, over the lifetime of the loan. If it does, your monthly payment can soar. A fixed-rate mortgage doesn't change, even in a period of high inflation and high interest rates. A good compromise is to get an ARM with a conversion feature, which gives you the right to convert to a fixed rate during the loan for a modest fee — usually less than $500.

Another option is a low or no-cost refinance. In this case, you agree to accept a mortgage rate that's above the current market rate but lower than you're paying. In return, the lender charges a very small refinancing fee. This is a wise choice if you've recently refinanced but rates have fallen further, or if you really are uncertain about how long you're going to stay in the house. A low-cost refinance is a bad deal if you're going to be in the house for a number of years.

If you have an FHA loan, you may be eligible for a "streamline" refinance, which is a no-cost refinance that gets you a slightly above-market rate of interest. Streamlines are good only if you don't change the amount left to be paid.

Another mortgage option that's become increasingly popular is the 5/1 or 7/1 hybrid. With these loans, you get the fixed rate for five or seven years at a lower rate than a 30-year fixed-rate mortgage, and then it becomes a one-year adjustable rate loan. Most people who get these loans do so because they expect to sell the house within five or seven years and pay off the mortgage.

Computers have allowed endless variations in loans, from 10-year fixed mortgages to 3/1 fixed/adjustable combinations. I bought my current house with a 3/1 mortgage, because I thought interest rates were relatively high when I bought it, yet I didn't want to be faced with a two-point increase from an ARM in just a year. When rates dropped in the next year, I refinanced.

If you're doing a refinance, it's very important to insist on a good-faith estimate of the costs up front, before you give the lender a penny. If you don't, you shift all the power to the lender and take unnecessary chances. You may find that a refinance doesn't make sense for you. If you find out too late, you could lose any money you've paid toward the refinancing costs. Another protection you have is the option of locking in the interest rate you're offered. That protects you in case rates rise after you've agreed to refinance.

Before you refinance, get a copy of your credit report to see if there's anything on it that could foul up the process. You don't want to lay out the money if a credit problem is going to keep you from refinancing. Get all documentation ready for the lender immediately. You need to document your employment, income, debt, and assets. When you provide the proper documentation, give the lender a dated, signed memo showing that you have given him the needed information. Make sure to keep a copy. This is to protect you later if the lender is slow to close the loan and causes you to miss out on getting a good interest rate. Lenders often are able to wiggle out of a commitment they don't like because the consumer was sloppy about handing over the required documentation.

MORTGAGE SERVICING

When you first get a mortgage, you might think you'll be doing business with the same lender for 30 years. That's rarely the case. Mortgage lenders often sell your loan to investors as soon as the ink is dry, take a fee for originating the loan, and use the money they get from selling your loan to make another loan. A single mortgage may be owned by a dozen companies during its life.

A lender has to disclose to you what percentage of its loans are sold and what percentage are kept in the lender's own portfolio. If the lender sells near 100 percent of its loans, you know you're dealing with a loan retailer.

Investors and lenders use mortgage servicing companies to handle the everyday business of collecting your payments, keeping track of your loan balance, and letting you know if you're late with a payment. So, in addition to having several owners over its life, a loan may be handled by several different servicing bureaus. Consequently, there is a large potential for mistakes, such as unapplied payments or errors in calculating your balance.

Mortgage servicing is a very profitable business and an area that causes a lot of consumer complaints. To add to the confusion, lenders often don't do the best job of handling loan problems when they do occur. The most important advice I can give you about your mortgage is to keep a copy of every check you ever write for your loan. I know that sounds like overkill, but if you have a loan for 5 or 10 years and there's a dispute about whether a particular payment was made, your best defense is to be able to produce the canceled check. Even if you pay on a mortgage for 30 years, you write only 360 checks. That doesn't take up much room.

All mortgage servicers must have an 800 number you can call for customer service. I've had quite a bit of experience calling these numbers, and I find it distressing how long I'm left on hold before I reach a human being. When you do reach a person, make sure you get his or her full name and write it down. You'll find a page in the Workbook chapter of this book to help you document mortgage and other consumer problems. If a lender makes a promise that isn't kept, you'll have someone you can call back and hold accountable.

If you find yourself in a dispute with a lender about a payment or another issue, don't send correspondence to the same address you send your payment. In most cases, this is merely a bill-processing center and clerks there will throw your letter away. Find out from the mortgage servicer where you should send correspondence. Start by sending your letters with a regular postage stamp. If the lender ignores the letters, start sending them by certified mail.

You can also get help by contacting the Mortgage Bankers Association office in your state. This trade association has a strong interest in seeing that your complaints are dealt with properly, because if they aren't, the state or federal government may decide to regulate mortgage lending activities.

The biggest dispute in mortgage lending is escrow practices. Escrow is the process whereby your lender collects a monthly fee from you to cover the cost of taxes and insurance on your property. The lender needs this protection, because if you were to let your homeowner's insurance lapse

and your home burned to the ground, the lender would lose its collateral on the loan. The same thing would happen if you failed to pay your property taxes and lost your house. While the lender has a legitimate need for escrow, many lenders have proven themselves to be extremely greedy by overcollecting escrow. Further, in most states, lenders are not required to pay interest on escrow, creating an incentive to overcollect.

Lenders are allowed to keep an amount equal to one-sixth your annual escrow needs in reserve. Let's say your annual bill for taxes and insurance is $1,200. The lender would be able to collect $1,200 annually, plus a $200 reserve. Many lenders play fast and loose with the numbers and collect far more money each year. I believe the most effective way to solve the abuses of escrow would be to require lenders to pay interest on these accounts. If your lender ignores your requests for an accounting of how escrow totals have been determined, tell the lender you're going to contact your congressman. Lending institutions fear congressional action more than anything else.

To give you an idea of how complex things can get, let me tell you about a loan I once originated with a small mortgage lender in Ohio. The loan servicing was handled by SunTrust Banks. The loan was sold repeatedly and moved around through a series of transactions and bank mergers and got all fouled up. After paying SunTrust every month for years, I decided to do a refinance on another property. The whole process came to a halt because, to my horror, my credit report said a company known as Society Mortgage claimed I was in default because I hadn't made a payment in five months. I had never even heard of Society Mortgage, and I certainly didn't know it owned the loan.

It took four weeks to get this mess straightened out. Eventually, I got an apology from

TIPS ON MORTGAGE SERVICING

- Mortgages typically have many different owners over the years and many different servicing bureaus, so it's not difficult for a mixup to occur over your loan balance. To protect yourself, keep a copy of every check you ever write for your loan.

- If you call a mortgage servicing bureau about your loan, make sure you get the full name of the person with whom you speak.

- If you find yourself in a dispute with a lender about a payment or another issue, don't send correspondence to the same address you send your payment.

- Keep an eye on how much money your bank collects to cover your annual property taxes and insurance. Lenders are allowed to collect your annual escrow needs plus one-sixth this figure, but many overcollect.

- One of the smartest things someone can do with a mortgage is to prepay on the loan. All you need to do is contact your lender and ask for its prepayment procedure. Then, once a year, check the loan balance the lender sends you to make sure the additional payments have been applied properly.

- Fee-based plans that charge $300 to $500 for administering a prepayment system are a bad idea; you can manage such a plan better and cheaper by yourself.

- If you reach 22 percent equity in your home, you can save a substantial amount of money by getting rid of private mortgage insurance.

INTERNET

www.irwinmortgage.com (Irwin Mortgage: mortgage information and calculator)
www.hsh.com/ (Mortgage information)
www.quicken.com/mortgage/ (Quicken mortgage information)
www.countrywide.com (Countrywide Mortgage: online mortgage application)

Society Mortgage, acknowledging that the company had been in error when it reported that my loan was in default. Even more maddening, Society Mortgage wasn't supposed to report my loan at all, because it was not the loan servicer. Only SunTrust Banks should have reported anything about the loan to the credit bureau. My credit report showed the same loan with both lenders and different balances.

One of the smartest things you can do with a mortgage is prepay on the loan. That's a lot simpler than it sounds. All you need to do is contact your lender and ask for its prepayment procedure. Generally, there'll be a box on your payment coupons for prepayment if you want to prepay. Just fill out the box and increase the amount of your check by whatever amount you choose. Some people prefer to write a second check and write "prepayment of principal" on it. Once a year, check the loan balance statement the lender sends you to make sure the payments have been applied properly. Instead of throwing several hundred dollars at your mortgage one month and nothing another month, I recommend prepaying your principal by a set amount each month. Try to pay $50 or $100 extra each month, or whatever you can afford.

It's remarkable the impact you can have on your mortgage by making prepayments. There are a number of Web sites that allow you to plug in your loan balance and interest rate and see how much you can reduce the length of your loan, and the total amount of interest you pay, by adding something to each mortgage payment. For example, if you have a 30-year $120,000 loan at 8.0 percent interest, adding $50 a month to your $881 payment would cut five years off the length of the loan and save you nearly $42,000 in interest over its life. Prepaying an extra $100 per month would cut nearly nine years off the loan and reduce the total interest paid by more than $67,000.

There are a number of Web sites with mortgage calculators that will show you how much you can save by prepaying your loan each month. Just plug in your loan balance, interest rate, and an amount you can afford to prepay, and it will show you the savings. Try www.quicken.com/mortgage/ or www.irwin mortgage.com.

I despise fee-based plans through which you prepay your principal. They charge $300 to $500 for administering a prepayment system you can manage better yourself. The typical plan collects half your regular mortgage payment every two weeks, which for the full year would amount to 26 half-payments, the equivalent of 13 regular monthly payments. These organizations forward a regular payment to the bank at the end of each month then add a 13th payment at the end of the year. Since you can do this yourself, there's no reason to pay a set-up fee to someone else. Just divide your mortgage payment by 12 and add that amount to your regular payment each month. You'll be making one additional monthly payment each year. If you do that early in a 30-year loan, it will cut seven to eight years off the length of the loan.

There are other reasons not to use fee-based prepayment plans. What happens if the company you're paying doesn't forward the payment to your lender, or doesn't pay on time? You could lose your money or suffer penalties. Finally, they're holding your money during the year and earning interest. If you prepay, those dollars should benefit you immediately, not up to a year later.

There's a philosophy among some financial planners that it's foolish to prepay on a loan and that you're better off putting the money in the stock market or some other investment. But most of us will spend the money rather than invest it. Prepayment of principal is a very clever method of forced savings and truly an investment in your future, because you reduce the length of your loan and the amount of money you pay on it.

Some people are trimming the length of their mortgage at the start. Some people are doing mortgages as short as 10 years. For most of us, that's not practical financially, and we're also frightened off by the monthly payment on a 15-year mortgage. If you can't swing a 15-year mortgage, look at a 20-year loan. While a 15-year loan may represent a significantly higher monthly payment than a 30-year, a 20-year loan represents only a marginally higher payment per month, and it dramatically decreases the amount of money you would pay over the life of the loan. For example, a

30-year $120,000 loan at 7.5 percent carries a monthly payment of $839. You get a lower interest rate for a shorter term, so you could borrow the same amount on a 15-year loan at 7.0 percent, with a monthly payment of $1,078. That $239 difference may be too much for many people to try the 15-year loan. But a 20-year loan on the same amount, at 7.0 percent, would be $930 a month, just $91 more than for the 30-year loan. By choosing a 20-year term instead of a 30-year term on this loan, you'd pay $103,286 in total interest instead of $182,061. A 15- or 20-year term lets you pay off the loan quicker, with a lower rate of interest and a lower total cost.

Another way you can save money on your mortgage is to get rid of private mortgage insurance (PMI), which you had to pay if you bought your home with a down payment of less than 20 percent. If you have a conventional loan (not FHA or VA), you were required to buy PMI, which protects the lender against the higher risk involved in your loan. You should dump the insurance when the value of your home increases, or you have paid enough on your loan that your equity in the house exceeds 22 percent (the amount you owe is less than 78 percent of your home's market value). If you have paid 22 percent of your loan, the lender is supposed to remove PMI automatically. Or, if you believe your home has increased in value substantially, you may be able to remove PMI by getting an appraisal. When you believe you have enough equity, contact your lender and ask what its procedure is for getting rid of PMI.

BEING A LANDLORD

Many people end up being landlords because they have a condominium or a house they can't sell. Because they go into renting property reluctantly, it's easy for them to get frustrated.

If you rent property, manage it as a business. First, set a rent that's fair for your market, not one that's based on your mortgage payment. People aren't going to rent your house or condo for $950 a month if they could rent something similar for $850, even if your mortgage payment is $950 or $1,000. By the same token, if your mortgage payment is $600 and the market price is $850, don't set your rent too low.

As prospective tenants come through your property, require those who are interested to fill out an application. You can get a standard financial application from an office supply store or bookstore. If you have friends at an apartment complex, ask if you can see one of their applications. You need to check a potential tenant's historical record. Does the person move constantly? Are there gaps in his or her employment? You're entering into a financial partnership with your tenant and you need to know if he or she will honor an obligation to you. Ask potential tenants to provide a copy of their credit report, so you can see if they've behaved responsibly in their other financial relationships. If someone has a lot of debt or recently declared bankruptcy, you may prefer a different tenant.

Choosing the wrong tenant can be a big mistake. I know of one case in which a landlord was left with a huge bill because a tenant failed to report a water leak. Under the lease, it was the tenant's responsibility to pay the water bill. But the tenant moved out without paying the bill and without telling the landlord about the leak. The damage to the property was significant, but the leak also increased water use. The water bill itself cost the landlord more than $1,000.

If a prospective tenant passes your screening test, set a realistic security deposit, but don't make it exactly the same as a month's rent. Make it a little higher or a little lower, so the tenant doesn't interpret it as a payment in lieu of the last month's rent. Get a standard lease and then include any special protections that are particularly important to you.

For landlords with just one or two properties, I strongly recommend you include a repair clause that makes the tenant responsible for the first $50 cost of any repair. Tenants who used to live in apartment complexes are conditioned to calling the management office to fix any problem. That's expensive for you because, unlike those complexes, you don't have a maintenance person on staff. You have to hire a contractor to do the work. Many little problems could be fixed by the tenant with a $3 part from a hardware store but might cost you $100 if someone has to come in to make the repair. If you have a repair clause, you may have to charge a little less in rent. But reducing the hassle and irritation

TIPS ON BEING A LANDLORD

- If you rent property, manage it as if it were a business. Set a rent that's fair for your market, not one that's based on your mortgage payment.

- Require prospective tenants to fill out an application, and ask them to supply a copy of their credit report.

- Make the security deposit a little higher or lower, but not the same as, a month's rent.

- For landlords with just one or two properties, include a repair clause that makes the tenant responsible for the first $50 cost of any repair. To do this, you may have to charge a little less in rent.

- Provide a $25 or $50 discount for early rent payment.

- Do a move-in inspection and a move-out inspection of the property to protect yourself in case you have to keep part or all of the security deposit to cover damage.

- If your tenants do not pay the rent, be prepared to evict them.

- If you're relocating far away from your property, ask a friend or relative to handle the rental, in return for some compensation, or consider hiring a professional management company.

CONTACT

Housing & Urban Development
Operations Division
Washington, DC
202-708-0547 (Ask to speak with the desk officer representing your state)
(Questions regarding landlord/tenant disputes)

Or:
The clerk of the court in your county

for you makes that worth it. I've done this with a condo I rent out, and it virtually stopped maintenance calls from my tenants. When they know they're paying the first $50, they don't bother me.

Another thing you should do is discount rent for early payment. You give somebody a discount, say, $25 or $50, if the rent is paid before the first of the month. This is very important for landlords who are new to the business, since most tend to be very slack about collecting overdue rent. The penalties and the process for eviction are such pains that you're much better off giving the tenant an incentive to get the money in early. I give tenants a $50 discount for paying before the first of the month. If they pay after the fifth, not only do they lose the discount, but they have to pay a $50 late penalty. I started doing this a few years ago and it changed everything. I used to get rent checks on the 10th or 12th of the month. Now the tenants always pay on time or early. No more problems.

Do a move-in inspection and a move-out inspection of the property to protect yourself in case you have to keep part or all of the security deposit to cover damage. Be clear up front what condition you expect the unit to be in when the tenant moves out.

If your tenants do not pay the rent, be prepared to evict them. Don't accept excuses. Don't be soft-hearted, because you're being walked on if you allow them to occupy a rental unit for free. To evict tenants in most states, you have to send them a letter demanding that they pay the rent or turn over the premises. If they don't do either, you can't just go in and set their stuff out on the street. You must go to the county courthouse and begin an eviction action. The clerk of the court will help you. The tenants will be served with an eviction notice and normally will have five to seven days to answer. If they answer and give a reason why they're not paying, a hearing will be held before a judge to give each party a chance to explain its side. In most cases, the tenants never answer, so the court authorizes the eviction. Then the county marshall or sheriff will go to the property with you, or with people you hire, permit you to enter the premises, and put the tenants' possessions on the street.

If you are speedy about an eviction, you can have it done within 30 days. Some landlords let tenants slide for months. Others start eviction proceedings by the fifth of the month if they don't have the money. Do what you are comfortable with. If you've requested the money twice and don't have it by the middle of the month, I recommend you start the eviction process.

If you're relocating far away from your property, don't try to manage it by remote control. If you do, you're asking for trouble. Instead, ask a friend or relative to handle the rental of the property, in return for some compensation. Don't ask for it as a favor.

Professional management is another option for people who are relocating out of state or who don't want to be landlords. Many real estate companies have divisions that will manage a property for you. The typical fee is half the first month's rent and a 10 percent commission each month. So the fee for an $800 condo would be $400 up front and $80 a month. That's well worth it if you're in Chicago and the house is in St. Louis. Rates may vary in your community.

Examine the agreement with the rental management company closely to see if you're protected if the company fails to do a good job collecting rent or securing tenants. And keep an eye on the quality of tenants the management company chooses. The company may not be as careful as you would be.

BEING A TENANT

The biggest mistake people make when hunting for an apartment is not asking enough questions. Before you write a check for an application fee or a deposit, get the specifics on the basic three — the length of the lease, the amount of the rent, and the amount of the deposit. If you have a pet, find out about the pet deposit. If you have any special needs, make sure they are met before you hand over any money or agree to rent the apartment.

Never sign an apartment lease on the spot. Take it home with you and read it. If you don't understand something, put question marks next to the item and get an explanation.

Don't pay an application fee or deposit before you take the contract home to review it. In most states, if you pay a deposit or application fee and decide not to rent the apartment, you forfeit the money you've paid. The feeling is the landlord may have taken an apartment off the market while you were considering it. If you do pay a deposit so that you won't lose an apartment you want, just be aware that you probably won't get your money back if you change your mind.

Always add a clause to an apartment lease giving you the right to terminate the contract before its normal expiration date if your circumstances change. You should have the right to terminate early, by paying a fee of perhaps one month's rent, because of a job transfer or if you decide to relocate to another city. In return for a larger fee, perhaps two months' rent, your lease should permit you to terminate for any reason.

It's important to have early termination rights to avoid potentially huge penalties. In most states, if you leave an apartment before the end of the lease, you remain responsible for the rent for as many months as it takes the landlord to rerent the property. If you're three months into a one-year lease, you could be on the hook for nine months' rent. You need this protection even if your intent is to stay the full year, because circumstances change and you should be prepared.

Most states have their own rules for people who occupy an apartment without a lease. Usually, the state has the equivalent of its own lease, which governs these "tenant-at-will" cases. Generally, under these rules, you can terminate at any time by giving the landlord a 30-day written notice. The landlord can raise the rent at any time, or demand the premises back, by giving you a 30- or 60-day written notice.

Many leases renew automatically unless you notify the landlord that you are leaving. Let's say you sign a year's lease that ends March 31. In many cases, you'll have to notify the landlord in writing by March 1, or pay rent for April. Sometimes the lease will renew for another 12 months.

In most cases, your landlord will conduct a move-in inspection before you move into an apartment. Make sure to be present for it, and note everything you can find wrong with the apartment. Whatever you don't note will be held against you at the time you move out.

At the end of the lease, there will be a move-out inspection. Be present for that as well, so you can dispute anything the landlord says that isn't valid. This is vital in order for you to get back your security deposit. In fairness, the landlord may notice something you didn't. Maybe the bathroom isn't terribly clean and the landlord wants to bring in a cleaning crew. If you're present at the inspection, you can offer to clean it.

Before you sign a lease, ask what condition the landlord expects the apartment to be in when you move out. This should be pretty revealing. If he hems and haws, you might have trouble getting back your security deposit. Some landlords, because of cash-flow problems, look for any excuse to keep a security deposit. Others use it only for legitimate purposes.

If a landlord doesn't give back your security deposit, you have specific rights, which vary by state. In many states, you have the right to sue for two or three times the amount of the deposit. Act quickly. If you don't have the deposit within 30 days of when you move out, send the landlord a letter demanding your deposit. If you don't receive it within 10 more days, sue the landlord in small claims court. Usually, in these cases, the landlord will dispute the condition of the unit.

If you have any reason to suspect the landlord is going to try to cheat you on the security deposit, take pictures that prove the apartment is in good condition. A roll of film costs just a few dollars. You don't even have to get the film developed if you get the security deposit back. If you want to prove you shot the pictures after you moved out, rather than when you moved in, photograph the front page of the local newspaper at the beginning of the roll of film.

Some people like the idea of renting a condominium or a house, rather than a unit at an apartment complex, because they prefer a true residential neighborhood to a transient one. The drawback to renting from a nonprofessional owner is that the management tends to be haphazard and inattentive. Maintenance requests go unanswered more often with nonprofessional landlords. The biggest risk is that the property owner will be foreclosed upon for nonpayment of the mortgage. In many states, you can be evicted on very short notice if that happens. Another danger with a private-owner condominium or house is that you may not be able to live there year after year. A private owner could sell the property and not renew your lease. An apartment complex is always going to be there.

Safety is an important issue for many renters. If you're considering a particular apartment complex, ask the apartment management company what security measures it has on site and if there have been any break-ins or violent crimes. In many states, the management company must tell you. It's also good to visit the property on a Saturday or Sunday afternoon, tell people who live there that you're thinking of moving in, and ask them if they feel safe living there. Ask them if their car or apartment has ever been broken into, or if they've heard about any violent crimes or break-ins in the complex.

Noisy neighbors are another common headache. If a neighbor is making your life miserable, try a friendly talk with him. If the neighbor doesn't respond, go to your apartment manager for help. If she doesn't do anything to solve the problem, call the police each time the noise level rises and have the neighbor cited for disturbing the peace. You have a right to live in peace and quiet.

On the other hand, people need to have some tolerance of normal noise levels. One of my callers moved into an apartment with her family and quickly learned that the people living beneath her thought her children were too noisy, even though she didn't think so. The neighbors kept complaining to management and banging on the ceiling with a broom handle, even though the noise wasn't out of the ordinary. The apartment complex eventually asked the caller to move to a different apartment in the complex. Because she had a lease, she didn't have to move. I recommended that she move only if she wanted to, and only if the apartment complex paid all her moving expenses, including the fees to reconnect her telephone and utilities.

Perhaps the most common complaint I hear from renters is that their maintenance requests are responded to slowly or inadequately. I strongly recommend that you show some faith in your landlord. But as soon as your landlord fails to serve you, start documenting every maintenance

Tips on Being a Tenant

• Before you write a check for an application fee or a deposit on an apartment, ask about the length of the lease, the amount of the rent, and the amount of the deposit.

• Never sign an apartment lease on the spot. Take it home with you and read it. If you don't understand something, put question marks next to the item and get an explanation.

• If you pay a deposit or an application fee for an apartment and decide not to rent the apartment, you probably will lose the money.

• Always add a clause to an apartment lease giving you the right to terminate the contract before its normal expiration date if your circumstances change.

• Many leases renew automatically unless you notify the landlord that you are leaving.

• Make sure to be present for the move-in inspection, and note everything you can find wrong with the apartment. Be present for the move-out inspection, too.

• If a landlord doesn't give back your security deposit, you have the right to sue in small claims court.

• Renting from a private owner is fine, but be aware of the danger of not being able to renew your lease, or of the owner being foreclosed upon.

• If your landlord fails to respond to maintenance requests, send written requests. If a landlord doesn't respond to a breakdown that makes the apartment unlivable, consider paying for the repair yourself and deducting the amount from your next month's rent.

• If you know you're going to be evicted, try to make arrangements to move your possessions, either to a friend's house or into storage.

CONTACT

Housing & Urban Development
Operations Division
(Questions regarding landlord/tenant disputes)
Washington, DC
202-708-0547 (Ask to speak with the desk officer representing your state.)

Or:
The clerk of the court in your county

request. If the landlord ignores your written requests, write "Request No. 2" and "Request No. 3" on subsequent letters, to reaffirm that you're having a continuing problem. If the landlord still ignores your requests, you may have to take the more drastic step of paying for the repair yourself and deducting it from the next month's rent. Do this only when the breakdown makes the apartment unlivable, such as for a burst pipe or a nonworking stove, refrigerator, or major appliance. Keep the repair receipt, and enclose a copy of it with the rent check.

Your explicit rights to repair and deduct vary by state, but you have an implicit right to a livable dwelling.

Let's say your water heater explodes and your landlord won't do anything about it. Hit the landlord with a written notice and let him know that if the water heater is not replaced within 24 hours, you will use the right of repair and deduct. One thing you cannot do is completely withhold rent because you don't like something. That will get you evicted.

Some landlords can be extremely gracious when there's a major repair problem. A few years ago, an upstairs neighbor of a friend of mine inadvertently set off the sprinkler system, saturating my friend's living room ceiling with water and causing the sheet rock to cave in. The apartment complex agreed to put my friend and his family in a hotel for four days while repairs were made, and they returned to find a bottle of champagne waiting in the apartment.

My friend's possessions weren't damaged, because there was enough time to cover the furniture with a tarpaulin. But that's a risk too many renters ignore. The landlord is almost never responsible for damage to your possessions, even from a burst pipe, unless you can prove gross negligence, which isn't easy. You thus need renter's insurance to protect against theft

and damage. It's not that expensive — about $15 a month — and it will prevent you from being wiped out. A few years ago, a friend of a friend lost all her possessions in a fire and had no insurance. She lived above a store and when the store caught fire, her apartment and all her possessions were destroyed. Losing photos and irreplaceable items was a given, but she was left with no clothes, except what she was wearing, and no furniture. It was terribly sad and unnecessary.

Although it's not required in many states, your landlord should provide you with smoke detectors. If the landlord doesn't, buy them yourself. Even though I'm cheap, I recommend spending a little more to get a smoke detector with a 10-year lithium battery. Most deaths in fires occur when the smoke detector doesn't work, often because the battery is dead. With a 10-year battery, there's far less chance that will happen. It's a real bargain if it saves a life. And you'll save the annual cost of regularly replacing batteries. If you have a cheap smoke detector, make sure it works, and check the batteries at least once a year, perhaps on New Year's Day. In a multiunit dwelling, there's a greater chance of fire than in a house, and smoke detectors are even more critical.

As I discussed in the chapter on credit problems, your mortgage or rent is the first and most important bill you have to pay, because eviction is a real danger. The eviction process is pretty standard in most states, although specific details vary. Some cities even have their own landlord/tenant laws. If you fear you may be evicted, check with the clerk of the court in your county to find out the specifics of the process in your area.

In most states, a notice will be delivered to you or tacked onto your door informing you of the eviction proceeding. You'll have a short time, approximately five to seven days, to pay the rent or explain why you should be allowed to remain.

If you don't pay and don't respond, you'll have little chance to stay in the apartment or house. But even if you do appear in court, don't expect the judge to be very sympathetic to a sad story. Landlords are not charities, and you have no right to live somewhere if you don't pay the rent.

Normally it takes about 30 days from the day the landlord begins the eviction action until the sheriff puts you out of the residence. If you know you're going to be evicted, try to make some arrangements to move your possessions, either to a friend's house or into storage. A small, self-storage rental unit will give you a place to keep your things until you find a place to live. If your stuff is put out on the street, it could be stolen or ruined by foul weather.

Money

Before self-service gasoline pumps became the norm, you had to rely on someone else to fill your tank. And before the Internet, you needed someone to help you with your money.

Technology has given us the ability to buy and sell stocks without a stockbroker and to monitor our investments ourselves. Full-service still is available, but self-service costs less and gives you more control.

To buy and sell stocks yourself, you have to know what you're doing, or you could be taken advantage of by a dishonest person, or end up making a bad buying or investment decision.

There's one golden rule to keep in mind whether you're buying something, investing your money, or using credit — treat time as your ally. The best way to avoid making a bad decision is to not make a quick decision.

In this chapter, I'll give you easy-to-understand information to help you get involved in investing for your future. I'll also give you tips about dealing with debt, protecting your money in a divorce, preparing a will, and choosing a lawyer and an accountant.

LONG-TERM INVESTING

Each year since I started answering consumers' questions about money, I've taken more and more questions about investing.

The trend shouldn't be very surprising. The baby-boom generation is moving closer to retirement age, working Americans who once had old-fashioned corporate retirement plans now have 401(k) plans, and the Internet has made it possible to check your portfolio and execute stock trades from the comfort of home. And more and more people, many in their 20s, 30s, and 40s, are becoming interested in making their money grow for the future.

The secret to building long-term wealth remains basic — put money aside regularly. Whether you deposit money in an investment account once a month or have a deduction taken from every paycheck, you'll create a strong financial resource for your future.

One of the best places to invest your money is in no-load (no-commission) mutual funds, which allow you to own a piece of corporate America with less risk than owning individual stocks. In a capitalist society such as ours, the wealth goes to those who own companies — the stockholders — not to those who work for them.

Your number-one investment priority should be funding your own retirement. No longer can you rely on the traditional vehicles that may have helped fund your parents' — or grandparents' — retirements. Their generations had a strong Social Security system and pension plans that were fully funded by their employers.

Today's working Americans will get only a small portion of the funds they need for retirement from Social Security, and the employer-paid pension is becoming a thing of the past. Without the government or a paternalistic corporation to fall back on, you have to be much smarter and more aggressive in planning for your retirement.

Despite the increased interest in investing, most people are still undersaving for retirement. That upsets me. Although most people probably won't starve in their old age, if they haven't saved sufficiently, they probably will have to work until they die.

To properly fund your retirement, you'll need to save about 10 percent of your pay throughout your working life. If you start saving in your 20s, you'll be leaps and bounds ahead of everyone else. But if you're 45 and haven't saved anything, don't be fatalistic and do nothing. Just start now.

There are several investment vehicles that you should consider when putting money aside for retirement, including the 401(k) plan, the new Roth IRA, the traditional Individual Retirement Account, and the Simplified Employee Pension (SEP). All charge a 10 percent penalty if you withdraw the money before age 59 1/2.

No matter which investment vehicle you select, you have to choose a specific investment. The list of choices includes fixed-income investments, like bank certificates of deposit, purchases of individual stocks or bonds, or mutual funds, which buy hundreds of stocks or bonds for you.

I'll describe the investment vehicles first, then the specific investments and how to buy them.

The 401(k) Plan

The principal retirement vehicle these days is the 401(k) plan. It's basically a tax-sheltered investment account, set up by your employer, to help you accumulate money for retirement. The 401(k) is the best way to build a retirement nest egg, because you can painlessly set aside money for your future, and you can take the money with you if you switch jobs.

The 401(k) provides several significant advantages. Most important, many employers match or partially match the money you contribute. So if you contribute $100 per month to the plan, your employer will contribute either $25, $50, or $100. With most investors trying hard to get a 6 to 10 percent return on their money, a vehicle that gives you an automatic return of 25, 50, or 100 percent, thanks to the employer contribution, is sensational.

The money you put into your 401(k) plan is deducted from your gross (before-tax) income, so participating in the plan lowers your tax bill for the year. In addition, you don't have to pay taxes on the interest or dividends your money earns until you withdraw the money at retirement. Sheltered from the corrosive effect of taxes, your investment can grow faster than money in a traditional savings or investment account.

Since 401(k) contributions are deducted from each paycheck, making the contributions is easy. Participating in a 401(k) plan is an incredible deal for those who are lucky enough to have the opportunity.

To best take advantage of the benefits of a 401(k) plan, you should put as much money into the plan as your employer will match. The more you put in, the bigger the annual tax deduction, the faster your retirement nest egg grows, and, up to a point, the more your employer contributes.

Each company's plan is different, but many will match your contribution up to 6 percent of your pay. Let's say that's the rule at your company, and the employer's match is 50 percent. If you earn $35,000 a year, you can put up to $2,100 into the 401(k) plan, and your employer will add in $1,050. Your total contribution for the year will be $3,150. In most cases, you may put in more of your pay, usually up to 15 percent. The extra money won't be matched, but it still will grow tax-deferred.

Many 401(k) plans permit employees to borrow against their accounts, but I don't recommend it. It's true that you're borrowing the money from your own fund and paying it back with interest to the same fund. But the money you pay back gives you a lower rate of return than if your money were fully invested in a stock mutual fund. So borrowing diminishes the size of the pot of money that will be available when you retire. Borrowing is an especially bad idea if the money is for something unnecessary, like a vacation.

There's also a danger in borrowing if you quit your job or are fired. When that happens, the borrowed money is due immediately. If you can't pay it back, the IRS treats the loan as an early distribution of your retirement money. You'll have to pay a 10 percent federal penalty on the total, plus ordinary state and federal income tax, for that tax year. On average, you'll have to pay 46 percent of the money you borrowed in taxes and penalties. If you've already spent the money, you may not even have what you need to pay the taxes.

The Roth IRA

I used to tell people to put as much money into their 401(k) plan as their company permitted. But the advent of a new retirement vehicle, the Roth IRA, has forced me to change my advice, because the tax advantage of the Roth IRA is superior to that of any other retirement vehicle.

Here's how the Roth IRA works. If you deposit money into a Roth IRA account and leave it there until retirement, you never pay taxes on the earnings. Never. With a standard IRA, the money grows tax-deferred — you pay federal and state income tax on it as you withdraw funds in your retirement years, which can eat up a quarter to a third of your money. But with the Roth IRA, the earnings grow tax-free. If you build a nest egg that contains $1 million 30 or 40 years from now, it's yours free of income taxes.

One disadvantage of a Roth IRA is that you don't get an income tax deduction in the year you make the contribution. So you pay taxes on it up front. But the tax-free compounding over the years makes that trade-off more than worthwhile. It's the best savings deal we've had since the income tax went into effect.

If you start a Roth account, or invest in any retirement vehicle, while you're in your 20s, you will be sitting pretty at retirement. In fact, if you set aside $150 a month beginning at age 25 and earn a conservative 8 percent on your money, you'll have nearly $1 million at age 65. If that money is in a Roth account, you'll get it tax-free. If it's in a 401(k), the employer match probably will make the total even larger. If you want to do some calculating on your own, visit one of the mutual fund Web sites, such as www.troweprice.com or www.vanguard.com.

I recommend that you put as much money into a 401(k) as your employer matches, then put whatever else you can afford into a Roth IRA, up to the limits allowed. Each person can put up to $2,000 a year into a Roth IRA, or $166 a month. Married couples can each deposit $2,000 a year into a Roth IRA, as long as they don't exceed certain income limits.

So if you earn $30,000 a year and your employer matches your 401(k) contribution up to 6 percent of your income, try to put $1,800 into your 401(k) and $2,000 more into a Roth IRA. If you earn $40,000, put $2,400 into the 401(k) and $2,000 into the Roth.

If you're still in a position to save more money, put as much into the 401(k) as your employer allows, even though the employer won't match any of the additional funds. You still get the tax deduction and the tax-deferred earnings growth.

Let's say you and your spouse both work and each of you earns $30,000. Each of you should put 6 percent into your 401(k)s, or $1,800, for a total of $3,600. (The employer match, at 50 percent, raises the contribution to $2,700 each, or $5,400.) Putting another $2,000 each into a Roth IRA increases the amount your family is saving for the year to $9,400, or 15.67 percent of your $60,000 family income. That's without the employer match on your 401(k)s. You could effectively stop there and do nothing else. If you want to save even more, put the maximum amounts your employers match in your 401(k)s.

If you work for a company that doesn't offer any retirement plan, your first priority for retirement investing should be to put the maximum $2,000 into a Roth IRA.

One of the advantages of a 401(k) over a Roth IRA is that the money comes out of your paycheck before you get paid. I encourage you to set up an automatic payment plan for a Roth IRA because, even with the best of intentions, people forget.

The Simplified Employee Pension (SEP)

If you're self-employed, or have some freelance or self-employment income, you have the right to take advantage of a fantastic retirement plan called a SEP, or Simplified Employee Pension. A SEP is a kind of super-IRA, a tax-sheltered plan that allows you to invest much more money than an IRA allows.

With a SEP, you can contribute up to 13.08 percent of your net earnings from self-employment for the calendar year, up to $30,000 a year in most circumstances. You figure your net income at tax time, after deducting expenses, and calculate your maximum SEP contribution from the net. You figure the amount you may contribute, deposit the money in your SEP account, and note the SEP contribution on your tax form.

Let's say you earn $50,000 annually as a full-time, self-employed individual. You can contribute up to $6,540 to the SEP. If you work part time for yourself as a landscaper and earn $10,000 after expenses, you can contribute $1,308 to a SEP — even if you have a 401(k) plan at your regular job. In most cases, you're not eligible to open a deductible IRA if you have a 401(k) plan — your eligibility decreases as your income rises.

The simple, one-page application form to start a SEP can be obtained from any discount broker, broker, or mutual fund company.

Employees of some businesses also may participate in a SEP. The law requires that if a business owner sets up a SEP, he or she must allow employees to participate in it. This type of SEP may be funded by the employer, the employee, or both. Employee contributions are tax-deductible. Employer contributions are not taxed until funds are withdrawn.

Self-employed people should put their first $2,000 into a Roth IRA and the rest of their retirement investment in a SEP.

The Individual Retirement Account (IRA)

Another option for retirement is the traditional Individual Retirement Account, although it's not a very attractive investment option anymore.

IRAs allow you to shelter up to $2,000 a year from income tax. The law also allows a nonworking spouse to deposit up to $2,000 into a separate IRA. Just as with a 401(k), the money is deducted from your gross income and grows tax-deferred. However, there is no employer match, and you must pay federal and state income tax on the money as you withdraw it in retirement.

If you have money in a traditional IRA, you might benefit by transferring it into a Roth IRA. You'll have to pay income tax on the money now. But you'll probably end up with far more money at retirement by taking the tax hit now and letting the money grow tax-free forever. It's a one-time special deal. You can't pay the tax out of the account, either. But it's such a great deal that it makes sense to borrow the money to pay the tax.

You might not want to transfer the money if you're over age 50, because you probably won't have enough years of compounding to make taking the up-front tax hit worthwhile. You also can't transfer the money if your gross income is more than $100,000.

Variable Annuities

Variable annuities are another investment vehicle that don't make much sense anymore, since Congress lowered the tax on capital gains in 1997. A variable annuity is like an IRA without any limit on the amount you may put in and without any current deduction from your income. It works only if you make a lot of money and you've already exhausted the other tax-advantaged ways to save for retirement. It makes sense only if you are 25 or more years from retirement and you pick an ultra-low-cost variable annuity, such as those from Vanguard, T. Rowe Price, Scudder, or Jack White. If you pick a higher-cost annuity, your investment will net you less money than if you put it into a no-load mutual fund in a traditional, taxable account.

I have one special warning about annuities. Some unsavory salespeople will try to con you into putting your IRA money into an annuity. Don't do it; moving your money will reduce the amount ultimately available for your retirement.

Saving for College

I like students to contribute to the cost of their college education themselves by working during their college years. I find it makes them more serious students who appreciate their education more.

I consider your retirement plan far more important than saving for your children's college education. That's because there are so many different ways to pay for college, but you can depend on only yourself to pay for your retirement.

I had a call once from a couple who were leaving the hospital with a two-day-old baby and wanted to put money aside for their child's college education. I was gratified to hear that they were thinking ahead. Unfortunately, they hadn't yet started saving for their own retirement.

Your first investment priority should be to put as much money into a tax-deferred plan as possible. If you've reached the limit of saving in these plans and you still want to put money aside, the next priority should be to develop a safety net for you or your family, in the event that you suddenly find yourself with unexpected expenses or a loss of income.

Any form of periodic savings plan will help you build a rainy day account. You can use a payroll deduction plan or an automatic transfer from your checking account. It doesn't matter if the money goes into a savings account, toward the purchase of savings bonds, or for shares of a mutual fund. The point is to put aside a certain amount each month. Money you'll need within five years should be parked, not exposed to the short-term risk of investments.

Your next priority should be saving for your child's education. Because of the recent cut in capital gains taxes, I have a new strategy about how to do this. If you're already investing properly for retirement, whether through a 401(k), Roth IRA, or SEP IRA, the best way to save for a child's college education is to deposit money in a no-load mutual fund in a traditional taxable account.

The capital gains tax is now a maximum of 20 percent for investments held for 12 months or longer, and as little as 10 percent for people in the 15 percent tax bracket. You can put money into a no-load mutual fund for 10 years, then give the money to your child as she reaches college age. You can give up to $10,000 a year. If you give the shares to your child and she then sells them, she'll pay 10 percent capital gains tax on the fund's earnings. If you sell the shares, you would pay a 20 percent capital gains tax.

Investing the money in your own name gives you more control than saving it in your child's or grandchild's name. A teenager may want to use the money to buy a motorcycle, and if the money's in his name, you can't stop him. Or, if he gets a full scholarship or elects not to go to college, you can continue to let the money grow and use it to help him buy a house. Keeping it in your name also makes it easier for your child to qualify for financial aid.

Parents used to like putting money in the child's name for tax reasons that no longer apply and because it made them feel they were supporting the child. If you put money in your child's name a few years ago, here's something to consider. If the child works part time or during the summer, she can transfer $2,000 each year to a Roth IRA. The money won't count in financial aid tests for college, because retire-

ment funds don't count, and she will get the money at retirement, after 50-plus years of tax-free earnings growth. Unfortunately, she won't be able to use it for college. You can't have everything.

You can withdraw up to $10,000 from a Roth IRA to pay for college expenses without paying a penalty, as long as the money has been in the account for five years or longer.

Parents should challenge their children who work part time to start saving for retirement. Tell your child that if he puts $500 or $1,000 a year into a Roth IRA, you'll put in the other $500 or $1,000. A child who invests $2,000 a year in a retirement fund starting at age 16 will have put enough aside by the time he's out of college to fund most of his retirement. That's because the money will have so many years to grow.

There are several alternatives to consider that can cut or ease the cost of a college education. One way is to have your child attend college year-round. That allows him to complete four years of school in three years, shrinking the total cost of housing and meals. If money counts, it's something to consider.

Another approach is to stretch out the length of college and have your child work to help pay the cost. Or she could attend a relatively inexpensive community college for two years, then transfer to a four-year college for the final two years.

Some people cringe at such suggestions, remembering their college years as a time of great fun, participating in fraternities and sororities. Your view may depend on whether you see college as a means to get an education or whether it should include a "life education" component, helping your teenager make the social transition to adulthood. There are a lot of local technical schools that are very successfully attracting students who want only the knowledge they get in the classroom.

Where Your Investment Dollars Go

Once you've selected your investment vehicle for retirement — 401(k), Roth IRA, SEP, IRA, or annuity — you need to choose a specific investment within the retirement fund. The best choice is stock and bond mutual funds, which give you the safety of diversity and the growth potential you must have to build a sizable retirement nest egg.

Stock mutual funds are the most efficient way to own companies — far better than investing in individual stocks. Mutual funds limit your risk by giving you a small part of a big basket of companies. So if one company fails or suffers a sharp decline in its stock price, it barely affects your diversified holdings. In that way, you benefit over time from the natural growth of corporate America and the profits it generates.

The problem for so many people is that they fear the short-term loss that can be generated from investing in stocks. Any mutual fund can have a bad year or two. But over periods of 10 years and longer, most good funds will easily beat "safe" fixed-rate savings vehicles. In fact, when you look at any 10-year period from the 1920s to today, stock market investors have received an average annual return of more than 10 percent. That includes the huge market losses in the Great Depression and the 1987 market crash.

The last decade has brought some huge run-ups in the value of stocks, as well as some scares about declines in value. I've gotten scared, too, from time to time. But these fears are irrational if your investment is for a long-term goal. I've made a pact with myself to review my investments only every 24 months. That reminds me that I'm investing to meet long-term goals. And it qualifies me under the law for lower taxation on capital gains. Under the 1998 tax law, money outside retirement accounts qualifies for lower capital gains taxes only if it has been invested for 12 months or longer. By reviewing my portfolio every two years, I'm ensuring that my investments will always qualify as long-term investments.

I also try to force myself to keep a long-term outlook toward money in retirement accounts, even if there's a calamitous decline in the short term. I know that long term in a capitalist society, stocks, and preferably stock mutual funds, are a wise investment strategy.

Having said that, don't expect the market to perform as well as it has over the past decade. Be realistic. A well-diversified stock portfolio should grow an average of 10 percent a year. Not in every year, but over the years, that's likely to be your average gain.

If you see your investments take a tumble and can't sleep at night because of it, switch to a more conservative investment strategy, such as a balanced fund, a lower-risk combination of stocks and bonds. It's not worth the potential reward if investing is going to seriously scare you.

You can enhance your chances of investing safely with a simple technique called dollar-cost averaging, which eliminates the dilemma of trying to time the market's peaks and valleys. You make regular contributions to a mutual fund, perhaps $50 a month, or divide a lump sum into 12 or 18 monthly deposits.

Without dollar-cost averaging, market dips are a real danger. If you invest $12,000 in stocks and the market plunges the next day, you're in trouble. But if you invest the same $12,000 over a 12-month or 18-month period, it doesn't matter what the market does. If prices go down, your $1,000 a month buys you more shares of stock. If prices rise, your portfolio increases in value. Over the long haul, given the historical tendency of the stock market to climb, you should do quite well. Dollar-cost averaging reduces risk dramatically.

Here's a great example of why you should use dollar-cost averaging. My brother invested $100,000 in a stock partnership in September 1987. The October 1987 stock market crash occurred a few weeks later and, when it did, he lost 40 percent of his money in three days. It took years for prices to climb to the point that he made back the $40,000 he had lost. If he had used dollar-cost averaging to invest over a 12-month period, he would have put $8,333 into the market in September 1987 and lost $3,333 — instead of $40,000 — when the market crashed. The second $8,333 he put in would have bought him a great many more shares, as would subsequent deposits, because the crash made each share of stock cheaper. When the market eventually took off again, he would have made a fortune. It's too hard to guess where the market is headed, and with dollar-cost averaging, you don't have to try.

Your 401(k) plan may offer anywhere from 3 to 10 investment options, including a money market investment, some form of fixed-income investment, a bond mutual fund, and one or more stock mutual funds. The worst thing you can do when you're saving for retirement is to put any money in a fixed-income investment. Fixed-income investments, like a bank certificate of deposit or a 401(k) plan's Guaranteed Income Contract, grow too slowly to meet your retirement goals. They're good places to keep money that you're going to need within a few years. But they will not be able to far outpace inflation and are a poor choice for a long-term investment. The best strategy is to choose several of the stock funds or combined stock and bond funds that are available in the 401(k) plan. There's nothing wrong with having a bond fund in your retirement portfolio, but it should contain 20 percent

or less of your money.

Your options in a Roth IRA, SEP, or traditional IRA are nearly unlimited. So you'll need some background to help you sort through the myriad of mutual fund choices. My best advice is to go to a bookstore and buy one of several excellent, comprehensive guides to mutual fund investing. Two of my favorites are *The Handbook for No-Load Mutual Fund Investors,* by Sheldon Jacobs, and the *Guide to Mutual Funds,* by the American Association of Individual Investors.

If you feel intimidated or overwhelmed by the prospect of reading an entire book on mutual funds, let me offer some basic strategies. These aren't the only right answers, but they are ideas that have worked well for people and keep them from being frozen by investment fear or apathy.

Index Funds

Most mutual funds have a professional manager, whose goal is to outperform the broad market by carefully buying top-performing stocks. For that service, mutual fund investors pay an annual management fee, which usually ranges from 0.5 percent to 2.0 percent of their investment in the fund.

One interesting kind of mutual fund, an index fund, operates with a different strategy. Instead of using a professional manager to pick stocks, the index fund aims for safety and growth by buying a very broad range of stocks or bonds, usually 500, 1,000, or 2,000 individual stocks or bonds. Instead of guessing where to put the fund's money, index fund investors own everything.

Some index funds aim to match the performance of the Standard and Poors 500 or other widely followed market indexes. Bond index funds often mix long-term and short-term government and corporate bonds.

The management costs for index funds are

near zero, and their performance often is very good to excellent. Buying a mixture of index funds is an easy, low-cost investment strategy.

Here's one idea that will give you a widely diversified number of stocks and investments in your portfolio. Put 30 percent of your money into a 500-stock index fund, 30 percent into a broad-market index fund (it will usually own 2,000 to 4,000 stocks), 20 percent into an international index fund, and 20 percent into a bond index fund. With that portfolio, you've bought the world — you've bought the biggest companies in the country; you've bought virtually all the publicly traded companies in the U.S., and you've balanced some of your equities with ownership of corporate debt, or bonds.

With this strategy, you can buy all your funds from one mutual fund company. You'll probably want to pick the company with the lowest costs. Vanguard is my favorite. Buying is as simple as calling one of the mutual fund companies and asking for a catalog of its funds. Or you could ask for a prospectus on its 500-stock fund, its international index fund, its broad-market index fund, or one of its bond index funds. If there are several bond index funds, ask for a prospectus on the intermediate-term fund. Such funds buy bonds with maturities from 3 to 10 years. I think an intermediate-term fund works best for people who are buying bonds just to balance their portfolios. Short-term bonds (less than three years) don't make sense in a long-term retirement portfolio.

You can put as much effort into assembling an investment portfolio as you want. Using an assortment of index funds is a low-tech answer for people who want to invest but are fearful of or uninterested in making lots of decisions.

To set up a portfolio, just call the mutual fund house you choose and ask for an application form. Fill it out and you're in business. If your money is already in an IRA account, you may be able to shift it by telephone into the investments you select.

If you have to transfer money from a bank IRA or roll it over from a 401(k) account, put the money into the mutual fund company's money market fund while you're deciding on your portfolio mix. Then call the company and move the money to the funds you choose.

You can move a lump sum directly into the investments you choose, but that carries some risk. Instead, use dollar-cost averaging. Put the lump sum into the company's money market fund, then transfer a portion every month into the specific investments you've selected.

You're not necessarily giving up anything in performance by choosing an index fund, because the fees are so low. Investment experts believe that an actively managed fund must outperform the market by 2 percentage points to compensate for the transaction costs and higher management fees. So a brilliant fund manager would have to achieve a 9 percent return just to keep up with an index fund that gains 7 percent, after fees are considered. However, some experts believe that a managed fund is a better choice if your investment window is less than five years.

Because index funds directly mimic the stock market, they're perfect in an "up" market and perfectly bad in a "down" market. That's one potential advantage of a professionally managed fund.

If you want to invest in mutual funds but are afraid to make any decisions, you can choose one of the catch-all "multifunds" available from several mutual fund houses. Vanguard's Vanguard Star has 62.5 percent stocks, 25 percent bonds, and 12.5 percent in money market funds. T. Rowe Price's fund is called the Spectrum fund. Several other no-load fund companies have similar products.

There are lots of choices in mutual funds —

TIPS ON LONG-TERM INVESTING

- Your number-one investment priority should be funding your own retirement.

- Put money aside regularly in a variety of stocks and mutual funds.

- Consider several investment vehicles when putting money aside for retirement: the 401(k) plan, the Roth IRA, the Individual Retirement Account (IRA), and the Simplified Employee Pension (SEP).

- When investing for retirement, stocks are a better bet, because of their growth potential, than conservative investments such as certificates of deposit, which barely keep up with inflation.

- To minimize the risks when investing in stocks, consider stock mutual funds. Mutual funds limit your risk by giving you a small part of a big basket of companies.

- Saving for a child's college education is a lower priority than saving for your retirement.

- One low-tech investment strategy is to invest in an assortment of index funds. Some of these funds aim to match the performance of the Standard and Poors 500 or other market indexes.

- Don't expect huge gains each year, and don't worry about huge losses in the short term. Keep your eye on the target, which is long term, 10 years or longer.

- If you see your investments take a tumble and you can't sleep at night because of it, switch to a more conservative investment strategy, such as a balanced fund, a lower-risk combination of stocks and bonds.

CONTACT

American Century
4500 Main Street
Kansas City, MO 64141
1-800-345-2021

Fidelity Investments
82 Devonshire Street
Boston, MA 02109
1-800-544-6666
www.fidelity.com

INVESCO
7800 E. Union Avenue
Suite 800
Denver, CO 80237
1-800-525-8085
www.invesco.com

Janus Capital
100 Fillmore Street
Suite 300
Denver, CO 80206
1-800-525-3713
www.janus.com

Morningstar, Inc.
225 West Wacker Drive
Chicago, IL 60606
1-800-735-0700
1-312-424-4288
www.morningstar.net

Charles Schwab Corp.
101 Montgomery Street
San Francisco, CA
94104
1-800-648-5300
www.schwab.com

Scudder
P.O. Box 2291
Boston, MA 02107
1-800-225-2470
http:\\funds.scudder.com

T. Rowe Price
  Investor Services
100 E. Pratt Street
Baltimore, MD 21202
1-800-638-5660
www.troweprice.com

USAA Life Insurance Co.
USAA Building
San Antonio, TX 78288
1-800-531-8000

The Vanguard Group
P.O. Box 2600
Valley Forge, PA 19482
1-800-662-2739
www.vanguard.com

REFERENCE

The Handbook for No-Load Mutual Fund Investors
by Sheldon Jacobs
1-800-252-2042

Guide to Mutual Funds
The American Association of Individual Investors
625 N. Michigan Avenue
Suite 1900
Chicago, IL 60611
312-280-0170

INTERNET

www.morningstar.net
www.quicken.com (investments, mortgage calculator)
www.fundalarm.com (links to dozens of other investment sites)
www.investorama.com (stocks, general)
www.hoovers.com (company and investment news)
www.bloomberg.com (business information, mortgage calculator)
www.netstockdirect.com (allows you to buy stocks direct from companies)
www.sdinews.org (allows you to buy stocks direct from companies)

Fidelity itself has hundreds — and if you like to read about all of them, have fun. But I want to caution you about becoming so overwhelmed by the choices that you do nothing.

If you want to spend a few hours getting some background, *The Handbook for No-Load Mutual Fund Investors* is very readable and will help you make decisions. In the meantime, here are some basics you should know.

The primary fees associated with mutual funds are sales loads, a hidden annual sales fee called a 12b-1 charge, and a management fee.

I don't think it ever makes sense to pay a significant load charge to buy a mutual fund. There's a vast selection of no-load funds, and your chances of doing well with them are as good as with a fund that carries a load.

You should never buy any mutual fund from a commission salesperson, such as a stockbroker. If you buy a professionally managed fund, you'll pay a management fee to the fund. Don't pay a second fee to a stockbroker for his advice. That goes double for an index fund. You get no professional advice with an index fund, so you certainly shouldn't pay a commission.

The loads you would pay if you bought from a stockbroker or a financial planner could be as high as 8.5 percent. So if you invest $1,000, $85 comes off the top as a sales commission and the remaining $915 goes into your account. That's a lot of money going to the broker. Fidelity has low sales loads on some of its funds — 3 percent or lower — and no loads on most.

Some brokers and financial planners will misrepresent a fund as no-load when it has hidden loads through the 12b-1 charge. Because you pay it every year, this fee, which might be 1 percent of your investment, could turn out to be more costly than an up-front charge. Plus, you pay not only on your initial investment but on your investment gains.

Over a 10-year period, a $10,000 investment in a mutual fund growing at 10 percent would be worth $25,937. The same investment in the same fund but with a 12b-1 charge of 1 percent would grow to $23,674. That's a difference of $2,263, about the same as investing in a fund with an 8.5 percent up-front sales load.

Some brokerage houses have said that they have "no-load" mutual funds, but the fine print in their ads shows an annual account charge or service fee of 1.25 percent. That's not a no-load fund.

Finally, all mutual funds have a management fee, which is the money you pay to have a professional money manager buy and sell stocks for your fund. You'll pay this fee annually on the total amount invested. It will be lowest for an index fund, for which management duties are insignificant. The management fee for index funds generally is less than 0.5 percent.

In addition to having low fees, index funds are very tax efficient and are a good investment choice for people who are investing outside a retirement plan. In many mutual funds, professional managers who are trying to produce strong results trade actively, and those trades create short-term capital gains on which investors have to pay income taxes. With index funds, you avoid that pitfall.

Paying more for a professionally managed fund could be worth it if the fund delivers. If a fund with a high expense ratio has greatly outperformed a fund with a lower expense ratio over a 5-year period and a 10-year period, it may be worth paying the higher fees.

Fidelity's heralded Magellan fund, managed for many years by Peter Lynch, has a 3 percent up-front sales load and a 1 percent annual management fee. But the fund was such a great performer — it grew at an annual average of 27.4 percent for nearly 20 years — that investors happily paid the charges.

However, Magellan points out the risk of

choosing a fund for its name-brand manager. Since Lynch retired in the late 1980s, the Magellan fund has had many managers and its performance has been questionable. If the manager of your fund leaves, there's no guarantee that the fund's performance will be similar to its past results.

If you choose your own mutual funds, it's a good idea to choose an assortment with different investment goals. So, although you might want some money in an international fund, don't put all your money into one. Putting some money into several different types of funds will give you better growth over the long term.

If your goal is to build a personal savings fund, for personal use or for a child's college education, a good strategy is to put a set amount of money into a mutual fund each month. A good choice would be one of the all-purpose "multifunds." Some mutual funds have a minimum monthly payment that's too high for many budgets. But four mutual fund families allow you to put in as little as $50 a month — Janus, INVESCO, T. Rowe Price, and American Century.

If you understand the basics I've discussed here, you won't be intimidated by anything you see in a prospectus or a book on mutual funds. If you want to study mutual funds in detail, subscribe to Morningstar, an information service that will provide you with all you ever wanted to know about mutual fund investing. Or check out Morningstar's Web site, www.morningstar.net.

No-Load Stocks

Mutual funds used to be an easy choice for long-term investing, because of the enormous costs that came with purchasing stocks individually. But it's now possible for people to buy individual stocks without the cost and bother of a stockbroker.

A change in federal securities regulations made it easier for companies to sell directly to the public, and improved technology has made it easier for companies to maintain their own customer accounts.

Several hundred companies now sell stock directly to the public, starting with the very first share, as long as the stocks are held outside retirement accounts. Unlike the old days when any purchase under 100 shares was considered an "odd lot," you can buy as little as one share with no additional expense. You can get information on buying stocks direct on the Internet at www.netstockdirect.com or www.sdinews.org.

Because investing in individual stocks doesn't give you the automatic diversification you get with mutual funds, I suggest you invest a minimum of $10,000 to start this kind of investment program. That gives you the ability to buy stocks in a wide variety of companies in different industries. I recommend buying a minimum of 10 different stocks, preferably 20, in unrelated industries. If you put all your money into technology companies and the technology sector runs into trouble, your investment would be very vulnerable.

If your investments in your retirement plan are widely diversified, your investments outside your retirement plan probably do not need to be as widely diversified.

If you have an extra $1,000 or so you want to invest in one or two companies you like, that's okay too. Just make sure you can afford to lose that money if the companies you choose fare poorly.

SHORT-TERM INVESTING

Investing for retirement is a low-risk proposition, because an investment window of 10 or more years smooths out the ups and downs of many growth-oriented investments.

Short-term investing is trickier. You need investments that fluctuate very little in value, so your money will be there when you need it. Let's say you put $5,000 into a mutual fund and, in the third year, the value of your investment drops 10 percent. That's no problem in a retirement portfolio, because the fund's value in 2002 is far less important than its value in, say, 2022, when you retire. But you could get burned if you have to cash in the investment in 2002 and take a substantial loss.

If you have an investment window of three years or less, stay conservative and consider yourself a saver, rather than an investor. A couple of good options are bank certificates of deposit and short-term Treasury securities, both of which are fully guaranteed.

Each of us has the ability to buy Treasury bills direct from the U.S. government, through the regional offices of the Federal Reserve Bank. Treasury bills are sold in a variety of terms: three months, six months, one year, two years, three years, five years, seven years, 10 years, and 30 years. The longer the term, the higher the interest rate you'll get, but the greater the risk that a sharp run-up in inflation could erode the value of your investment. Most people buy Treasury bills with a term of five years or less. That makes a lot of sense if the purpose of the investment is to park your money for a few years.

Treasury investments compete with banks for your money. There are times when Treasurys will pay more than banks, and there are times when Treasurys will pay less.

To buy Treasurys, you open a Treasury Direct account at a regional office of the Federal Reserve Bank. If you live in a city with a Federal Reserve branch, you walk in, fill out a short form, and hand it to a teller with a check. A minute later you'll get a receipt and you're done. If you don't live near one of the 36 regional Federal Reserve branches, you can do the transaction by mail. Call or write to the nearest Fed office, or to the Bureau of the Public Debt in Washington, and ask for a kit.

The beauty of buying Treasurys direct from the government is you pay no commission. Some people who don't know about this program needlessly pay a commission to a stockbroker or a bank. That could eat up most of the advantage of buying them.

There are some conditions to bear in mind with the Treasury Direct program. You need a cashier's check if you're buying T-bills with maturities of one year or less. Otherwise, a personal check is fine. Treasurys of one year or less have a $10,000 minimum. Two-year and three-year Treasurys have a $5,000 minimum, and Treasurys with maturities of five years or longer have a $1,000 minimum. In addition, the hours you can buy Treasurys direct are somewhat narrow, usually from 9 A.M. to 2 P.M.

If you think Treasurys are for you, buy the *Wall Street Journal* and check the approximate interest rates for three-month and six-month T-bills. The rates are listed in a daily chart called the Treasury Yield Curve. The rate you will receive is based on the amount investors bid at auctions. Three- and six-month Treasurys are usually sold each Monday. The longer-term Treasurys are sold monthly or quarterly. Two-year and five-year Treasury notes are issued during the last week of each month. Three-year and 10-year notes usually are issued on the 15th of February, May, August, and November. Thirty-year Treasury bonds usually are issued on the 15th of February and August.

Most people who buy Treasurys in person buy the morning the securities are auctioned or the day before. If you're buying by mail, you might have to buy a week before the auction.

Treasury bills, notes, and bonds differ primarily in their maturities. Three-month, six-month, and one-year Treasurys are called bills. Two-year,

TIPS ON SHORT-TERM INVESTING

• If you may need your money in a few years, it's more important to choose less volatile investments.

• Good options for people with an investment window of three years or less are bank certificates of deposit and short-term Treasury securities.

• Under the government's Treasury Direct program, you can buy Treasury bills, notes, and bonds directly, either by mail or at any regional branch of the Federal Reserve Bank.

• A good strategy with certificates of deposit is "laddering," buying certificates of different maturity and constantly rolling over the funds.

• If you have an investment window of three to 10 years, you could try short-term bond funds or "balanced" funds, which own both stocks and bonds.

• Tax-free municipal bonds are generally a good idea only for investors in the top tax bracket.

CONTACT

Bureau of the Public Debt
Division of Customer Services
Washington, DC 20239
202-874-4000
www.publicdebt.treas.gov

three-year, five-year, and 10-year Treasurys are called notes, and 30-year Treasurys are called bonds. There's one other significant difference. T-bills are sold at a discount from their stated value. So, just as with a savings bond, you pay less for the T-bill than its face value. A $10,000 six-month T-bill might cost $9,700. The difference between what you pay and the face value is the "interest."

If you can't meet the minimum deposits for the Treasury Direct program, or you simply prefer bank certificates of deposit, you'll get the best return by "laddering" your savings. If you're investing $5,000, use $1,000 to buy a one-year certificate of deposit (CD), $1,000 for a two-year CD, $1,000 for a three-year CD, $1,000 for a four-year CD, and $1,000 for a five-year CD. When the one-year CD matures, use the $1,000 to buy a five-year CD, and do the same the next year when the two-year CD matures. If you continue this process, each of the CDs will be for five years, giving you the best interest rate on your money. But instead of having all $5,000 locked up for five years, you'll have access to one-fifth of your money each year.

Investment decisions are more difficult if you want to put money aside for a moderate period of time — three years to 10 years. Experts traditionally have advised "safe" stock and bond investments for this investment window. But you can get burned even with these investments. Many people who invested in short-term bond funds, for example, suffered dramatic losses a few years ago when their value dropped unexpectedly. People who tried short-term bond funds for a 4 percent yield, instead of 2 percent in an interest checking account, were stunned when they lost 6 percent of their money. That was unusual, but it can happen.

More often, people with an investment window of three to 10 years will do well with short-term bond funds or "balanced" funds, which own both stocks and bonds. But you still have more risk than with a long-term investment horizon.

I see a lot of advertisements for tax-free municipal bonds, but I'm not at all sold on them for most taxpayers. A lot of people buy municipal bonds because they hate to pay the government taxes. It's fine to feel that way, but disliking taxes shouldn't be the basis for an investment decision. If you're in the 15 or 28 percent tax bracket, you may be better off with a taxable investment than with a tax-free investment. You get a lower yield on a tax-free municipal bond than with a taxable corporate bond, and the tax advantage often isn't sufficient to make up the difference. Tax-free municipal bonds are a good choice if you're in the top tax bracket and want an investment that produces a steady, current income. But the top tax bracket includes less than 2 percent of all taxpayers.

If you're 60 to 70 years old, there are several factors to consider when making investments. You have a short investment window, because you might need access to your money in less than 10 years. You also want your investments to generate income. But you need growth, too, because there's a good chance you could live another 20 years.

The solution is to invest a portion of your money to generate income, through high-dividend stock or bond funds, and a portion with an eye toward the future. In *The Handbook for No-Load Mutual Funds,* mutual funds expert Sheldon Jacobs suggests that even someone in retirement should have 60 percent of his investment portfolio in stocks (and 40 percent in bonds). You might find that too aggressive for your taste.

Jacobs suggests a retirement portfolio with 35 percent in a variety of stock funds, 25 percent in internationally oriented stock funds, and the remaining 40 percent in bond funds.

For investors within 10 years of retirement, Jacobs suggests a more aggressive approach: 50 percent in stock funds, 25 percent in international stocks, and 25 percent in bonds. And in a younger person's "wealth-builder" portfolio, he suggests 65 percent in stock funds, 30 percent in international stocks, and 5 percent in aggressive growth stock funds.

STOCKBROKERS AND OTHER INVESTMENTS

The Internet has eliminated the need for you to buy or sell stock through a full-commission stockbroker.

If you want to buy stock, you can buy direct, from the first share, from hundreds of companies. There are several Web sites to check out for stock buying, including www.netstockdirect.com and www.sdinews.org.

You can also use technology to sell stocks you own, or buy through a discount broker. Alternatives to a full-commission broker include a discount broker, a discount broker using electronic trading, or a pure electronic trading firm. Discount brokers such as Charles Schwab, Fidelity, and Waterhouse have offices around the country, so you can do transactions at the office. You can also perform transactions electronically. Discount brokers cost more than all-electronic brokers, but you have the advantage of dealing face-to-face with people if you want or need to do that.

A typical trade with a full-commission stockbroker might cost $200. By contrast, trades with an all-electronic firm range from just $7.95 to $28.95, no matter how many shares you trade. You just send the company a check and set up a money market account, or send the company your stock certificates.

In the online world, you have to be sure you're dealing with reputable people. Make sure electronic trading firms are members of the National Association of Securities Dealers (NASD) and the Security Investor Protection Corporation (SIPC), which means they have standard industry coverage in case they go out of business. Don't take their word for it. Call the national NASD office or the NASD office in your city to verify that the company is a member.

If you make a trade electronically and the transaction isn't carried out, file a complaint immediately with the brokerage's compliance officer and with the NASD. However, that's probably not going to happen. Both the discount brokers and electronic brokers know they have to service the customer to stay in business. I have never had a complaint from anybody using an electronic broker, and I get a lot of complaints about full-commission brokers.

If you don't have Internet access, you can also buy and sell stocks through a discount broker by using a touch-tone telephone. You get a discount on trading by doing that.

Full-Commission Brokers

Buying shares of stock in a single company is a risky investment, and it's riskier still if you deal with a stockbroker.

Stockbrokers may seem like unbiased investment advisers. In truth, they are commissioned salespeople, whose job is to get you to buy and sell stocks, because these trades generate commissions for the broker and for the brokerage firm. There is an inherent conflict of interest between the investment products that would be most suitable for you and the ones that generate big commissions for the brokers.

If you choose to do business with a full-service broker, make certain to state your investment objectives very clearly on the brokerage agreement you will be asked to sign. If you're a conservative investor who does not like risk, state it. If you like a moderate amount of risk, state that. And if you have no fear of risk, indicate that you're willing to try risky investments. If you fail to state what level of risk you're willing to take, you can get burned later.

If you ever notice an unusually high level of trading activity in your account, you must act immediately. This rip-off, called churning, is done to generate commissions from unnecessary trades. If trades are made that you have not authorized, or if the broker is doing anything else you don't like, rush a letter to the stockbroker stating that the activity in your account is unauthorized by you and all trading activity should stop immediately. Have someone at the brokerage sign to acknowledge receipt of the letter. Then send a letter to the brokerage house demanding an immediate meeting with the branch manager. Document every phone call that takes place with the broker if you feel the broker has violated your trust. Finally, if you feel you have been cheated because of the churning, immediately send a certified letter to the brokerage house stating that your account has been churned and that you want all money returned to you, including all commissions unfairly earned and any losses suffered on unsuitable investments.

When you sign your agreement with the stockbroker, it probably will contain a clause saying you will not sue the brokerage firm and you agree instead to arbitration to resolve any disputes. Make sure you cross that phrase out, put your initials by it, and insert the following sentence: "I reserve the right to sue XYZ brokerage in the event that I have a dispute with the firm." That's very important.

Complaints against brokerages are staggering, and victims almost never get their money back. Bob Brennan of First Jersey Securities is alleged to have stolen $70 million in clients' money. He filed for bankruptcy and is alleged to have moved the money to Gibraltar, on the coast of Spain.

The problem is that stock brokerages are really just sales organizations, not investment houses. The branch manager is judged by how much volume he pushes through his office. Each broker is judged by how much commission he drives through. At sales meetings, new investment products are introduced and the manager tells the brokers to sell these products hard because extra commission is being paid on them. The brokers then get on the phone and work their accounts, telling clients why this or that product is such a great deal and will make a fortune for the client.

The moral is, be careful when you're investing money. Don't buy securities from someone who isn't registered with both the National Association of Securities Dealers and the regulating authority in your state.

I've had a number of experiences, both good and bad, with investments. I invested in a video rental concession in a major supermarket and lost all my money when the general manager embezzled from the investors and skipped town. I also was involved in an experimental car company in which I lost my investment.

I've been involved in other ventures that were very successful. I invested in a commuter airline that went from being privately held to publicly traded. I've done quite well as one of the original investors in a community bank. And I've done extremely well buying troubled real estate, including foreclosures, relocations, and even estates.

Here are a few of the things I've learned:

• Don't invest in businesses you don't know anything about.
• Don't buy individual stocks unless you just think it's fun to do or you widely diversify your holdings. Placing your money in just a few companies can be extremely risky.
• If you're going to take a major stake in a business, don't do so without having some voice in how that business is operated.

My most important advice on investments is the simplest: if you do not understand an investment, do not buy it. Just because a friend, a relative, or an investment counselor tells you to invest in something, don't do it unless you fully understand the investment. People violate this investment rule often, even though it makes the most basic sense. Then they're shocked when their money disappears. People get seduced by risky, trendy, and confusing investments, such as oil and gas limited partnerships, wireless communication limited partnerships, futures, and commodities trading. Don't rely on promotional literature for such investments. Investigate before you buy.

The most important time to be conservative with your money is when you win the lottery or receive an inheritance or a large settlement from a lawsuit or claim. People who are lucky enough to come into large sums of money have a tendency to gamble with it. That's just what you shouldn't do. The best approach is to be as conservative as possible. If you receive a large amount of cash, you shouldn't increase your spending or change your lifestyle dramatically, or that money will soon disappear. If others know about your windfall, everybody's going to be at your door trying to sell you the greatest new business venture, the greatest new investment, or a resort property you don't need. So batten down the hatches. This is the one time when it's okay to lock the money in the bank and let it earn the market rate of interest.

One fellow I met seemed determined to give away a large amount of cash. He had just won the lottery and came to talk to me at a trade show about the three-wheel car company I was involved with. He told me he wanted to invest in the business because he believed it was producing the fuel-efficient car of the future. Here I was, one of the owners of the company, and we needed money. But although I would have loved to have had his money in the company, I told him it was a risky venture and that he should rethink his plans. He didn't appreciate the advice, but it was the best advice I could have given him. I've long wondered what ever happened to that man and whether he blew all his money.

The reverse sometimes happens, but not often. I've heard of people who invested their winnings in a business and wound up with 10 times the original sum. But for every entrepreneur who successfully invests his or her new money in a start-up company, there are probably 100 who fail and wind up with nothing.

401(K) PAYOUTS

If you quit a job or are fired, you may have to decide what to do about the money in your 401(k) retirement plan. Once upon a time, you would get a check from your company and have 60 days to put the money into an Individual Retirement Account, or another company's 401(k) plan, or face severe tax penalties. But so many people spent the money that the government changed the rules. Now if you take a pay-out check from your employer, 20 percent of your 401(k) money will be withheld to cover your potential tax liability. With 20 percent withheld, it's very difficult to put the full amount into an IRA.

Let's say you've had $10,000 in a 401(k) plan. You have 60 days to roll over the full $10,000 into another retirement plan. Because $2,000 of your $10,000 was withheld by the government, you have to redeposit not just the $8,000 you received but write a check for $2,000 to make up the balance. If you don't, the $2,000 you haven't rolled over will be considered a withdrawal and will be subject to a 10 percent early-withdrawal penalty ($200 of the $2,000) plus normal federal and state income tax. The withdrawal penalty doesn't apply if you are 59 1/2 or older.

If you don't roll over any of the 401(k) payout into a retirement plan, then all $10,000 is subject to tax and the early-withdrawal penalty. For most of us, that means $4,000 to $5,000 of the $10,000 would be eaten up.

One way to avoid any of these complications is to do a trustee-to-trustee transfer of your money. If you leave your job, instruct your former employer to send the retirement money directly to an IRA account at a particular mutual fund house or to any other financial institution that manages IRAs. Or if your new employer has a 401(k) plan, have the money deposited directly into your new account. If you follow this procedure, no money is withheld, no taxes are due, and your money continues to grow until your retirement.

Sometimes people are tempted to spend their 401(k) payouts after being fired from a job or suffering other financial setbacks. They worry about how they're going to pay the rent, buy food, and take care of their family. They spend the retirement money and then end up with a huge tax bill equal to 40 to 50 percent of the total payout. Sometimes people find a job in

CONTACT

National Association of Securities Dealers
   (investments)
Disciplinary history: 1-800-289-9999
Licensing information: 301-590-6500
www.nasd.com

INTERNET

www.investorama.com (stocks, general)
www.netstockdirect.com (allows you to buy stocks
   direct from companies)
www.sdinews.org (allows you to buy stocks direct
from companies)

three or four months and decide they don't need to spend the money. But they're still stuck with the tax bill if they've taken their money out of the tax-sheltered environment and allowed 60 or more days to pass before rolling it over.

Here's what you should do if you're afraid you're going to need the money. Transfer the money directly from your employer's 401(k) plan into an IRA. Make sure the IRA account is totally liquid — that is, money can be withdrawn from it at any time. If you use a mutual fund account, choose a money market mutual fund. Then, if you find you must have some of your IRA money to live on, pull out what you need and leave the rest in the plan. If you do it that way, only the portion you've withdrawn will be subject to tax.

Here's another trick. If you lose your job late in the year and expect to have a lengthy period of unemployment, try to leave your money in an IRA until at least January 2. There are two advantages to doing this. First, your tax rate will be much lower if you don't earn much that year, so pulling your retirement money won't cost you as much in taxes. Second, the tax won't be due until the following April 15, almost 16 months after you withdrew the money. So you'll have some time to get back on your feet. Make every effort not to spend more than half your retirement money if at all possible. That way, you'll always have the other half to cover you in case you end up with a huge tax bill. Someone I know was unemployed and spent all her retirement money during her unemployment. She ended up having to borrow money to pay the IRS.

When you roll retirement money into an IRA, I recommend you do it using a procedure I outlined earlier called dollar-cost averaging. First, deposit the money into a money market account in the IRA. Then, with all the money safely under the IRA umbrella, divide it into roughly equal amounts and transfer portions of it over a 12- or 18-month period from your money market account into stock mutual funds. If you have $12,000 to invest, you transfer $1,000 on the same day each month from the money market account into the stock mutual funds, or $667 a month for 18 months. That way, you're protected from the sudden ups and downs of the market.

I got a pension fund distribution once and deposited all the money with the Charles Schwab discount brokerage house, which allows customers to purchase certain no-sales-commission mutual funds. Schwab's plan is called the Mutual Fund OneSource. Customers buy without any sales cost, just as if they were buying directly from the mutual fund house. But they have the convenience of dealing with a brokerage firm.

I transferred my money into Schwab's money market fund and periodically buy into nine different mutual funds. My plan was set up so that I made an initial investment in each of the nine funds and put the rest in the money market fund. Each month for 18 months, a portion of my money is transferred into the nine funds. The minimum amounts I invest are very low, but there are some perks for investing a larger sum. Under Schwab's plan — and these rules are subject to change — if you transfer $10,000 from a 401(k) plan or an IRA, you pay no IRA custodial fees for life. And with the Mutual Fund OneSource, I can keep my account with one institution but buy mutual funds from a number of different mutual fund families.

Another strategy is to do a direct transfer of your retirement money and instantaneously buy the same holdings you had in the company-sponsored plan. You don't even have to worry about dollar-cost averaging because you've already done that by making payments into the company's mutual fund out of every paycheck.

One word of caution: if you transfer a 401(k) payout into an IRA, you might want to keep it separate from any previous or future IRAs you may have. If you keep the 401(k) money separate, you will be permitted to move it into another company's 401(k) plan later. If you mix funds, you lose that option.

I've heard horror stories from people who've been waiting for years to get their 401(k) payouts. There are no rules requiring the employer to distribute the money within a certain number of months. Each plan has its own rules, listed under the distributions section of the summary plan and description. You can request a copy of the plan from your former employer or go to the employer's office and read it.

When I sold my travel agencies, the buyers wanted to continue contributing to the retirement plan. Then they decided they wanted to liquidate it. Incredibly, the process of handling the paperwork and coordinating among the new owners, myself, and the insurance company took 4 1/2 years. People were inconvenienced, but at least no one lost money because of the delay. The money remained in the retirement plan, and the holdings of the employees continued to grow.

Finally, many employers will continue to manage your retirement money for you even after you leave the company. If you don't want the hassle of investments, it may be smart to leave your 401(k) money in the care of your former employer.

TAXES AND INVESTING

People make a huge mistake when the primary reason they invest is for the tax benefits. You never know when such a decision will come back to bite you.

TIPS ON 401(k) PAYOUTS

• If you leave a company and take your retirement money, 20 percent will be withheld to cover potential federal taxes. But if you don't redeposit 100 percent of the money into an IRA account or another 401(k) plan within 60 days, you will lose nearly half of it to federal and state taxes.

• You can avoid withholding taxes if you do a trustee-to-trustee transfer of your money. If you leave your job, instruct your former employer to send the retirement money directly to an IRA account or to the 401(k) plan at your new employer.

• Don't spend your retirement money, or you'll end up with a huge tax bill. If you think you may need the money, put it in an IRA, then withdraw only what you need.

• Use dollar-cost averaging if you're going to put your money into a stock or bond mutual fund. Put the money into a money market IRA account, then transfer the money gradually into other funds over 12 or 18 months. This protects you from the ups and downs of the market.

• If you transfer a 401(k) payout into an IRA, keep it separate from any previous or future IRAs you may have. If you do, you'll be permitted to move your money later into another company's 401(k) plan.

In 1993, I bought a variable annuity, which was the smartest tax move I could make at the time. Then, in 1997, Congress changed the tax law, and the economic benefit of the variable annuity disappeared. What seemed like a smart move in 1993 became a stupid move four years later.

This was yet another lesson that the underlying investment should first be sound. If it has tax advantages, that's a bonus. Making an investment decision solely for tax reasons leaves you exposed to loss.

Here's another example. Many banks encourage people to borrow against their house, through a home equity loan, for a vacation, a boat, or a car. Many people consider this a smart loan, because you can deduct the interest paid on the loan from your income tax. On consumer loans, there is no interest deduction anymore.

This is another tax decision that appears to be smart but in most cases is dumb. Your house should be treated as security. If you use it as a piece of collateral for a loan and you're unable to pay back the loan, you don't lose the boat or the memories of the vacation you took. You lose your house. To put your house at risk because of a tax advantage is an unwise decision. It's an even worse decision if you're borrowing against your house for something that retains no value, like a vacation. The only reason to borrow against your house is to increase the worth of the house, for example, to add a bathroom or renovate your kitchen.

The purchase of a home is another instance of an investment for which the tax advantages are frequently overstated. Home ownership is part of the American dream and a measure of our success. But from a financial standpoint, buying a house is not always the smartest decision. The standard deduction is so large now that the benefit of itemizing deductions on your tax return — the main financial benefit of home ownership — has been significantly reduced.

Let's take the example of a family that earns $60,000 a year and owns a $120,000 house. Say they put $10,000 down and borrowed $110,000 on a 30-year, 7.25 percent fixed-rate mortgage. By itemizing their deductions, the family would owe about $6,388 in federal income tax. If the family took the standard deduction, it would pay $7,907 in federal taxes. So the federal income tax savings from buying the house, for this family, is just $1,519 annually. There would be additional savings on state income taxes. But that's not a huge amount of money compared with the cost of the house.

Congress has changed the law to help you when you sell a house. Before the change, you had to put the proceeds from a home sale into your next house, or pay tax on the increase in the price of your house since the day you bought it. Now you can sell your house and the proceeds are tax-free, up to a ceiling of $250,000 for an individual and $500,000 for a couple. So if you paid $80,000 for a house and sell it years later for $150,000, the money you earn from the sale will not be taxed. Instead of being forced to put all the money into a larger, more expensive home, you can use some as a down payment on your next house — a smaller house if you prefer — and invest the rest however you choose.

The new tax treatment also makes a house a good way to build savings for the future, if you have trouble saving through other vehicles. But as I've warned, tax laws are subject to change.

Sometimes, people have a sufficient sum of money to pay cash for a car or even a home. I've had calls from people who've received an inheritance and wonder whether they should use it to buy a home without taking out a mortgage. My best advice is, go over the numbers with your accountant to see if you'd be helping yourself by paying cash for the house instead of putting the money into some other investment.

The interest on a car loan is no longer tax-deductible, so unless you love paying interest, buying a car with cash is a great idea if you can afford it. My attitude is, we'd be a lot better off if people still bought cars for transportation, the way we did 30 years ago. Too many people today buy cars as personal statements. If you can pay cash for a decent used car and therefore don't have to make a monthly car payment, you can do really well. Take the amount you would have used for the monthly payment, stash it in a piggy bank, and use it to pay cash for the next car you want to buy.

One of the most troubling tax decisions people make when April 15 rolls around is not filing their tax return because they don't have the money. If you can't pay, you should file anyway and attach an explanation. You're treated much differently if you fail to file than if you file but can't afford to pay. Those who don't file can face potential criminal charges.

If you do file and can't pay, you should enter into negotiations with the IRS and your state to set up a payment plan. Generally, they will be reluctant partners in this process, so you need to provide a complete explanation for why the plan is justified. You will have to give a lot of information about your finances, but this is far preferable to burying your head in the sand.

Once people don't file one year, they become afraid and don't file in subsequent years. If you find

TIPS ON TAXES AND INVESTING

- In choosing an investment, be sure to choose one that is sound. If it has tax advantages, that's a bonus.

- Don't take out home equity loans. If you use your house as collateral for a loan and you're unable to pay back the loan, you lose your house.

- From a financial standpoint, buying a house is not always the smartest decision. The standard deduction is so large that the benefit of itemizing deductions on your tax return — the main financial benefit of home ownership — has been largely negated.

- You no longer have to reinvest the proceeds from a home sale into a new house, so a house has become a good, tax-advantaged way to save money.

- If you can't pay your income taxes on April 15, file your tax return anyway and attach an explanation.

- If you have problems with the IRS, try the IRS problem-resolution office. If that doesn't work, call or write your congressman or U.S. senator's constituent service office for help.

CONTACT

IRS Problem Resolution National Office
Taxpayer Ombudsman's Office
1111 Constitution Avenue NW
Room 3017-C:TA
Washington, DC 20224
1-202-622-6100

yourself in this situation, you can go to the IRS and turn yourself in. The IRS will help you recreate your tax return for the years you didn't file. Surprisingly, in many cases people fail to file when they are due a refund. So you may not be facing the financial albatross you suspect, and there is a tremendous feeling of relief when you do settle up.

Of course you may get some other feelings from dealing with the IRS. The agency has a reputation for being uncaring and uncooperative, and many people believe that reputation is well deserved. For this reason, Congress forced the IRS to set up a problem-resolution program. Congressional constituent service offices had become de facto problem-resolution centers. If someone had a problem with the IRS, he'd call his congressman, and his or her staff would work to resolve it. Congress got tired of dealing with so many IRS problems and forced the IRS to set up this program to provide better service to the public. The problem-resolution office is supposed to improve communication and find solutions.

If the problem-resolution program doesn't get you satisfactory results, call or write your congressman or U.S. senator's constituent service office for help. If you don't know the name of your representative in Congress, call another one and a staffer will tell you how to reach him or her. Or call one of your U.S. senators.

CREDIT CARDS

As people have carried more and more credit cards, many have dug themselves ever-deeper financial holes. It's incredible that, even in a booming economy, we keep setting new records for bankruptcy filings. Currently, more than a million consumers file for bankruptcy each year.

I look at debt as a disease and credit cards as one of the easiest ways to get sick. Nobody ever got

wealthy borrowing money for gifts, clothes, dinners out, entertainment, or travel. When you purchase lifestyle with credit, you end up with huge obligations and no tangible assets. The meal is eaten, the trip is taken, and most of the clothes you bought end up sitting in your closet.

Credit cards are seductive. When you first get one, it seems to be a new source of wealth. But that wealth really is an illusion, because misusing a credit card actually lowers your standard of living over time.

It's so heartening to hear from people who have been fortunate enough to emerge from overwhelming debt and are determined not to make the same mistake again. A few years ago, I met a fellow at a convenience store who told me a remarkable story. Two years earlier, when he started listening to my show, he had $26,000 in credit card debt and he hated to answer his telephone. In those two years, he completely changed his lifestyle, wiped out all his credit card debt, and bought his own home. That made me feel great. In two years, someone who was drowning in debt and whose life was out of control wiped out the debt and reclaimed his life.

Credit cards are okay if you use them for safety or convenience. In high-crime cities, it's good to carry a credit card rather than cash because, if your card is lost or stolen, the maximum cost to you is $50. Having been a victim of crime, I almost always use credit cards and carry only a minimum of cash. But I use credit cards only as an alternate method of payment, and I pay the bill in full each month.

Two-thirds of all credit card holders use their cards the wrong way. They purchase merchandise with their cards and then carry a balance, financing this new debt at extremely high rates of interest. Paying that interest is what siphons away your money. If you have $1,000 in a bank in a savings account earning 3 percent and you are

TIPS ON CREDIT CARDS

• Debt is a disease, and credit cards are one of the easiest ways to get sick. Nobody ever got wealthy borrowing money for gifts, clothes, dinners out, entertainment, or travel.

• Credit cards are okay if you use them for safety or convenience.

• Two-thirds of all credit card holders use them incorrectly. They buy things with money they don't have and finance this new debt at extremely high rates of interest.

• If you don't carry a balance, get a card with no annual fee and a 25-day grace period between the day of a purchase and the day the interest meter starts running.

• If you frequently carry a balance, get a card with a low interest rate. The annual fee matters very little.

• Don't carry more than two or three credit cards. They're unnecessary and can cost you up to $50 per card if they're lost or stolen.

CONTACT

Ram Research
Card Trak
460 West Patrick Street
P.O. Box 1700
Frederick, MD 21702
1-800-344-7714
www.cardtrak.com

(For a comprehensive guide to low-interest credit cards, no-fee credit cards, and secured credit cards)

Some experts say you should pay for everything with cash. But as long as you track what you buy, how you pay doesn't matter. If you feel your spending is out of control, take a little notebook along with you and record every expenditure you make for two weeks. Then put a code by each item. Put an "A" next to purchases you absolutely had to make. Put a "C" down when you're not really sure if you had to have the item, and put an "F" by anything that you truly didn't need. The reason I use those codes is because people can relate them to school grades. You get an "A" for spending money correctly and an "F" for spending money incorrectly.

If you can discipline yourself to use credit cards only for convenience, choosing a card is easy. All you need to do is get a card with no annual fee and a 25-day grace period between the day of the purchase and the day the interest meter starts running. That way, you can have the convenience of credit cards with no cost at all.

If you frequently carry a balance, the annual fee matters very little. Far more important is the interest rate, which will end up costing you a lot more money on a high balance than any annual fee. Certain banks now specialize in credit cards with variable interest rates. These cards tend to have high annual fees and the rates are not fixed, but the interest rates tend to be lower than those for most cards. If you can't avoid carrying a credit card balance, at least pay a lower rate to finance it.

If you must have a variable rate card, avoid those that attract you with an ultra-low teaser rate. Pick one that calculates the interest rate using a widely followed rate, such as the prime lending rate. You'll know in advance how the rate is figured. I received a mailer recently from a credit card company offering a very low interest rate — 6.9 percent. But that rate was applicable for only 90 days. After that, the rate jumped to 17.5 percent. So that card had no advantage.

paying 17.5 percent interest on your $1,000 credit card balance, somebody's doing real well and it's not you.

One other point: if you pay in full some months and carry a balance during other months, avoid any card, such as the Discover Card, that has a "two-cycle" billing method. Using this technique, the lender adds the balance together for two months before computing interest and therefore severely punishes people who pay their bills in full some months but carry a balance other months. You're better off taking a card with a higher rate of interest than going with a card that uses the two-cycle method.

A lot of people still carry too many credit cards. It makes sense to carry a VISA and a MasterCard, but skip department store cards and gasoline credit cards. Department store cards have very high interest rates and are primarily tools to get people into the stores to spend money. These cards are really invitations to increase your debt.

Gasoline cards are similarly useless. Generally a business that takes a gasoline credit card will also take a VISA or MasterCard. Using a gasoline card or a department store card means there's an additional bill you have to pay, and if that card gets stolen, you're liable for the same $50 on it as on any other card. If your wallet is stolen and you have two credit cards in it, your maximum risk is $100. If you have seven cards, your maximum risk is $350.

You don't want to carry just one card because if the lending institution decides to lift your card for some reason, you are without credit. No two banks use the same credit standards, so you're better protected if you carry a VISA and a MasterCard, each from different institutions. I carry a VISA from my insurance company, a MasterCard from my credit union, and a Discover Card so I can use it at Costco, which doesn't take any other cards.

CREDIT PROBLEMS

If you misuse your credit cards, trouble is inevitable. Eventually, you'll be heavily in debt and just making minimum payments on your credit card bills. By paying the minimum, you never work off the balance. All you're doing is paying interest on the early debt you took on.

Some advisers say you can tell you're in credit trouble if your debt payments exceed a certain percentage of your take-home pay, but I don't think anybody ever figures out those ratios, except when applying for a mortgage. You know how you feel. You need help if you're afraid to answer the phone or open the mail, you have trouble sleeping at night, or you're eating too much or too little.

I've seen more people in credit trouble over the years not because they were making less money but because they were taking on more debt. Because couples have come to need both spouses' incomes, if either loses a job or gets sick, or they divorce, a money crisis may soon follow.

When you get into financial trouble, you need to create a pyramid of priorities. Your most important priority is to pay your mortgage or rent. Your next priority is to pay your car loan, and the third is to pay your utilities, which keep your house functioning. After that you pay your unsecured creditors — credit card and loan companies.

Ironically, the most ferocious and frequent phone calls you'll receive when you fall behind on your bills will be from credit card and small loan companies. Mortgage companies tend to react more slowly because their loans are secured by your home. Car loan people are a little quicker but not real quick, because their loan is secured by your automobile. Because of these calls, people in credit trouble often throw money at the wrong source. Paying your credit card bills should always come last.

You have strong rights under federal law to prevent collection agencies from harassing you, although the law does not apply to the creditors themselves. The Fair Debt Collection Practices

Act bars collectors from threatening to harm you, your reputation, or your property and from using profane language or falsely claiming to be an attorney or a government representative. The law also prohibits collectors from claiming that you will be arrested or imprisoned if you don't pay, and it prohibits late-night phone calls and repeated phone calls intended to harass you.

You can stop collection agencies from contacting you at home, at work, or at all by sending them a "drop dead" letter. You'll find a prewritten drop dead letter in the Workbook chapter of this book. It's a good idea to send it by certified mail, and don't forget to keep a copy. Once a collection agency receives it, the company can contact you only to acknowledge that it won't contact you again or to notify you that it is filing a lawsuit. Under the law, if a company continues to harass you, you can sue it for actual damages and punitive damages of up to $1,000. The law is enforced by the Federal Trade Commission.

Beware of companies that claim they'll help you get out of debt. A caller told me she was considering such a service. She was supposed to send a check each month to this company. The company would then subtract its fee — $15 a month plus $5 per credit card or loan — and distribute the rest to her creditors. The red flag was a line in the contract saying she wouldn't hold the company responsible if it didn't send the money to her creditors.

A legitimate consumer service is available to help you when you can't keep the wolves from your door. It's called Consumer Credit Counseling, and it's available in most areas. Consumer Credit Counseling is provided by a network of nonprofit organizations. They're funded, ironically, by the credit grantors for the purpose of offering people a method to honor their debts. Call the National Foundation for Consumer Credit Counseling to find a location near your home.

People who go to credit counseling generally fall into one of three categories. A third are so far in debt or have such little income that credit counselors cannot be of help to them. These are the people for whom bankruptcy is a real option. The next third are not in nearly as bad shape as they think they are and just need help in preparing a budget and setting new spending priorities. These folks are helped through counseling at little or no cost to them.

Consumer Credit Counseling Service is best known for the way it helps the third group of people, those whose debts are no longer manageable but who are able to repay them within three years, with some help. A repayment plan negotiated by Consumer Credit Counseling requires some give on both sides. It requires the consumer to cut spending or increase income through a part-time job or more work hours. It requires the department stores and other lenders to reduce the amount of money owed or create more favorable terms for repayment.

When you feel your financial situation is hopeless, Consumer Credit Counseling can give you an honorable way to meet your obligations. That's what most people want. The sudden power people feel when they regain control over their lives is wonderful. I remember one man who had just finished his repayment plan with Consumer Credit Counseling Service. He was near tears as he talked about the burden that had been lifted off him. That's the beauty of the process. It does not promote bankruptcy as an easy way out, like the seductive TV ads, but it enables people to make a fresh start with dignity and hard work.

For a while, I heard about credit grantors who refused to comply with the terms negotiated by Consumer Credit Counseling. Very few do that anymore, and those that do show themselves to be extremely foolish. If someone is right

TIPS *ON* CREDIT PROBLEMS

- By paying the minimum amount on your credit cards, you'll never work off the balance. All you're doing is paying interest on the early debt you took on.

- When you get into financial trouble, create a pyramid of priorities. Your most important priority is to pay your mortgage or rent. The next priority is to pay your car loan, and the third is to pay for your utilities, which keep your house functioning. After that you should pay your unsecured creditors — credit card and loan companies.

- If you need help, don't file for bankruptcy immediately. The best option is to contact Consumer Credit Counseling Service, which can help you work out a debt repayment plan.

- If you've had credit trouble and want to reestablish your credit, try a secured credit card, which lets you charge up to the amount you place on deposit with the lender.

CONTACT

Federal Trade Commission
Publications Division
Washington, DC 20580
202-326-2222
www.ftc.gov
(Ask for a copy of the brochure *Fair Debt Collection Practices Act*.)

National Foundation for Consumer Credit Counseling
8611 2nd Avenue
Suite 100
Silver Spring, MD 20910
301-589-5600
1-800-388-2227
www.nfcc.org

Ram Research
Card Trak
460 West Patrick Street
P.O. Box 1700
Frederick, MD 21702
1-800-344-7714
www.cardtrak.com

(For a comprehensive guide to low-interest credit cards, no-fee credit cards, and secured credit cards)

on the edge of being able to work out a successful repayment plan through Consumer Credit Counseling, and a shortsighted, mean-spirited credit grantor doesn't go along, it's going to push the debtor into bankruptcy court and then the credit grantor will probably get nothing.

At one time Citibank was completely uncooperative with Consumer Credit Counseling, but now it's on the team. When Citibank pressured customers too aggressively, more filed for bankruptcy. So it changed its approach.

Some people worry that going to credit counseling will hurt their credit rating. Most of these people already have flawed credit reports and credit counseling really has a neutral impact. Plus, once you've completed a repayment plan, Consumer Credit Counseling will help you obtain one mortgage loan, one car loan, and one credit card. So, rather than being a negative, credit counseling has a reward at the end — the establishment of a responsible level of credit with the service's assistance.

If you have had credit problems and are trying to reestablish credit, I suggest you get a secured credit card. You get a secured card by posting a deposit with the lender, say $500. Then you're able to charge up to the $500 you have on deposit. The money you have on deposit earns interest, and you have a credit card you can use like any other VISA or MasterCard holder. A lot of organizations offer secured cards with very unfavorable terms, and precious few offer secured cards at reasonable rates. The best ones tend to have moderate annual fees, $35 or less, no application fees, and grace periods from the purchase date until interest charges begin. To get a list of lenders that offer reasonable terms on secured cards, contact Ram Research, whose address and phone number are listed on page 27, or check its Web site (www.cardtrak.com).

Perhaps you haven't reached the point of going to Consumer Credit Counseling and your financial situation has begun to improve. Maybe you got a job or a raise. Start digging out of debt this way: First rank your unsecured debts by interest rate. Pay the monthly minimum on all credit cards and credit lines, except for the card with the highest interest rate. Throw every penny you can at that card each month until you've paid it off, then go to the second highest and extinguish that one. If you have six lines of credit, motivate yourself to cut it to five. That's much easier and more satisfying than trying to get rid of all of them at once. Try to set a realistic time period — within three years — to get rid of your debt.

CREDIT REPORTS

Your credit report may be one of the most important documents with your name on it. The information it contains can affect whether you qualify for a home mortgage, get a car loan, rent an apartment, or get hired for a new job. So a mistake on your credit report can lead to very big problems.

Getting a credit report corrected is one of the most difficult and frustrating chores consumers ever face. There are three major credit bureaus — Equifax, Experian, and Trans Union — and they don't share information. So even if you correct an error with one bureau, you will have to do the same with the other two. After a month-long battle to get an item removed from your Equifax credit report, Experian and Trans Union may still show you to be a deadbeat.

Fortunately, you now have greater clout to have mistakes on your credit report corrected. Because Congress has changed the Fair Credit Reporting Act, credit bureaus now must act within 30 days after you tell them about an error. If you have independent information proving that a debt listed on your credit report is not correct, the credit bureau must give as much weight to that as information provided by a credit grantor. Also, you now have the right to talk to a human being at the credit bureaus. One of the biggest frustrations people have had in dealing with the bureaus is having to talk to an automated system.

But perhaps the biggest change may be the power you have if a bank or credit grantor, or a credit bureau, fails to correct an error after you have properly notified it to do so. You can now sue — a huge change from the bad old days. Your suit depends on the amount of harm you've suffered. In most cases and in most states, you sue in small claims court. But if the harm is major and you're going to seek a great deal of money in damages, you'll need a lawyer.

One of the ways to determine damage is to calculate how the credit error has harmed your ability to get a loan. The way you are evaluated for credit has changed significantly. You used to be accepted if you had good credit and rejected if you had bad credit. Now you're given a letter grade based on your credit payment history. The worse you're graded, the higher the interest rate you'll be expected to pay for a loan, and the greater the down payment you'll be expected to pay. So a mistake on a credit report can result in costs that are easy to measure.

I get calls from people who have 10.5 percent mortgages because they've had a great deal of credit trouble in the past. Even though their credit isn't completely clear, they may be able to refinance their mortgage at 8.75 percent interest when the lowest rate in the market is 7.25 percent. The lower the score people get, the more fees will be involved in closing the loan, because people who have bad credit tend not to shop as much for a loan. They're happy they can get one at all, and they're not as worried about having to pay fees.

Credit card lenders have a technique called predictive analysis they use to determine whether you're likely to file for bankruptcy. They can send you a notice raising your interest rate, in one case I heard to as high as 34 percent, even if you haven't done anything wrong. They're just guessing that you will. The lenders are reacting to the increase in bankruptcies and the increasing tendency of people to file for bankruptcy even when they're not missing payments. A few years ago, people started to choose bankruptcy because they had too much debt to pay off, even if they were not behind on their payments.

One reason mistakes have been hard to fix in credit reports is the way information is supplied to the credit bureaus. Let's say a credit card company incorrectly says you're a deadbeat but you convince Equifax to correct the error. A month later, the credit card company may send a new report to the credit bureau with the error still on your credit record. If that happens, you have to ask the credit bureau to use something called "suppression technology," which will prevent an item from ever reappearing on your report once it's been cleared up.

I've had many callers tell me their credit report listed a loan they knew nothing about. Someone else borrowed the money and didn't pay it back, and somehow the default on the payment wound up on their credit report.

TIPS ON CREDIT REPORTS

• There are three major credit bureaus that issue credit reports to lenders — Equifax, Experian, and Trans Union — and they don't share information. So even if you correct an error on one credit report, you'll have to do the same on the other two.

• You have the right under federal law to challenge items on a credit report. The credit bureau then has 30 days to decide whether the item in question should be removed.

• If a credit bureau refuses to correct a mistake, you can sue it.

• Get copies of all three of your credit reports six months before you apply for a home loan. An error on a report can take months to clear up. If your time is ticking away on a home closing and you can't get approved for a loan, you're going to lose the house.

CONTACT

Equifax Information Service
P.O. Box 740123
Atlanta, GA 30374
770-375-2500 or 1-800-685-1111
www.equifax.com

Experian (formerly TRW)
P.O. Box 2350
Chatsworth, CA 91313
1-800-682-7654

Trans Union
P.O. Box 7000
North Olmstead, OH 44070
1-800-916-8800

I strongly recommend that you spend the money to get all three of your credit reports six months before you apply for a home loan. Federal law now sets an $8 limit on the amount you can be charged for a copy of your report. Some states allow you to get a copy for free.

I receive so many distressing phone calls from people who are trying to get approval for home loans and are stymied by credit report problems. I had a call from one fellow whose credit report was so messed up that he had to take two weeks off from work to straighten it out. He discovered, while refinancing his house, that someone he didn't know had used his Social Security number to obtain 10 credit cards. The crook had fraudulently racked up several thousand dollars in charges.

An error on your credit report can take months to clear up. If your time is ticking away on a home closing and you can't get approved for a loan, you're going to lose that house. With a car loan, time is less important. You should go into your bank or credit union and get preapproved for a car loan just before you're ready to buy. You'll know immediately if there is a problem. It's not as much of an earth-shattering crisis if you can't buy a new car. When you get knocked out of the housing market, it's traumatic.

One way to avoid potential disasters is to guard your Social Security number. Consider leaving your Social Security card at home, rather than carrying it in your wallet, in case your wallet is ever lost or stolen.

DIVORCE

People often get so caught up in the emotions of a divorce that they forget its financial implications. I think that's human nature. I can tell you from personal experience that a divorce is one of the most painful experiences you can go through.

Still, during this period when you are vulnerable emotionally, you are also vulnerable financially. You have to protect your financial interests

by terminating not just the marriage but all joint financial obligations.

If you have credit cards that are jointly owned, the accounts must be paid off and closed, and each party should obtain credit in his or her own name. This is essential so that neither spouse is responsible for the other's bills. Even though the divorce decree may say your ex-husband is supposed to pay the credit bills, sometimes he doesn't and the credit card companies come after you. I take calls about this all the time.

If the credit card accounts are not closed, you can be hurt in two big ways. First, even though you may have paid all your bills and maintained a great credit rating, your credit can be ruined and you can get knocked out of the credit market. That's trouble if you want to buy a home or a car.

Second, though you may not realize it, you are financially responsible for your former spouse's credit card debt, even if he or she gets the merchandise. That's because a credit card agreement, like any joint credit agreement, is legally superior to the divorce decree. The contractual obligation continues regardless of what the decree says. If you pay off and close those accounts, you have nothing to worry about. Otherwise, you have a time bomb waiting to explode, sometimes months or years later.

Your only recourse if your former spouse runs up debts and then reneges on the obligations is to call your divorce lawyer and file an action based on the divorce decree. But that doesn't change the fact that you owe the money to the credit grantor.

Another important asset to think about is your house. It doesn't matter if you sign over your rights to the house to your partner. You're at risk because of the obligation on the mortgage. Before reaching a final agreement on the divorce, you need to know whether the person keeping the house can qualify for a new mortgage on his or her own. If he or she cannot, the house should be sold so that neither party is responsible. If both of you remain on the loan, the one who moves out has no advantages and lots of disadvantages. You really have a problem if you can't sell the house.

If you're both listed on a car loan, the same problems can occur as with a house or credit cards. But there's a complication. If it's a five-year loan and you're early or midway through paying it off, the vehicle usually is worth less than the amount owed. If that's the case, you will need additional money to refinance the loan or need to sell the car and pay off the existing loan.

Lawyers hate when I say this, but I believe strongly that couples should try divorce mediation, rather than getting separate lawyers immediately, going into enemy camps, and duking it out. Divorce takes such tremendous emotional tolls on the individuals involved, and the legal process, being adversarial, only increases the hurt, distrust, and anger. Some municipalities now require that mediation be used in all civil cases, including divorce, before the parties may appear in court.

If children are involved and the parents are fighting about the divorce, both spouses have something to lose as the process goes forward. I know of one couple who wound up in a shoving match at a shopping center after the father made off with the couple's two-year-old son in front of their young daughter. That's a tragedy for the whole family.

Another couple I know of tried mediation and now share joint custody of their five-year-old daughter. She spends four days each week at Mom's house and three days at Dad's house, and everyone gets along very well. The parents live close to each other and in the same school district. Forget money for a minute and consider your relationship with your children and your children's future well-being. Mediation is a great tool to try during a divorce and creates much less hostility.

TIPS ON DIVORCE

- You have to protect your financial interests in a divorce by terminating not just the marriage but all joint financial obligations. That includes credit card accounts, mortgages, and jointly held loans. Refinance the loans or sell the house or car.

- If joint accounts are not closed, you are legally responsible if your ex-spouse doesn't pay, no matter what the divorce decree says. Your credit can be ruined, and you can get knocked out of the credit market.

- Consider divorce mediation, a less adversarial process than using lawyers, in which a mediator tries to get the two parties to reach a fair agreement. But be sure to have any mediation agreement reviewed by a lawyer.

- If your ex-spouse is months or more behind in child-support payments, consider using a collection agency. But don't pay more than one-third the amount due in collection agency fees.

CONTACT

Child Support Enforcement
370 L'enfant Promenade SW
4th Floor East
Washington, DC 20447
202-401-9373
www.acf.dhhs.gov/programs/cse

Divorce mediation is not the entire answer, however. A mediator merely tries to get the two parties together to reach an agreement they believe is fair. But before a mediation agreement is final, each party should have it reviewed by an attorney who specializes in family practice law. In the end, you need a lawyer's expertise to point out elements of the proposed agreement that may be unwise or unfair to you. If you skip this step, and I know of at least one person who did, you could get burned.

Child support is a major financial issue of divorce. It's almost a cliché now that the noncustodial parent doesn't pay child support. Lots of parents do pay. But collecting child support, either because of underpayment or nonpayment, has become a major national problem. Generally, it's the mother trying to collect child support from the father.

Many states have child-support recovery offices, but as a group they are abysmal failures, mostly because the caseloads are so enormous. They can be good sources of information, however. You can find out, for example, that the law allows you to collect back child support even after a child turns 18 and that you can go back to court during the child's lifetime and request an increase in support payments. But actually collecting the money can be next to impossible if the parent truly doesn't want to pay.

The difficulty in collecting child support has spawned a booming industry — child-support collection agencies. Some are traditional collection agencies that have gone into this as a sideline. Others do nothing but collect overdue child-support payments. For a mother who's dealing with a father who has never paid or has not paid for months or years, seeking help from one of these agencies is an excellent idea to consider. You will give up a portion of the child-support money in collection agency fees — a third is typical — but if you haven't been getting checks, every dollar you get is found money. If a collection agency wants more than one-third of the total due, you should probably look elsewhere.

Finally, there's the problem of what to do about income taxes. One spouse generally accepts responsibility in the divorce decree for income taxes that may result from audits of tax returns that were filed before the divorce. If your spouse is involved in a business, you may want to indemnify yourself in the decree from the business's tax responsibilities. But the IRS doesn't recognize such division of responsibility and may go after either spouse if more taxes are owed.

If the tax return hasn't been filed for the year prior to the divorce, you have the option of filing jointly or separately. You pay a higher rate if you file separately, but doing so can protect you from your spouse's tax liabilities for that year. After the divorce, of course, you are single and file separately.

WILLS

As important as it is to have a will, it's amazing how many people of all income levels don't have one. I think it's because people prefer to avoid the reality that they're going to die someday. They'd rather not think about their mortality.

The greatest favor you can do for your survivors is to stipulate, in your will, what you want to happen to your assets.

When you die without a will, most states write a will for you. In a legislated will, the state distributes your assets to your family based on its own formula. The thought of your money going to a relative you can't stand should be motivation enough for you to do a will. If not, think of the person to whom you would like to give most or all of your assets. He or she might not get the money because you haven't designated it in a will.

I remember one case involving a utility executive who had divorced and remarried, then died without writing a will. He left an estate worth $700,000. Because he had no will, the state divided the money equally among his two children and his second wife; each received about $225,00 after expenses. He might have wanted it split some other way, but without a will it was impossible to follow his wishes.

TIPS ON WILLS

- Creating a will is simpler than you think. In most states, you have to be at least 18 years old and of sound mind for a will to be legal.

- The will must be written, signed by you, and witnessed by two people who won't receive anything from your estate.

- You can draw up your own will, using a kit or a computer program, or have a lawyer prepare one. Do what's comfortable for you. But if you start doing your own will and become confused, stop and seek the advice of a lawyer.

- If you have lots of assets, especially more than $625,000, don't prepare a will yourself.

- A living trust is an alternative to a will that allows you to pass your assets immediately to your designee when you die. It's a complicated and expensive document to prepare, and few people need it.

Another case also illustrates the importance of having a will. A husband and wife with two small children were killed in a car accident, leaving insurance payments and other property worth $2 to $3 million. Because the couple had a will, a trust was set up to manage the inheritance, and custody of the children was decided according to the parents' wishes. Had there not been a will, the state would have appointed a guardian for each child's property. Court permission would have been needed for many financial decisions, a cumbersome process that would have produced legal expenses of several thousand dollars per year for perhaps 15 years.

Creating a will is simpler than you think. For a will to be legal in most states, you have to be at least 18 years old and of sound mind. The will must be written, signed by you, and witnessed by two people who won't receive anything from your estate. That's all you have to do. End of the mystery.

If you want to have a will done by a lawyer, that's fine. Lawyers' fees for doing a will vary widely, depending on the complications of your estate and how much the particular lawyer charges per hour. To write my most recent will, I used a computer program called WillMaker. There are four or five other programs for personal computers that make the process very easy. Mine took about 10 minutes to do. Then I had the will reviewed by my lawyer. It costs significantly less to have a lawyer review a will than to have a lawyer draw one up. Here's the kicker. My lawyer did not suggest one change in the will I drew up using the computer program.

A will kit from any good bookstore generally costs less than $20, and a computer program generally costs less than $50. A lawyer may charge as little as $150 or as much as several thousand dollars.

You should do whatever is comfortable for you; either draw up your own will, using a kit or program, or have a lawyer do it. But if you start doing your own will with a kit or a computer program and you reach a point where there's a question you don't understand, or there's a procedure or some language that doesn't make sense to you, stop right there and go to a lawyer. If you have substantial assets or there are children involved, it can be disastrous to accept language in a will that you don't understand, or to make decisions that you haven't fully thought out. Those are the two big variables with wills that you have to be really sure about.

If you have a lot of assets, especially more than $625,000, don't do a will yourself. It is critical, to avoid very high estate taxes, to plan your estate with a lawyer who specializes in wills, estates, and trusts. Most people laugh at the thought of having more than $625,000 in assets. But many times people forget the value of their life insurance, their home, and the money in their retirement plans. It can add up quickly.

The state processes your will after you die, and your assets are distributed through a procedure called probate. Probate usually is quick and routine, especially if the assets are less than $500,000 or $600,000. But in some states, probate can be inefficient, expensive, or corrupt; it can take months or years, and court costs can seriously erode the value of an estate.

Some assets pass directly to a spouse or child if they are jointly owned. In the case of a house, the deed must list one individual as owner and the other as "joint tenant with right of survivorship." If you merely list two people as co-owners, the deceased's 50 percent share of the house will pass to his or her heirs as specified by the will. It works the same way with a car.

For a bank account, generally joint ownership is all you need for the co-owner to have immediate access and ownership after the other dies. For stocks or mutual fund accounts, include "joint ownership with right of survivorship" on the papers. With life insurance, it doesn't even matter what's specified in your will, because the insurance contract is a superior document. The payment automatically goes to the designated beneficiary.

There are lots of unscrupulous folks out there who will try to convince you that a will is terrible and a living trust is a godsend. In fact, less than 1 percent of the public needs one. A living trust is a method of avoiding probate and having your assets pass immediately to your designee outside the probate process. A living trust is appropriate only in very rare circumstances, such as when someone owns property in several states and wants to avoid multistate probate. For example, you might own a home in Michigan and a retirement home in Florida.

A living trust also can be appropriate if a person is in failing health and wants to turn over effective control while he or she is still able to do so. There generally is no tax advantage to having a living trust, because the same inheritance taxes apply. If you do have a specialized situation that calls for having a living trust, have a lawyer prepare it. A living trust is a very complicated document and, consequently, the cost will be many times more than the cost to draw up a will.

There's another document you may have heard referred to as a living will. It's a form you fill out that lets hospitals know whether they should use extraordinary measures to keep you alive if you are critically ill. The Supreme Court has ruled that hospitals must accept these written medical care instructions.

You should complete a living will so your family won't have to agonize over your treatment. Ask your doctor or hospital for a living will, also known as a durable power of attorney for health care, or an advance directive. Or check with the American Association of Retired Persons (www.aarp.org).

FUNERALS

Another topic people avoid thinking about is the arrangements for their funeral. Most of us die keeping those thoughts to ourselves and leave our grieving loved ones to decide if there will be a funeral or a memorial service, a burial or a cremation. At their weakest moments, when they are often overcome by sadness or guilt, these loved ones have to make some very difficult and personal decisions.

I've been on the funeral home sales tour, and it's an awful experience. The funeral director, usually someone who is very pleasant and low-key, often starts by taking you through the casket area. The caskets are arranged from the most expensive, in the front and very well displayed, to the least expensive, in the far end of the room, gathering dust. In many funeral homes, the least expensive caskets aren't even on display.

In the funeral home environment, you're encouraged, gently but persuasively, to spend more money than you would have anticipated, at a time when you're most vulnerable. Typically, you have absolutely no chance to comparison-shop, because you've already designated the funeral home and had the body of the deceased transported there. You are a captive in negotiations over costs and services.

Do yourself and your family a favor by making funeral decisions yourself, ahead of time. The most effective way to hold down the costs and improve the chances that your wishes will be carried out is to join the Memorial Society in your area. You pay a one-time fee to join and can list your wishes and get negotiated prices for caskets and burial or other services. You set the budget and pick what you want. When you die, your family goes to the funeral home you designated and

someone there pulls the file specifying the arrangements you made and the preset costs. Funeral homes are willing to give great prices to Memorial Society members in exchange for the high volume of business generated through the relationship.

I don't recommend that people prepay for a funeral or a cemetery plot. We've become such a transient population that it's foolish to prepay for arrangements in a particular city. Circumstances could change and you might move to a different city. Not only that, but what happens if the funeral home goes out of business? Your money could go down the tubes. By joining the Memorial Society, you make all the necessary decisions, and prices are set, but funeral expenses are not paid until you die.

TIPS ON FUNERALS

• Most people die without making funeral arrangements, forcing their grieving families to make tough decisions and overpay on funeral costs. Join your local Memorial Society and make those decisions yourself, ahead of time.

• Don't prepay for a funeral. You could move to another city or the funeral home could go out of business.

CONTACT

Funeral and Memorial Societies of America
6900 Lost Lake Road
Egg Harbor, WI 54209
414-868-2729
www.funerals.org/famsa/

(For a directory of memorial societies in your area)

CHOOSING A LAWYER OR AN ACCOUNTANT

I get very upset when people choose a lawyer based on a television ad. If you do that, there's no way to be sure you're getting a quality person. I don't recommend taking a referral from the bar association, either.

If you've ever used a lawyer for any reason and it was someone you liked and respected, ask him or her to suggest someone with the expertise you need. Don't take the referral on blind faith, but it's a good first step. Another way to find a lawyer is to ask friends, relatives, and colleagues to suggest someone they have used and liked.

In all cases, interview the attorney as if you were interviewing someone to fill a job. Make it clear that the interview is to help you decide whether you are going to hire him or her. Most attorneys will give you 30 minutes of their time for this purpose at no charge. It's well worth the effort, because it's far easier to hire a lawyer than to fire one.

Be particularly cautious if you're hiring someone to represent you on a contingency basis. Typically in these cases, the lawyer will receive one-third of any settlement you receive but won't charge you an hourly rate along the way. It seems like a no-lose situation. But if you fire a contingency lawyer, he or she can bill you for the hours spent working on your case. That means that if a lawyer puts in 20 hours on your case and charges $200 per hour, he or she could send you a bill for $4,000 and you would have to pay it.

If you fire one contingency lawyer and hire another, make sure you obtain a signed release from the first lawyer relinquishing any claims to the final settlement. As hard to believe as this may be, the first lawyer could claim he or she is owed one-third of the settlement. You might have to pay a third to the first lawyer and a third to the

second lawyer because you didn't get a release from the first lawyer.

Even if you're paying a lawyer on an hourly basis, you need to be careful whom you hire. The law has become extremely specialized, and no single lawyer can handle every job for you. You don't want to pay for a lawyer's on-the-job training. If you need specialized legal help, you want a lawyer who knows that particular field. If you are getting a divorce, you need a divorce lawyer. You don't want a general practice attorney who once handled a divorce for a cousin. If you need a will, you should choose a lawyer who specializes in wills, estates, and trusts. If you're going to sue somebody, you want a litigator. And if you're doing a real estate transaction, you need a real estate lawyer.

Chances are that nothing awful will happen if you pick the wrong lawyer to handle your case. It might cost you more in legal time because the lawyer's lack of knowledge means he or she will need more hours to get the job done. On the other hand, the lawyer could botch the case.

I dealt with one case in which the lawyer messed up badly enough that my caller could have lost $5,000. When my caller originally sold her house, the buyer didn't have all the money needed to buy it. So the buyer entered into a second mortgage agreement with the seller for $5,000. That meant that if the buyer didn't pay back the $5,000, the seller had the right to get her house back. But the lawyer forgot to record the second mortgage at the courthouse, so when the buyer resold the house, he never repaid the $5,000 to the original seller. When the seller called me, I pointed out the error to the lawyer and, to his credit, he paid the $5,000 debt out of his own pocket.

Another lawyer spent 11 months in prison after embezzling money from clients. The clients had come to him to sue Audi over the Audi 5000,

TIPS ON CHOOSING A LAWYER OR AN ACCOUNTANT

• Don't pick a lawyer based on a television ad or a referral from the bar association. There's no way to be sure you're getting a quality person.

• If you've ever used a lawyer and it was someone you liked and respected, call him or her and ask for a referral to someone with the expertise you need.

• Always interview a prospective attorney as if you were interviewing someone to fill a job. Most attorneys will give you 30 minutes at no charge for this purpose.

• Be particularly cautious when you're hiring someone to represent you on a contingency basis.

• In choosing a CPA, individuals or small businesses often do best with small to medium-sized local practices.

• If you interview CPAs who tell you how clever they are and how they are going to beat the IRS, hire someone else.

CONTACT

American Bar Association
www.abanet.org

American Society of CPAs
1211 Sixth Avenue
New York, NY 10036
1-800-862-4272
www.aicpa.org

the car that was alleged to accelerate unexpectedly in some circumstances. The lawyer took up-front fees from victims and settlement money from Audi, and pocketed all of it. One couple I talked to was referred to him by a lawyer the couple found in the telephone book. The crooked lawyer took a $2,000 retainer from the couple and pocketed $7,000 in settlement money without the couple's knowledge. He apparently bilked hundreds of people of millions of dollars.

More commonly, disputes occur over bills. If you are concerned, ask the lawyer for more information. Law firms today are being asked to justify every penny that's billed, and you have a right as a customer to demand a full accounting. If that doesn't resolve the problem, call the American Bar Association and ask about fee arbitration.

If your relationship with your lawyer turns adversarial, which is most unfortunate, you need to document everything in writing, just as he or she would do to you.

I get so many complaints about lawyers and only a few about accountants. Still, it's a good idea to make the effort to find a good CPA. One of the best ways is to ask people who own their own businesses.

I have a built-in bias against individuals or small businesses that use large accounting firms. You're a low priority to them, so you'll be placed with someone who is very inexperienced. There's so much turnover at the lower levels that you'll never get the attention you need. The ultimate insult is paying high fees for uncaring and inattentive service.

An individual or small business often can do best with a small to medium-sized local practice. Like a lawyer, a CPA will generally give you 30 minutes of free time for an interview, if you ask for it. The most important questions you can ask are "How many CPAs are there in the firm?" and "How long has each been with the firm?" If you hear that the people have been there a good long time, that speaks well for the firm. If there's a great deal of turnover in personnel, that's an important warning sign to stay away.

It's important what questions a CPA asks you. You want to make sure the CPA is interested in your situation and is asking questions that address the concerns you have.

If you interview CPAs who are trying to sound like heroes, telling you how clever they are and how they are going to beat the IRS, that's a red flag. If, instead, they talk about prudent ways to reduce your tax exposure and liability, that's good.

Technology

The Internet has completely changed the way I do consumer research for my radio show and the advice I give to listeners.

You can use the Internet to find the value of a used car, figure out how to shop for a mortgage or pay one off early, look for a job, get a price quote on life insurance, or check the value of stamps and coins in a collection. You can even post complaints about a company. By providing an open marketplace of information, the Internet totally shifts the balance of power between seller and consumer.

Getting information from the government sure is a lot easier. Information that once took days to get is now available instantly at government Web sites.

As the Internet era continues to dawn, people are getting more and more excited about its benefits. But as the ultimate in free speech, it also provides a forum for unsavory characters promoting schemes and rip-offs. Be very careful with "information" you get in cyberspace. There are a lot of very impressive Web sites that are impressive mainly in their cunning.

Another danger is that material on the Internet can be objectionable or harmful to children. There are a variety of computer software "filters" available to help parents protect children from adult-oriented content and violence, but I'm not sure any of them work very well yet. I think parents have to be the ultimate filters of what their children view on the Internet. As the parent of a nine-year-old girl, I know there are sites where there is the possibility of danger, but until there's an effective way to filter what she sees, it's my responsibility to monitor and control her Internet use.

Technological change makes the need for information even greater. In this chapter, I'll help you buy a computer, get a wireless phone or pager, choose between cable and satellite television, and tell you a little bit about long-distance calling, E-mail providers, online banking, and Internet access.

BUYING A COMPUTER

Who would have thought just a few years ago that you would be able to buy a sophisticated computer, complete with monitor, for less than

TIPS ON BUYING A COMPUTER

- Plan on spending $500 to $800 for a computer, but be prepared for your computer to be obsolete about three years after you buy it.

- Buy a computer based on how you plan to use it.

- If money is very tight, consider buying a used computer.

- Buy when you need to buy, because no matter how long you wait for the best deal, the computer you bought will be much cheaper in six months.

- If you're an experienced computer user, consider buying from a burn-in shop, which will build your computer to order. If you're a first-time buyer, choose a store that will provide more hand-holding.

- Unless you have a very specialized need, buy a Windows-compatible computer, not an Apple.

$500? A good-quality computer used to cost at least $2,000, and anything less expensive was probably a cast-off.

Price is now more important than details such as the speed of the microprocessor or the size of the hard drive, because of a change in the industry's marketing philosophy. With most buyers now looking for computers in the $500 to $1,000 range, that should be your target as well.

Be careful when you go to a computer store, or wherever you're thinking of buying your computer, if the salesperson starts trying to talk you into more and more expensive hardware. Don't fall for the pitch, because you probably don't need all those extras. Buy a computer based on how you plan to use it, not on all its bells and whistles. Just about any computer can do a marvelous job with word processing. If you're going to use your computer mostly to access the Internet, make sure it has a good modem, whatever that may be at the time. If you're going to use your computer mostly to play video games or to do desktop publishing, make sure the computer meets the specifications for the game or publishing software you plan to use. For up-to-date details on a good basic configuration, check my Web site (www.clarkhoward.com).

Because technology is advancing very rapidly, you'll probably have to replace your computer in three years. Some buyers think that if they pay twice as much, they won't have to replace it as quickly. That's a fundamental error. Paying $1,500 instead of $750 may buy you only six more months of use. It's better to spend $750 now and another $750 in three years for a new, more advanced computer.

Buy a computer when you need to buy it, because no matter how long you wait for the best deal, the one you bought will be much cheaper in six months.

If money is very tight, consider buying a used computer. There are a lot of people out there who are so taken with the latest technology that they discard nearly new computers that are just fine for most uses. You probably can buy a used computer that will do just about everything you want for about $300.

Where to Buy

Another key question when buying a computer is where to shop. People who have owned computers have become much more comfortable at buying by mail order or at "burn-in shops," which build computers to order. Burn-in shops use off-the-shelf components to make a computer with the central processing chip, hard drive, RAM, modem, and CD-ROM drive that you specify, and the computers are very inexpensive. Prices may change several times a day, because the price is based on how much the shop has to pay for computer components.

There's no hand-holding at burn-in shops. If you won't need a lot of help in how to use your computer, you'll get a good one at a great price. If you've never owned a computer or used one at work, you're probably better off paying more and buying from a computer store.

The caliber of customer service usually isn't very good at burn-in shops. But if you take the computer home and there's an immediate problem with one of the components, they're generally very good at taking care of it. Normally the problems you will have will appear when you first turn on the computer.

To comparison-shop at several burn-in shops, you have to write down the specifications you want. Include the hardware you want and whatever software you want the shop to preload. You have to be able to compare apples to apples. Call several shops and give them your specifications, and they'll give you their prices.

I get almost no complaints about burn-in shops, because the people who buy from them tend to be experienced computer users and know what they're doing. First-time users often don't understand a basic phrase like "booting a computer up," which means turning it on. If that's you, you need technical support, even if you have to pay extra for it.

The other major place buyers are turning to is mail-order houses, such as Dell Computer. They're exactly the opposite of burn-in shops in that they overcome the obstacle of distance by offering exceptional service. Even a first-time buyer probably would be okay buying a computer from Dell.

When you buy a computer by mail order, the reputation of the seller becomes very important. If you buy from an unknown company and have a problem, and the people there don't care, you can't drive across town to talk to someone. Traditional computer stores like CompUSA are becoming a blend of mail-order houses and burn-in shops. You can pay a computer store to come out and set up a computer at your home or office and provide technical support. Or you can skip this service and save the fee.

If you buy from a burn-in shop, you won't get a brand name like Compaq on the computer box, and the processing chip may be from AMD or Cyrix, rather than industry leader Intel. In my opinion, that absolutely does not matter. Most computer manufacturers are just assemblers of other companies' components, so a Compaq or a Gateway computer will be essentially the same as a no-name brand. Compaq became the number-one computer seller because the company figured out the right combination of price and customer service.

A few years ago, you paid more for a Compaq computer because it had a reputation for being a better-quality product. But as people became more sophisticated computer buyers, the company decided that its market segment was getting smaller. So Compaq decided to build the best computer it could and sell it for the lowest price. Sales took off. Compaq didn't cut corners; it just became more efficient and cut prices.

Most people today are buying Windows-compatible computers, and that's the right choice given Apple's small market share. But buy a MacIntosh if you want the absolute easiest computer to use, or if you need it for a specialized application for which Apple's technology is superior. That's primarily true for graphics-heavy programs. Apple has always been a favorite of graphic designers.

There's a real trade-off here. There's a huge amount of software available for the Windows computers, but they're harder to use. Apple computers are easy to use, but you may not be able to use them for what you want.

E-mail

Not everyone with a computer chooses to be connected to the Internet. But even those who aren't can take advantage of electronic mail, or E-mail.

At least half a dozen companies offer advertiser-supported, free-to-the-consumer E-mail. If you don't mind putting up with the ads, you get excellent service. And even if you are connected to the Internet, you can switch to free E-mail and keep your E-mail address no matter which Internet service provider you're using. That's an advantage for people who don't want to switch providers because they'll have to notify friends, family, and colleagues that their E-mail address has changed. The same thing happened when 800 numbers became portable. People felt more free to switch companies, and rates fell.

Advertiser-supported E-mail also enables you to check your E-mail from virtually any computer in the world. You can access the provider via a dial-up or go to the company's Web page.

The most famous of the free companies is Juno, which you can check out at its Web site, www.juno.com, but there are many imitators. I've never had a complaint about any of these companies.

Online Banking

Traditional banks are both excited and terrified of the Internet, because they've invested a lot in expensive buildings. Internet banks, with their very low cost structure, pose a major threat to traditional banks because they can charge less for services and pay higher rates for savings accounts, checking accounts, and certificates of deposit.

There's nothing dangerous about using an Internet bank, even one that has no bank building nearby. Just make sure the bank is FDIC insured. To be safe, check with the local FDIC (Federal Deposit Insurance Corporation) office before you transact any business. A lot of Internet banks are opening single offices in a variety of communities, to give people places to go if they have a complaint and to give them a higher level of confidence in the idea of Internet banking. But you never need to visit the office. To open a CD, you just mail the bank a check.

Online bill paying, which people have been talking about almost since the birth of the personal computer, is closer than ever to becoming a good consumer tool. Not long ago, banks were charging $10 a month for online bill paying, and the system still relied on a check being mailed from the bank to the utility company.

We're close to having a free or nearly free service that will enable you to transfer money directly from your account to the computer at the gas or electric company. Such a service would eliminate the cost of postage and the danger of your payment getting lost in the mail. You could send the payment the day it is due and know that it was received.

I just got a notice from Discover saying my wife and I didn't make our payment. Oddly, I not only remember when I mailed the bill, but from which mailbox. My wife and I were in Park City, Utah, the day after Christmas, and we found several bills we had forgotten to mail before we left home. I dropped them in the mailbox in the Park City Post Office, and every check cleared except the one to Discover. Who knows where it went, but we had to pay interest and late payment penalties, even though we had done nothing wrong. Unfortunately, the postal service is not flawless.

The potential savings from a true electronic bill-paying system are enormous for credit card companies and others who send out lots of bills and receive lots of payments. There are many incentives for them to create a system that works.

WIRELESS PHONES

Owning a wireless telephone and making calls with one is getting a lot cheaper.

For 13 years, the country was divided into small cartels and two wireless telephone companies shared a monopoly. In that noncompetitive environment, there was no incentive for the operators to lower prices. Calls were very expensive, the rate plans were very expensive, and you had to sign a very unfavorable contract that committed you to one company for as long as two years.

Thanks to new technology and an opening up of the markets, rates are plummeting almost monthly. Most large cities in the country now have five or six players, and smaller markets will end up with three or four.

Rates have fallen so low and call quality has improved so much that in some cities it's possible to disconnect your traditional wired telephone

TIPS ON WIRELESS PHONES

• The cost of wireless phone service has dropped so much, and the quality has improved so much, that it's possible to use wireless all the time.

• Look for rate plans that do not require a contract, and choose a plan that includes the number of minutes in your flat rate that you expect to use each month.

• Choose digital wireless service, not analog, to get the best prices, quality, and privacy.

and do everything via wireless. My brother in Arizona has done that. He's on a plan that includes so many minutes of calls at a monthly flat rate that he can't even use them all.

As I write this, about a fourth of the people in the nation uses wireless service — more than 50 million adults. That's a huge change from the days when the minutes you spent on a wireless call were precious and expensive.

Wireless phones are incredibly convenient and, for good or bad, enable people to reach you more easily. My wife used to complain that she could never find me. Now, with digital technology, wireless phones include voicemail and paging, and with some you can even access and send E-mail, which scrolls across a screen. My brother gets more than 100 E-mails a week on his wireless phone. It's been an enormous help to him.

Some cities offer wireless Internet access, at about $10 more than wired access. With wireless, your computer is always connected to the Internet, so there's no need to dial to get online. With a laptop computer and a wireless connection, you can create and transmit a document from almost anywhere, without having to plug the computer into anything.

There's been a lot of fuss about the need to increase competition in local telephone service so that consumers could choose from several local phone providers, instead of just their local Baby Bell company. But even if there are never several local providers, some form of technology could break open the local phone monopoly.

Because things are changing quickly in this area, it's difficult to give you advice. But I do recommend that you study your options carefully if you're looking to buy wireless phone service or if your contract for wireless service is about to expire. It wouldn't be far-fetched to create a spreadsheet to compare plans. If you want a phone only for emergencies, there are "lifeline" plans around the country that have dropped to $10 or less a month. Keep the phone in your glove compartment or purse, and take it out for emergencies only. Safety still is the number-one reason people want a wireless phone, and the falling rates have made it possible for almost anybody to have one.

If you use a wireless phone more frequently to make personal or business calls, you can take advantage of market prices that are moving toward a nickel a minute, an incredible drop from recent years when rates typically were 35 or 45 cents a minute. It's amazing what competition can do.

If you use your wireless phone a lot, the rate cuts have led to tremendous savings. I talked to a couple in the interior design business who used to spend the day on the road, calling suppliers and going to see customers. They had wireless phone bills of $1,800 a month. Now they pay $200 a month. Opening up competition was like giving a lot of people who depend on wireless phones a tax cut.

Look for a plan that does not require a contract and that includes the number of minutes in your base rate that you expect to use. A plan might include 600 minutes for $50, or 8 cents a minute. If you need 600 minutes, that's the plan to pick. If you need more time, you might choose a $70-a-month plan that gives you 1,000 minutes, a rate of 7 cents a minute. You get a volume discount for buying more minutes. But don't pay $70 or more a month if you're not going to use the minutes. My wife uses her phone a lot, and she ends up using about 300 minutes, or a total of five hours, a month.

Eventually, you'll be able to buy unlimited minutes for a flat monthly fee, just as you do with wired service, and prices will be roughly the same for wired and wireless.

Digital service still isn't perfect, and you'll still lose a call occasionally. But call quality has improved to the point that, as long as you're not moving, most people can't tell the difference between a wired and a wireless call. Wireless calls using analog technology aren't as clear, and I expect that analog technology will die off in the not-too-distant future. It's too expensive to transmit analog calls, so analog systems won't be able to approach the low prices of digital.

Digital phones are still rather expensive, $50 to $200, because they have to be capable of switching to analog in areas where there's no complete network or digital transmission tower. But digital call plans include far more minutes than analog services, since the company's cost of transmitting each digital call is far lower. The analog phones you got for free ended up being pretty expensive, because you were handcuffed by an expensive contract. Digital calling also offers private wireless calling. Analog is not private at all.

Batteries also can be a bit of a headache for wireless phone users. I put mine in the charger each night, and it's good for 40 hours of use. My wife has a car charger, so her phone charges while she's driving around town. If you're a wireless user, you just have to remember to charge your phone.

Finally, if you use wireless phones a lot in your business, consider a technology offered by Nextel (www.nextel.com). It essentially allows free, private conversation among members of your own work group.

PAGERS

Paging has become the inexpensive, easy-to-use choice for reaching people quickly.

Although digital cell phones include paging functions, some people don't want or need wireless calling. Pagers are now available for as little as $3 to $7 a month.

A few years ago, a teenager who had a pager might have been using it to make drug deals. Now a lot of parents give their kids pagers to keep track of them, and the child is grounded if he doesn't immediately return a page from Mom or Dad.

I use a pager because I don't want to give out my cell phone number to everybody. So friends and family get the cell phone number and business associates get the pager number. Everybody can reach me, but I maintain some privacy.

You can usually get a pager for free or nearly free in return for a one-year service commitment. I recommend getting the pager and paying for the year's service in advance. The largest cost for the paging company is collecting payments and dealing with people who don't pay. Normally, a paging company will give you a huge discount for paying in advance. You could lose out if the company goes out of business, but the risk is small. Normally if a company gets into financial trouble, it just sells its accounts to another company.

> ## TIPS ON PAGERS
>
> • Look for deals on pagers in the alternative newspaper in your town.
>
> • You can get a discount by paying for a year's service in advance.

The best place to look for deals on pagers is in your town's alternative newspaper. The business market has moved away from pagers to wireless phones, so the business is targeting young people.

LONG-DISTANCE CALLING

The best approach to choosing a long-distance service for home or business use is to look for the lowest per-minute price you can find. Don't put up with monthly minimums, monthly fees, or restrictions.

In most cities, a good rate is 8 cents a minute 24 hours a day seven days a week. But because it's so inexpensive for companies to transmit long-distance calls, rates probably will get cheaper.

I got an offer in the mail recently for 10-cents-a-minute calling, 24 hours a day, for a monthly fee of $4.95. It just doesn't make sense to pay that much. If you make 240 minutes of long-distance calls a month, the equivalent of four hours, you would pay $28.80 at 12 cents a minute. If you made the same number of calls but paid 10 cents a minute, plus $4.95, your long-distance bill would be $28.95. So even for four hours of long-distance calls a month, you're better off with a slightly higher rate than paying a monthly charge. At 250 minutes a month, the $4.95 is equivalent to a charge of an extra two cents a minute. Most

TIPS ON LONG-DISTANCE CALLING

• Choose a long-distance provider that gives you the lowest rate for each minute of calling. Don't pay monthly fees or agree to make a minimum number of calls.

• Pay telephones and phones at hotels and hospitals often are run by alternative operator services, and the rates to use them can be exorbitant.

• To avoid the AOS rip-off, connect to your long-distance provider by dialing an 800 number. AT&T is 1-800-CALL-ATT. MCI is 1-800-950-1022. Sprint is 1-800-877-8000.

• Prepaid calling cards offer several advantages. Figure the cost per minute before you buy.

CONTACT

American Telecom Network
1-800-477-9692
www.callatn.com

people don't have anywhere near that kind of long-distance volume.

One company that has offered very good rates is American Telecom Network. It has excellent rates for outbound calls, toll-free inbound calls to your house, which are great if you're traveling or have children in college, and calling-card calls, and there are no fees for any of the products. As I write this, American Telecom charges 8.9 cents a minute, flat rate, if you pay your bill by bank card and 14.9 cents for calling-card calls, with no setup charge. If you call from a pay phone, all calling-card companies are now passing along a charge of 28.4 cents. That charge, levied by the pay-phone operator, applies for any call to an 800 number from a pay phone. It appears on your phone bill.

When you make a long-distance call away from your home, you have to be very careful. Public phones often are owned by alternative operator services (AOS) and can charge astronomical rates for long-distance calls.

You may think that because you dial the number and punch in your AT&T, Sprint, or MCI calling-card number, you are using one of those systems. An AOS merely bills through those cards and can charge as much as it wants. I've heard examples of charges that were 10 times the rates of a legitimate long-distance company.

Keep an eye out for this rip-off when you use any public phone, but particularly those at airports, universities, hotels, and hospitals. If you fall prey to an AOS, you could pay $1 or $2 a minute, compared to 15 cents a minute with your own long-distance service. For a 15-minute call, that's $2.25 with your system versus $15 to $30 for a rip-off AOS.

Owners of public phones are now required to disclose who provides the long-distance service, both in writing and through a short audio message. If you don't recognize the name of the company that's posted, dial the 800 number provided by your long-distance service.

Here are the 800 numbers for the major long-distance companies:

• AT&T
1-800-CALL-ATT
• MCI
1-800-950-1022
• Sprint
1-800-877-8000

You have to deal with AOSs because, after deregulation, phone companies saw long-distance service as a giant profit maker. People had no way of knowing when they used an AOS that they were going to pay more, or how much more, until they got their bills. An AOS is a complete rip-off. The last thing people think about when they're making a call from a hospital bed is which long-distance service they're using. Although hospitals continue to be among the worst offenders in this rip-off, there has been such a backlash of consumer complaints about AOSs that many of the big hotels are going back to legitimate phone services.

I've found a better deal on calling-card-type calls by using prepaid phone cards. I carry one that charges 14.9 cents a minute.

Before you buy a prepaid card, figure its cost per minute. You do that by dividing the cost of the card by the number of minutes you may use it. For example, a $15 card that gives you 100 minutes of calls is charging 15 cents a minute. I bought some cards on sale recently that cost 10 cents a minute. I bought every one the store had. You can get a good deal if you shop around because companies that offer prepaid cards don't have to pay for the cost of billing you each month and don't have to worry that you won't pay for your calls.

One minor annoyance with prepaid cards comes when the card runs out of minutes. You might have three minutes left on your card but need to make a 10-minute call. I was calling my daughter from a ski trip in Utah and just told her that at some point the call would click off. She understood. And if you lose a $20 phone debit card, you lose $20. So if you have one, treat it like cash.

A greater danger is that the card company could go out of business and your card could become worthless. You can limit your risk by buying from a well-recognized retailer or a well-known long-distance company. I buy an MCI card from Costco.

Prepaid cards make lots of sense for international travelers. I find that I get the best rates on calls to the United States with prepaid cards. Each card comes with a tiny brochure listing rates and codes.

I expect the cost of long-distance calls to continue to fall as we move further away from a system in which long-distance revenue subsidizes the cost of local phone service. That was certainly true in the 1960s, when picking up the phone to make a long-distance call was a big deal. That's because the Bell system, which was dismantled in 1984, heavily subsidized local service with long-distance revenues. But even in 1998, the local Bell operating company was getting 45 percent, on average, of the money you paid for a long-distance call. As those subsidies are reduced, local phone rates may go up — although the declining cost of wireless calls will place a brake on fees for local service — and long-distance calling is going to get steadily cheaper. People who make very few long-distance calls will end up paying more. Those who make a lot, who like to call friends and family around the world, will pay much, much less.

If you're a heavy user of long distance and a computer user, consider several of the technologies that allow you to make long-distance calls via the Internet. The technology is getting better and better, and it can be a big money saver. With Internet telephony, you pay as little as 4.9 cents a minute, 24 hours a day, seven days a week. You get this much lower price in return for having your calls routed over the Internet. But you will see what I consider to be a small decline in quality. I've often been willing to accept lower quality to save money. That's just the way I am. But some people find it annoying. Try one of the nickel-a-minute companies, such as IDT or QWEST, and see what you think.

Wireless will also have an impact on long-distance rates. Wireless companies in Texas already provide customers with toll-free calling throughout the state, and one wireless company in California is providing its wireless customers with nationwide long-distance calling for just one cent a minute. Long distance for one cent a minute is essentially free. Someone who makes 1,000 minutes of long-distance calls each month, a pretty fair amount, would pay a total of only $10 for those calls.

SATELLITE TV

I had really hoped that satellite-delivered television would provide the kind of competition for cable television for which a lot of us have been yearning.

Virtually nowhere in the country do people have a choice of cable TV providers and, in spite of their pledges to provide better service, the monopoly cable companies continue to be a constant irritant to many cable customers and a source of numerous complaints. Rates for cable service are escalating at several times the national rate of inflation.

Satellite service has turned out to be more of a niche product than a direct competitor. As I write this, 6 million homes in the nation have satellite dishes. Until that figure reaches 20 million, satellite service won't pose a major threat to cable TV and provide the real competition we need.

Satellite TV is completely different from cable TV. Satellite TV gives you far superior choices in programming, a better picture and sound, and a lower price. At the same time, it has some severe drawbacks. In most cases, you can't get local channels, including your local television news, if that's important to you. And it's far more expensive if you want to watch different programs in different rooms of the house. If Mom and Dad want to watch a movie on satellite TV and the kids want to watch the Disney Channel, you need two separate satellite receiver boxes. A second box now costs about $100 but is likely to get cheaper. My brother has satellite TV on his main TV and basic cable for the other televisions in the house.

I've had satellite TV for several years, and when I watch cable TV in a hotel room, it strikes me as incredibly inferior. With satellite, when you flip to a channel, you immediately see what you're watching, when it started, and what it's rated. The digital picture and sound are incredibly sharp, more like what's on a computer screen than on cable TV. Satellite TV really shines if you have a home theater setup in your house. When we moved into our new house, we had a few days of cable service left from the previous owner. When we hooked up the satellite service to the same TV, the difference in quality was like night and day.

TIPS ON SATELLITE TV

- Satellite TV has exceptional picture and sound quality, choice in programming, and customer service, but it also has drawbacks.

- There's a greater up-front cost for satellite TV if you want to watch different programs in different rooms of the house.

- In most cases, you can't get local channels on satellite, including local news programs.

And customer service from the satellite company is exceptional.

Satellite TV gives you many different variations of HBO, Showtime, and the other premium channels. We get six HBOs for $10 a month, which is a great deal. Two are East Coast feeds and two are West Coast feeds, so they carry the same programs at different times. The other two channels have different programming. So you have all kinds of choice in when you watch and what you watch.

If you're a sports fan, satellite TV offers an incredible number of choices. You can get every NFL, major league baseball, NBA, and NHL game from anywhere in the country, along with a lot of college sports packages. My father-in-law was over at my house one time and my wife and her mother were out. I was watching five football games at once, going back and forth to each game. He was so frustrated, not being able to relax and watch one game, that he finally got up and went for a walk.

If you don't watch much TV and can't get a good signal with a regular antenna, basic cable is still a better buy. But if you like to watch TV, satellite is incomparable. Until there's competition from some other source, and telephone companies have been unable to provide it, I think it's an excellent choice.

The Basics

The essence of my radio show is helping people solve problems. Many callers I talk with have been mistreated by a company or government agency and don't know what to do about it. I don't have a magic wand that forces companies to admit they're wrong and make amends, but I know what works.

In this chapter, I'll tell you some simple techniques to make your voice heard. You'll be surprised at how effective they are and how easy they are to use.

When cajoling and prodding don't work, you may have to go to court. I'll tell you how to file a case in small claims court — and how to collect on your judgment if you win.

This chapter also includes some important tips to guide you in returning merchandise to retailers, choosing a dry cleaner, and signing a contract. I'll tell you when it's critical to use a credit card and what you need to know when you purchase major items such as furniture, carpeting, beds, and jewelry.

SOLVING PROBLEMS

Part of the trick to solving consumer problems is having a strategy you can use to get results. Too often, consumers get frustrated and just go away mad, and going away mad is not a solution.

Whether it's a business or the government that's confounding you, the first strategy is to try to talk to somebody at a higher level than where the problem originated. If a higher-level official is unresponsive, go still higher in the organization. Go as high as you can, either by phoning, writing, or visiting the organization. If a salesperson won't help you, go to the manager. If it's a chain, go up the ladder to the regional vice president or the home office. To get results, you have to get out of the normal loop and go straight to the decision makers who can actually solve problems.

One of the big problems in corporate America is that those who have the most direct contact with the public have the least amount of power to solve customer complaints. I always shake my head when someone in the customer service department says there's nothing he or she can do. More and more, the companies that succeed are those that connect with the public and solve problems. When front-line employees don't have the latitude to find solutions, customers get angry and sales plunge.

If you reach nothing but dead ends on the phone, or you can't even find out whom to speak with, your next strategy should be documenting your attempts to solve the problem. Keep a log of the phone calls you make, with whom you speak, and what is said. In the Workbook section of this book, you'll find worksheets to help you document these calls.

One of the newest and more interesting ways to handle problems with a company is to blanket it with E-mails and post complaints on bulletin boards and in chat rooms. Depending on how technologically oriented the company is, you may get results this way. Some companies may try to block your E-mails with filtering programs that reject messages from customers who aren't already on a pre-approved list.

Traditional letters are also a very powerful tool. I take dozens of calls from people who have complained repeatedly by telephone and then gave up. I had one call from an apartment renter who wanted to move out after a problem arose with her landlord. She had tried to resolve the dispute by phone but got nowhere. At that point she had no solid evidence that she had made any effort to find a solution. Writing letters not only gets attention but is a great method of documenting your efforts.

In your first letter, list whom you've spoken with about the problem, what attempts you've made to solve it, and what specific action you would like from the recipient of your letter. Give the person a specific period of time to deal with the problem. If you don't get a response in the allotted time, immediately send a second letter with a copy of the first attached. This takes very little time but is effective at working toward a solution.

TIPS ON SOLVING PROBLEMS

- If you're having trouble resolving a problem with a business or government office, talk to a higher-level official. Go as high in the organization as you can.

- If phone calls or E-mails don't work, write a letter detailing the problem and requesting some action to resolve it. If you don't get a response, send a second letter with a copy of the first attached. Always keep a copy of your letters, and always keep the tone positive and friendly.

- If a government agency is not serving your needs, call the constituent service office of your congressman, U.S. senator, or local elected official.

- If your problem is with a private organization and all attempts to resolve it have failed, try sending one last letter by certified mail. If that doesn't work, you may have to sue the business in small claims court.

Always keep a copy of your letters, and always, no matter what the situation, keep the tone positive and friendly. Never write a nasty, angry letter. Words can hurt or help. Angry words send a powerfully negative message and may prevent you from getting any cooperation.

If you have tried to contact people by phone, E-mail, letter, and in person and have gotten nowhere, it's time to look for another pressure point. If a U.S. government agency is ignoring you or not serving your needs, call the constituent service office of your congressman or U.S. senator. If it's a state agency, call one of your state legislators. And if it's a city, county, or town issue, call the elected official who represents you in those governments. Your elected officials know they can gain a loyal voter by taking care of your needs. That's why you turn to them.

I know of a fellow who found out when he applied for a credit card that the Department of Veterans Affairs claimed he had defaulted on a mortgage loan in another state. In fact, it was a case of mistaken identity. He had never defaulted on the loan — he had never even been to that part of the country. He wrote to the V.A. explaining that there was a mix-up, but the agency insisted he had defaulted. Then he wrote to one of his U.S. senators, whose vote on federal appropriations helps decide the department's funding. The senator's office then contacted the agency on the fellow's behalf and, not surprisingly, the matter was cleared up rather quickly.

If your problem is with a private organization and all attempts to resolve it have failed, try sending one last letter by certified mail. It's not necessary, in fact it's undesirable, to send your first couple of letters this way, because sending a certified letter is often seen as a hostile gesture. Assume that the company has been negligent toward you, but not malevolent, and that your letter will get proper attention. Usually, if you are persistent, you will get results.

Even if a company doesn't satisfy you, remember that you have the power to vote with your wallet. If a business treats you poorly, spend your money elsewhere. In a consumer-driven society such as ours, that's the ultimate power.

SMALL CLAIMS COURT

With the proliferation of high-profile legal cases in recent years and the advent of cable channels such as Court TV, Americans are getting a lot more familiar with procedures in the courtroom.

When phone calls, meetings, and letters have failed to resolve a dispute with a company or an individual, small claims court is a great place to turn. Cases in which two parties have an honest disagreement are likely to be resolved most effectively. The process does not work as well if your adversary deliberately set out to cheat you.

Taking a case to small claims court is fairly easy. Before you file a case, send a letter by certified mail to the other party. The letter has to cover a few basic elements, including:

- How you've been harmed.
- Why that particular person or company is responsible.
- How much money you seek and why it is justified.

Use a friendly tone in the letter, because it may be read later by a judge. You want the judge to view you as a reasonable person who tried but failed to solve a problem and has turned to the courts for help.

You sue in the county in which your adversary lives, the county in which you were injured, the county in which the business in question is located, or the county in which the product in dispute was manufactured. You need an exact address so the party can be served notice of the suit. If the defendant is served and doesn't show up to argue his or her side, you win by default.

Call the clerk of the court in the county in which you'll be filing your case to find out that court's procedures. Some courts have a kit or brochure to help you. You'll pay a filing fee — generally less than $100 — that you may recover if the judge rules in your favor. In most cases, you don't need a lawyer. In fact, some states prohibit lawyers in small claims court. The rules vary on other aspects of the process. New York State allows either party to appeal a small claims court verdict, but Hawaii and Arizona are among those that bar such appeals. Louisiana allows the losing party to pay in installments.

Tips on Small Claims Court

• Small claims court procedures are most effective in resolving disputes in which two parties have an honest disagreement. They don't work as well if your adversary deliberately set out to cheat you.

• Before you file a case, send a letter by certified mail to the other party. Write this letter in a friendly tone, because a judge eventually may read it.

• You sue in the county in which your adversary lives or, if it's a business, the county in which it is located. You'll pay a filing fee — generally less than $100 — that you may recover if the judge rules in your favor.

• If the judge finds in your favor, be prepared for the hard part — collecting on your judgment. A judgment means you have a license to search for money. You can garnish the person's checking account or paycheck, put a lien on the person's house, and seize cars or other assets.

• If someone is unemployed or self-employed, or skips town, you may find your judgment is worthless.

REFERENCE

Everybody's Guide to Small Claims Court
(Nolo Press)
1-800-992-6656

On average, you can sue for up to $5,000 in small claims court. But the limits vary by state, with some as low as $1000 and some as high as $15,000.

There's a wonderful book available to help, *Everybody's Guide to Small Claims Court* (Nolo Press), which explains the process in great detail.

Once you get your trial date, it's time to prepare your case. The most important points to remember are to be well organized and bring strong documentation. The judge wants to hear a short version of your story, so carefully think through the three basic elements you included in your certified letter. Try to provide documentation for each point: (1) how you have been harmed; (2) why the other per-

son or the company is responsible; and (3) how much money you seek and why it is justified.

Bring letters you've written in the past, records of phone calls you've made, and, if you can, photographs. Let's say someone put sod in your yard and the sod didn't take. Take pictures of the yard and bring the pictures to court. Or, if you had repairs done to your house and the repairs were done poorly, take pictures that illustrate the sloppy work.

If the judge finds in your favor, be prepared for the hard part — collecting on your judgment. If you're dealing with an honest individual or business, you'll get a check right on the spot. If the other guy is going to fight tooth and nail not to pay you, your ability to collect what is owed you will depend on your persistence. A judgment means you have a license to search for money or other assets. If you can't find any, the judgment is worthless.

Depending on the state, you may have the right to take money from the person's paycheck or checking account, put a lien on his or her house, or seize the person's automobiles. Mississippi even provides help in collecting on your judgment. Check with the clerk of the court to see what the rules are in your area.

It's possible that you won't be able to collect, particularly if someone is unemployed or self-employed or skips town. The only way you'll ever have a chance to get your money is to try. If you're trying to locate someone's checking account, try to remember whether or not you've ever written the person a check, or the person has ever written you one. If so, you can find the name of the person's bank and account number either on the back of your canceled check or, if you deposited a check written to you, on your bank's microfilm copy of the check. If you've never exchanged checks, have a friend write the person a small check. You'll get the account information when the check clears and is returned in your friend's bank statement. With your judgment, you'll be able to garnish the person's bank account before he or she knows it.

It's easiest to garnish someone who works for a large employer or the government. The clerk of the court will be able to provide the forms and tell you how to garnish someone's wages or checking account.

Collections attorney Gary Jackson tells some great stories of the lengths he has gone to in order to collect on a judgment. One of Gary's clients took his car into a mechanic for a major repair, then became ill and couldn't come back immediately for the car or call the mechanic. Three weeks later, after he was feeling better, the fellow came back in to settle his bill and pick up his car. But the mechanic, having neither seen nor heard from the car owner, had sold the car to pay the repair bill. Under local law, he couldn't do that without first filing a lawsuit, so the car owner took the mechanic to small claims court and won a $5,000 judgment.

The mechanic refused to pay, and because the garage didn't take checks, Gary couldn't locate the mechanic's checking account. He did find out through a records check that the mechanic owned a camper, so he had the sheriff seize the camper and it was auctioned off for $1,000. That didn't come close to covering the judgment, so the sheriff went back and seized some engine hoists, a cash register, and a set of golf clubs. On the third trip, the mechanic refused to let the sheriff onto the premises. Gary protested to the judge, but local law at the time allowed the mechanic to keep the sheriff off his property. Gary solved the problem by contacting his state legislator and getting a new law passed that allowed the sheriff to enter. A year later, Gary presented the judge with a copy of the new law and the judge ordered the mechanic, who was in the courtroom, to let the sheriff take anything he wanted from the mechanic's garage. The mechanic immediately stood up and paid the car owner a portion of what he owed — $500. He eventually paid the full amount.

In another case, a woman went in for breast-reduction surgery and the insurance company mistakenly sent the benefits check to her instead of the doctor. She cashed it and refused to pay the bill, so the doctor sued and won a judgment. She refused to disclose information about herself and was called before a judge. She walked into court wearing a neck brace from an auto accident in which she was hit by another driver. Gary Jackson asked the judge to force her to disclose who had hit her, then garnished both drivers' wages and both insurance companies. Because the woman wouldn't pay directly, Jackson intercepted the money due her from the auto accident and collected on the judgment.

RETURNING MERCHANDISE

Few qualities inspire confidence and loyalty among customers more than a retailer that is willing to pay refunds or exchange merchandise cheerfully. If you buy something in the wrong size or color, or you just don't like it as much as you thought you would, it's great to know you can bring it back. It's also very disturbing if you can't.

In many states, retailers are permitted to adopt any return or exchange policy they desire, as long as they let customers know the policy. A retailer may refuse any refund or exchange and post a notice that all sales are final. It can provide refunds under certain conditions, such as requiring you to return a television in its original packaging. Or it can provide exchanges or in-store credit but refuse to give cash refunds. Notice can be provided in any of several ways. The refund/exchange policy can be printed on sales slips or clothing tags or posted on a sign by the cash registers.

It's a good idea to find out a store's policy on returns and exchanges before you buy there. Be aware, too, that return policies and refund policies are different. A store may be very liberal about allowing you to bring back merchandise and exchange it for other merchandise or receive an in-store credit. But it may be inflexible about giving you your money back. Many items that you purchase cannot be returned for cash and you're simply expected to know that policy. The best example is an airline ticket, which is almost always nonrefundable.

You have to make your own decision about whether to patronize a store with a rigid refund or exchange policy. If you are willing to take your chances in return for a better price, then go in with your eyes open. If you often buy something and change your mind, then be selective about where you shop. If you're buying a gift, be fair to the recipient. You may believe it's the best gift ever, but he or

TIPS ON RETURNING MERCHANDISE

• In most states, retailers are permitted to adopt any return or exchange policy, as long as they let the customers know the policy. That includes refusing any refund or exchange.

• The refund/exchange policy may be printed on sales slips or clothing tags or posted on a sign by the cash registers.

• It's a good idea to find out the store's policy on returns and exchanges before you shop there. Be aware, too, that return policies and refund policies are different.

• You have to make your own decision about whether to patronize a store with a rigid refund or exchange policy. If you are willing to take your chances in return for a better price, then go in with your eyes open.

• If you're buying a gift or shopping by catalog, make sure the item can be returned for a full refund.

she may disagree, or may already have something exactly like it. Buy gifts only from stores that have liberal return policies.

I don't recommend buying floor samples or clearance merchandise marked "all sales final" if the item is not packed in its original factory carton. Then you really are at risk if you've spent money and, when you get the item home, it's damaged or doesn't work.

When you buy from catalogs, be certain you understand the company's return policy. There's a big difference between buying from a catalog, where you can see only a picture of an item, versus buying in a store, where you can see and evaluate the merchandise. You buy from a catalog at your own risk if you don't have the right to return it for a full refund.

The fastest-growing retailers in the nation all have very customer-friendly return and refund policies, and I don't think that's a coincidence. Treating customers fairly is just good business. It's a shame that some stores are so unbending, and it's sadder still that those policies are adopted because a few customers abuse return privileges. Think about how harshly you're often treated when you write a check. Blame it on the very few people who write most of the bad checks.

DRY CLEANING

As much as I love a bargain, I have to tell you that price is not the most important factor in every consumer decision. It's more important to choose a dry cleaner that will do a good job of cleaning your clothes and will be fair to you if problems ever develop.

Clarify the dry cleaner's policies before you bring your first garments in to be cleaned. Tell the dry cleaner you don't ever expect to have a problem but you're curious what the cleaner will do if a piece of clothing is lost or damaged, because you've heard so many horror stories. The answer will help you decide if you should take your clothes to this particular dry cleaner.

If there's a change in ownership, talk to the new owner and see what his or her attitude is about service. If you don't like what you hear, you may want to switch cleaners. It's a good idea to get to know the owner or manager in any case. If a problem ever develops, it's easier to resolve if you already know someone in charge. If the only person you ever speak with is a clerk, you may have trouble getting satisfaction.

Just as with a doctor, lawyer, or accountant, one of the best ways to find a dry cleaner is to ask friends and neighbors whom they use and whether

---

TIPS ON DRY CLEANING

• Choose a dry cleaner that will do a good job of cleaning your clothes and be fair to you if problems ever develop. Price is less important.

• If an item is destroyed in the cleaning process, the cleaner does not owe you the amount of money needed to replace the garment. The company owes you a depreciated value based on the number of years the item is expected to last.

• If there's a dispute over how a garment was damaged, the cleaner can submit the item to the International Fabricare Institute for testing.

• If it turns out to be the manufacturer's fault, most retailers will either give you a credit or put you in touch with the manufacturer, which will generally reach some form of accommodation with you.

CONTACT

IFI Garment Analysis Laboratory
12251 Tech Road
Silver Spring, MD 20904
1-800-638-2627
www.ifi.org

---

they're happy with the service. I prefer to use a cleaner that does the work on the premises. It will have immediate access to spot-removing chemicals and will be able to test a stain immediately. Also, if the work is done on site, there's less chance an item will be lost.

If clothes are cleaned on the premises, ask how often the cleaning fluid is distilled. There's no way to know if the cleaner's being truthful, but it's a good idea to ask anyway. A good cleaner should distill the solvent daily, because clothes cleaned in dirty solvent can become dingy and discolored. You wouldn't wash clothes in dirty water, and a dry cleaner shouldn't use dirty solvent.

Most of the calls I get about dry-cleaning problems concern white or off-white garments that become dingy after being cleaned. One caller won a $263 judgment in small claims court because a dry cleaner refused to make good on a white suit that was discolored. Once a garment is cleaned in dirty solvent, it's ruined. The original color can't be restored.

If you notice that an item you've had cleaned has been damaged, go back to the dry cleaner as soon as possible and show it to the manager on duty. A lot of times he'll ask to clean or press it again or to repair a button or zipper. Or a manager may want to show it to the owner. That's fine. But if the item is still unsatisfactory after that second cleaning, it's time for the cleaner to take responsibility and come up with some money.

If an item has been destroyed in the cleaning process, the cleaner does not owe you the amount of money needed to replace the garment. The company owes you a depreciated value based on the item's expected life span. If it's a shirt you would normally keep for five years and you've owned it for two years before it is destroyed, you deserve 60 percent of the value of the shirt. If you normally keep an item for two years and it's damaged in the second year, you may not be entitled to any money at all, since it was near the end of its useful life. You'll have to negotiate with the cleaner over how much you deserve as compensation for a ruined item.

A cleaner might have been doing a good job and take responsibility for damage but seem unable to cough up any money. You could cut a deal for some free cleaning in exchange for the loss suffered because of the damage.

If the cleaner claims that an item has been damaged because of improper manufacturing and you believe the cleaner has damaged it, you may want to turn to a third party. If the cleaner is a member of the International Fabricare Institute (IFI), you can have an evaluation done of the item by the IFI testing laboratory in Silver Spring, Maryland. IFI will issue a report on the cause of the damage. IFI's fee may be paid by the cleaner or the customer, or both may agree to split the cost. According to IFI, manufacturers are responsible for the damage in 47 percent of the items the lab tests, consumers for 37.5 percent, and dry cleaners for 15.5 percent. The dry cleaners' share is low because dry cleaners send problems to the lab only when they believe they are not responsible, the IFI says.

If an IFI report says damage is the manufacturer's fault, most retailers will either give you a credit or put you in touch with the manufacturer, which will generally reach some form of accommodation with you. I once had a suit that bunched up after being cleaned. The cleaner said the cause was a specific defect in a manufacturing process called fusing. I went back to the store, which was a retail outlet for a manufacturer. The salesperson recognized the defect, knew it was the store's responsibility, and immediately offered to give me a new suit. A number of Better Business Bureaus offer dry-cleaning arbitration programs.

One solution to dry-cleaning problems in the future may be do-it-yourself dry cleaning. There is a technology now that lets you dry clean your clothes by putting them into a plastic bag with a chemical "pill" and tossing the bag around in a regular clothes dryer. However, some of my staff members didn't like it because you have to press the clothes yourself.

CHARGEBACKS

When you pay for something in advance, such as an airline ticket or a custom-made sofa, you're taking on some risk. What if the airline or furniture store goes bust, as so many have over the past few years? What if you order from a catalog and the merchandise never arrives? If you prepay and don't get the merchandise or service, you could lose your money.

If you write a check or pay cash to a merchant who fails to deliver, the only way to get your money back is to sue. If the merchant goes out of business, you become a claimant in bankruptcy court, where you'll wait forever and, if you're lucky, collect a few cents on the dollar for what you're owed.

There's a simple way to protect yourself from these risks — use a major credit card. That way you offer yourself the privilege of a chargeback, a refund paid by your credit card company.

Banks, credit unions, and other credit card issuers are deluged with requests for chargebacks and in many cases refuse to honor them. However, the limited rights you have to receive a chargeback from your card issuer are bolstered by broader protections provided by VISA International and MasterCard International. Contact VISA or MasterCard if your bank, credit union, or other card issuer denies your request for a chargeback.

If you pay a deposit to order furniture and the store shuts down before you receive it, VISA or MasterCard will refund your deposit. But you must follow the right procedure. Here's the key. If

---

TIPS ON CHARGEBACKS

• When you pay for something in advance, such as an airline ticket or a custom-made sofa, you're taking on some risk. If you prepay and you don't get the merchandise or service, you could lose your money.

• If you use a credit card when you prepay, you give yourself the privilege of a chargeback, a refund paid by your credit card company.

• If you order something and don't receive it, file a chargeback claim before 60 days have passed. If you receive the merchandise later, tell the credit card company to drop the chargeback claim.

CONTACT

VISA International Customer Service
P.O. Box 8999
San Francisco, CA 94128
1-800-227-6811 (traveler's checks)
1-800-847-2911 (lost or stolen credit cards)

MasterCard International
Public Affairs Department
888 7th Avenue
New York, NY 10106
212-649-5476

you haven't received your furniture in 50 days, write to your credit card company and file a chargeback claim. Once the 60-day window closes, so has your right to do a chargeback. Go ahead and put the item in dispute no later than 60 days from the date of the original charge. Later, if the furniture is delivered, just contact the credit card company and it will release your chargeback request.

Whether the chargeback is permanent or the amount is reposted to your bill should be determined by the facts of your case, but whether this happens will depend on the fairness of your card issuer. You find out about your credit card company's loyalties when you do a chargeback. Some consider the merchant, not the consumer, their most important customer.

INFREQUENT PURCHASES

It's easy to sympathize with a young couple buying a new sofa. Buying items such as furniture, jewelry, and carpet can be daunting, indeed; we make these purchases so infrequently that it's difficult to know how to shop. Here are some tips.

When buying furniture, deal only with reputable retailers — healthy businesses with knowledgeable salespeople. Also think through how a piece of furniture will fit into your home. If you're considering a sofa with an unusual pattern or color, ask if you may take home a cushion for a few hours and look at it with the rest of your furniture. Many times something that looks like a perfect match in the store will look like a sore thumb at home.

Don't ever feel you need to make a snap decision, even if an item is on sale. Furniture sales scream at you every week in the newspaper.

There are a few things to look for to determine if a piece of furniture is well made. For wood pieces, such as a desk or dresser, the top should have a very smooth finish, ideally hand rubbed. If you see tiny bumps and craters, like the surface of an orange peel, the finish is of poor quality. Solid wood is great, but veneer, a thin piece of wood applied to another piece of wood or particle board, is good, too. Many fancy pieces with intricate inlays in the top are veneer. What you don't want is a plastic top with a wood-grain finish that's photo-applied to particle board. This piece is basically plastic with a picture of wood on it.

Next, open a drawer and look at the connection between the front of the drawer and the side. You want something that's dovetailed — that is, connected firmly by a series of stubby, interlocking fingers on both the front and side. In a cheap piece, the drawer fronts may be stapled or nailed to the side and eventually will pull right off. The inside of the drawer should be smooth enough that if you rubbed a piece of gauze on it, the gauze wouldn't snag. Also, the drawer should be deep when measured from front to back. Sometimes manufacturers cut corners by using shorter drawers.

It's harder to judge the quality of upholstered furniture. You could place a $399 sofa next to a $1,399 sofa and not see much difference. One thing to look for is whether the patterns line up correctly. Just as the stripes on a shirt pocket should match up with the rest of the shirt, so should the patterns on furniture. It costs more to have the pattern on the back match up with the rest of the piece, because that takes more fabric. Ask the salesperson about the springs. "Eight-way hand tied" — in which the springs are tied together with twine in eight directions — is a classic way to put furniture together. Another spring design, an independent Marshall unit, is okay, too.

If you're buying furniture and taking it home with you immediately, it doesn't matter how you pay. But if you're putting down a deposit or hav-

TIPS ON INFREQUENT PURCHASES

• When buying furniture, deal only with reputable retailers — healthy businesses with knowledgeable salespeople.

• If you're considering a sofa with an unusual pattern or color, ask to take home a cushion and look at it with the rest of your furniture.

• Wood furniture should have a very smooth finish. With upholstered furniture, make sure the patterns line up.

• If you're putting down a deposit for furniture or having it delivered, pay only by credit card. With your credit card chargeback rights, you are protected if the furniture doesn't arrive.

• Always try out a bed before you buy it, even if you shop, as I do, at warehouse discount stores.

• Experts recommend that you look primarily at mattresses and box springs made by one of the four major bedding manufacturers: Simmons, Sealy, Serta, or Stearns & Foster.

• It is important to buy a mattress with the proper firmness. A full-size mattress needs to have at least 312 coils to provide good support.

• When you buy carpet, it's important to buy from a good dealer, to get a good-quality carpet yarn, and to make sure the carpet is properly installed.

• It doesn't matter if you buy carpet from a carpet store or a department store, just don't buy over the phone.

• Buy a carpet made from a premium carpet yarn, such as Du Pont's Stainmaster, Monsanto's Wear-Dated, or Allied Fibers' Worry-Free.

• Get a guarantee in writing that the carpet will be power stretched to ensure proper installation.

• Buy jewelry because you like it, not because you hope it will increase in value.

• Buy jewelry only from stores that allow you 72 hours to inspect it and, if you choose, to return it for a full refund.

INTERNET

Better Business Bureau
www.bbb.org

Coins and Stamps
www.collectorsauction.com
www.stampsonline.com

ing the furniture delivered, pay only by credit card. In the last few years, a lot of furniture stores have closed up shop without filling orders or delivering goods. I've had to tell too many callers who prepaid by cash or check that they won't be getting any money back. Some eventually get their merchandise or partial refunds, but they are lucky. Many others learn an expensive but important lesson: If you pay by check or cash, you could lose your money. If you buy with a credit card and the furniture store fails to deliver the merchandise, you are protected by your chargeback rights.

Beds

I've had a number of questions in the past few years about how to buy a bed. My own solution is pretty low-tech. I go to my favorite warehouse discount store with a book or magazine and read awhile, in different positions, to see if I'm comfortable. If I am, I buy it. If I'm not, I don't. The most recent mattress I bought, a Sealy, is the best one I've ever owned. I've never had a problem with a bed I purchased in this manner.

The book answer is somewhat more complex and probably will end up costing you somewhat more. But the experts say spending a bit more for a bed is pretty reasonable when you consider that you spend one-third of your life in it and that a good set of bedding should last for 10 to 15 years.

It's recommended that you look primarily at mattresses and box springs made by one of the four major bedding manufacturers: Simmons, Sealy, Serta, or Stearns & Foster. Look for a mattress that's priced in the middle of the manufacturer's product line. The most expensive will be loaded with bells and whistles you don't need. The cheapest won't be of adequate quality.

The most important characteristic a mattress should have is proper firmness. A soft mattress won't give your body the support it needs, and you'll wake up feeling achy, like you slept in a hammock. A mattress that doesn't give at all will make you feel like you slept on the floor.

The right mattress should give enough to accommodate the contours of your body, yet provide good support. A 200-pound man will need more support than a 130-pound woman, so it's absolutely necessary to try a mattress out before you buy it. Wear comfortable clothes, and see how each mattress feels. If you're married, go shopping with your spouse. Any reputable store is fine.

You'll hear a lot about mattress construction when you talk to salespeople or read product materials. The most important part of all that gibberish has to do with the coils and the upholstery, which determine the firmness of the mattress and its ability to react to your body. A good-quality full-size mattress will have 400 to 800 separate coils. Queen- or king-size mattresses will have more coils than their full-size counterparts of the same brand and model, and twin-size mattresses will have fewer. Ask the salesperson how many coils the full-size version has, and use that figure to help evaluate quality. Don't buy a full-size mattress with fewer than 312 coils.

At least one top-of-the-line mattress has coils that are individually wrapped in cloth pockets, which I'm told enables it to adjust better to shoulders and hips. That's great, but there are plenty of excellent mattresses with the more standard, open-coil design.

The surface layer of a mattress isn't just cosmetic. Manufacturers use materials from horse hair to high-density foam, in combination with cotton batting, to help adjust the level of firmness. But don't worry too much about the content or design of the upholstery fabric. A silk surface will cost a lot more, and you'll have it covered most of the time with sheets and blankets. Another worthless extra is a spun Dacron filler some manufacturers use to give the surface 7 to 10 inches of extra puffiness. It isn't worth the extra cost.

It's strongly recommended that you buy a new box spring at the same time you buy a new mattress. Some people try to save money by buying just the mattress. But experts say box springs wear out just like mattresses, although not as visibly. Putting a new mattress on an old box spring may cause the new mattress to sag. Some new box springs have metal frames, rather than wood. That adds weight, but it may add strength as well.

Any bed frame will do, as long as it has a center support bar or enough horizontal slats to support the bed.

Carpet

When you buy carpet, it's important to buy from a good dealer, get a good-quality carpet yarn, and make sure the carpet is properly installed. It doesn't matter if you buy from a carpet store or a department store, just don't buy over the phone. Generally someone who tries to sell carpet over the phone is trying to rip you off, selling cheap-quality carpet at inflated prices.

When you buy from a carpet store, make sure the showroom is neat and well kept, not a sloppy warehouse. An owner who takes care of his showroom is more likely to insist his installers do a good job in your home.

Choosing the carpet itself is relatively easy. Buy a carpet made from a premium carpet yarn, such as Du Pont's Stainmaster, Monsanto's Wear-Dated, or Allied Fibers' Worry-Free. Zeftron from BASF and XPS from Hoechst Celanese Corp. are two other good yarns. It's less important which mill turns those yarns into carpet, but you should look for a finished product whose yarn has a good twist to it. If you look closely at the carpet fibers, the tips should have a sharp, pencil-point appearance. That means the carpet's been properly twisted. Poorly made carpet will have very little twist and the tips will look frayed. Quality carpet

should look good for 5 to 10 years, but cheap carpet can look ugly in as little as six months.

Installation is critical to the way the carpet will look in your home. Most carpet dealers use contractors, rather than their own employees, to do the installation, and most contractors are poorly trained and use sloppy procedures. Ask the dealer what kind of guarantee is offered on installation. Ninety days to one year is normal. More than one year is a plus.

For proper installation, carpet should be power stretched into place so it is drum tight. Most installers use a knee-kicker to stretch carpet, a technique that won't achieve the right tautness. Loose carpet looks terrible and wears unevenly. When you buy, get a written guarantee that the carpet will be power stretched. As for padding, the best kind is half-inch, six-pound rebond, a dense padding made from chopped, pressed foam.

If you live in the southeastern U.S., consider taking a trip to Dalton, Georgia, northwest of Atlanta, where most of the nation's carpet is made. Dalton has a number of outlets, and they sell massive volumes of carpet. The best deal is to buy factory seconds, but there are some seconds to buy and some to avoid. Usually the best irregulars are the ones whose colors don't match those of the store samples, and those pieces usually are from the beginning and the end of a production run. The piece you buy will be uniform in color — it just won't match the national sample exactly. That doesn't matter at all if you like the color. My wife and I bought carpet in Dalton for $3.99 a yard and $5.99 a yard, and it's great carpet.

Buy only from a store that unrolls the carpet you want to buy. Then get on your hands and knees and inspect it. A good outlet will have a very well-lit area for you to check its carpet. Don't buy carpet that's irregular because of a stitching problem. One example is a weave defect called "chicken feet."

You can figure the number of yards of carpet you'll need by dividing the square footage of your room by nine, then adding 10 percent to account for waste. If you pay $15 a yard, it would cost about $460 to carpet a bedroom that measures 12 feet by 21 feet, or about $3,300 for an entire 1,800-square-foot house. Even if you don't buy irregulars, carpet prices have declined, probably because of the influence of mass-market discounters such as Home Depot and Costco.

Make sure to get a few quotes on the number of yards you will need. Telephone salespeople and other unethical installers commonly mislead customers by quoting cheap prices but overestimating the yardage. It's no bargain to pay $12.99 for 195 yards (total price: $2,533) when another dealer, charging $15.99, says you need only 150 yards (total price: $2,399).

One company no longer in business quoted its prices in "units" that were actually equal to half a yard. A buyer who needed only 27 square yards wound up paying for 54 "units" at $12.99 a unit. In other words, she bought cheap, builders' grade carpet at the outrageous price of $25.98 a yard, paying more than $700 for cheap carpet when she could have bought good carpet for $500 or less.

Ask the installer how much carpet he has brought and make sure it's the amount you've purchased. Also check the manufacturer's name on the carpet and look at the padding. Some dealers will pull a fast one by giving you cheaper carpet or padding than what you bought or by selling you one quantity of carpet and sending the installer out with less.

Jewelry

When it comes to jewelry, some consumers see a purchase as an investment that could increase in value. But buying jewelry with that goal should be done only if you're an expert in the industry. If you're buying jewelry as a gift for yourself or a loved one, determining the true value of the item will be very difficult. Plus, jewelry bought at retail loses a lot of its value as soon as you purchase it.

I recommend buying jewelry only from stores that allow you 72 hours to inspect it and, if you choose, to return it for a full refund. This gives you the power to buy a piece that you like and then have its value estimated by jewelry appraisers.

Jewelry generally is an emotional purchase, not a financial one. It's possible to buy jewelry now in warehouse clubs with concrete floors, but you might not want to tell an admiring friend that your diamond ring came from a warehouse. But if you consider money more important than love or emotion, consider buying jewelry from a warehouse club or buying a used piece, perhaps from a pawn shop.

The Better Business Bureau publishes an excellent booklet on how to understand the various quality grades of diamonds, gold, and other jewelry. I recommend you read it before making a major jewelry purchase.

Coins and Stamps

The Internet has forced me to change completely my advice on how to buy or sell coins, stamps, and other collectibles.

Before the widespread use of the Internet, I recommended that you visit stamp and coin shows, talk to several dealers, and see what kind of prices you were quoted. Then you could settle for the price you were offered or advertise the collection for sale in the newspaper.

But there's a great Web site now, www.collectorsauction.com, that lets you see current bids for coins and stamps from buyers all over the world. Check what buyers are asking for and getting for their collectibles and you can more easily determine what to ask for yours. If you're not computer savvy, or don't have Internet access, ask a friend to help.

CONTRACTS

Most people don't bother to read the contracts they're asked to sign when they buy a car or rent an apartment. But you do yourself a disservice when you sign a contract without knowing all its contents. Ask for time to take the contract home and read it.

If the party trying to get you to sign a contract refuses to let you leave with it, or pressures you to make a decision right then, don't sign the contract and don't do business with the organization. Pressure tactics are used a lot at health clubs, which often try to push you into signing expensive, long-term deals.

It's important to remember that a contract is a negotiated document, not a unilateral declaration. Many standard prewritten contracts are very one-sided: the consumer has all the responsibilities and the other side has all the rights and privileges. If necessary, you can insist on changes. Or if an organization says the terms and conditions of a contract aren't negotiable, think about doing business with somebody else.

If you read a contract and something sounds unfair, or you don't understand something, mark out the item with a pen and put your initials by it. Don't agree to any clause you don't understand or don't like. Once you sign the contract, you have to live with its provisions.

FRANCHISES

Many people see buying a franchise as a quick way to go into business for themselves, without having to build up a business's reputation from nothing. Buying a franchise isn't necessarily bad or good in itself, but it requires planning. Any time you're thinking of going into a business or an industry you know little about, you shouldn't immediately set up shop or buy a franchise.

TIPS ON CONTRACTS

• A contract is a negotiated document, not a unilateral declaration. Always ask for time to take a contract home and read it.

• If the party trying to get you to sign a contract refuses to let you leave with it, or pressures you to make a decision right then, don't sign the contract and don't do business with that organization.

• If you read a contract and something sounds unfair, or you don't understand something, mark out the item with a pen and put your initials by it.

The best approach is to go to work in the industry, either for an independent operator or the franchise you're evaluating. Work in the industry for at least six months, preferably one year. I don't care if it means you're taking out the trash. Go in with your eyes and ears open so you can learn as much as possible. By doing this you'll learn two things. First and most important, you'll find out if it's a business you like. Second, you'll learn enough as an insider to know if the promises the franchisor makes are genuine. You'd be amazed how many people do this and then completely drop any thoughts of getting involved in the business.

Before I went into the travel business, I went to work in an agency for six months. I did everything you do as a lower-level employee in a travel agency, including writing and delivering tickets. The only mistake I made was doing it for only six months. A year would have been better. But because I had some experience, my agency started turning a profit in its fourth month of business. It was terrific to start making money that quickly.

If you find after working in an industry that you like it and want to buy a franchise, think about these questions: Is the name readily recognizable in

TIPS ON FRANCHISES

- Before buying a franchise, go to work in the industry, either for an independent operator or the franchise you're thinking about buying. You'll learn plenty about the business and may decide it's not for you.

- Find out the answers to these questions: Is the franchise name readily recognizable in your area? Does that name brand have a good reputation in the general community and in that trade? Does the franchisor provide strong support?

- Call franchisees in a nearby town and ask them what they like and don't like about owning their franchise.

- Evaluate your territory and make sure the company won't put another store close to yours.

your area? Does the name brand have a good reputation in the general community and in that trade? Does the franchisor truly provide the support its glossy literature promises?

The best way to find out about franchise support is to call franchisees in a nearby town. People in your own town may not be truthful because they may see you as a potential buyer for their business. You also need to evaluate the cost you pay for support, including the up-front fees and the percentage of your sales you'll pay the franchisor. Make sure your business will be able to support that level of royalties.

Another thing to evaluate is territory. Some franchisees, just as they become successful, are stunned to find out that the franchisor is placing another franchise right down the street from their business. A famous sandwich shop chain has made many of its franchise holders unhappy by opening too many stores close to others, making it difficult for the franchises to be profitable.

Other franchises have been criticized for spending too much effort on opening new stores and thus generating up-front fees, or letting corporate leadership lapse because a founder sold out or became less involved. Some say the Wendy's hamburger chain enjoyed a resurgence because founder Dave Thomas became a more visible leader.

One of the big advantages of a well-recognized franchise name is that your company is easier to sell if you decide to leave the business. It's much harder to sell an independent, nonbranded business. However, the fact that a franchise remains on one street corner for years does not mean it's successful. Often a franchisor will buy back a troubled franchise and run it until a new owner is found, rather than let anyone know it has failed. The industry rule of thumb is that 90 percent of franchises succeed. But one franchise consultant I spoke to believes that at any given time only one-third are successful, one-third are getting by, and one-third are failing.

MULTILEVEL MARKETING

Multilevel marketing organizations want you to believe that you can become wealthy with very limited expense on your part but a great desire to win. If you're thinking of going to work for a multilevel marketing organization, beware of all the hoopla and be on guard for possible illegalities.

TIPS ON MULTILEVEL MARKETING

• You make money in two ways in a multilevel marketing organization: you buy products from the company and resell them to customers, and you recruit people into the organization and earn a commission off their sales.

• Don't join a multilevel marketing organization unless you have sales ability, you believe in the product, and the product is priced fairly.

• Don't join if the main purpose of the organization is rounding up new recruits. Such an organization may be an illegal pyramid.

• If you're an outstanding salesperson who would do well at multilevel marketing, you would probably do better by selling through a traditional sales channel, in which you won't have to split your commissions.

CONTACT

U.S. Office of Consumer Affairs (For consumer and insurance questions and to ask for a free copy of the *Consumer's Resource Handbook*)
202-565-0040

Multilevel marketing organizations recruit individuals to sell a variety of products, including items such as household cleaners and diet aids.

You make money in two ways in a multilevel marketing organization. The first is by serving as a combination retailer and sales representative — you buy products from the company and resell them to customers. The second way is by recruiting people into the organization and earning a commission off their sales. That's where the term multilevel comes in. If I recruit you and you recruit a friend, I get commissions off both your sales and your friend's sales.

A multilevel marketing presentation is something like a high school pep rally. You'll hear testimonials from people who say they were near the financial abyss and found the ticket selling purple oranges. Now they're rolling in money and have a fancy car and a retirement home at the beach.

If you're thinking of joining such an organization, consider whether you have any sales skills, whether you believe in the product, and whether the product is priced fairly. You should be confident you will be able to go up to strangers or acquaintances — because you're going to exhaust your friends and relatives very quickly — and convince them of the virtues of the product and get them to buy. A lot of people can't or don't want to do that.

If you're going to sell a product, it should represent a fair value. It's no fun to justify why you sold someone, particularly a friend, a product that was more expensive than a similar product at the store. As consumers, your customers won't want to and shouldn't buy something that's overpriced.

I don't recommend joining any multilevel marketing organization that requires you to pay a substantial up-front fee to participate.

It's also very important to determine if the emphasis of the company is on selling its products or on recruiting people into the organization. If you hear a lot about the virtues of the products, the organization is on sound footing. However, if its main purpose is rounding up new recruits, it may be an illegal pyramid. One caller told me about a meeting she went to at which the product was never mentioned. All they ever talked about was recruiting.

In the spring of 1998, the Securities and Exchange Commission got a judge to appoint a receiver for International Heritage, a North Carolina organization that the SEC alleged was engaging in fraud. The SEC charged that the organization was not engaged in traditional selling, only in running a pyramid. The company took in $150 million, an incredible amount. Several states have been working with International Heritage to come up with a procedure to make refunds to customers. As we go to press, it's unknown how much of the $150 million will be returned.

International Heritage charged people an entry fee of $1,850 for a "buying center." People in the organization received commissions from every new member, and a number of members made fortunes.

A pyramid organization can succeed only as long as it recruits new members, but as it does so it requires more and more members to support its ever-expanding base. Normally, it will just collapse. But let's say, hypothetically, it is remarkably skilled at recruiting and has no difficulty signing up members. Eventually it will run out of people in the United States or on Earth and collapse. Pyramids are illegal because only the scam artists who start them make any money.

One more word of caution about multilevel marketing. If you're an outstanding salesperson, you would probably do better by selling through a traditional sales channel, where you won't have to split your commissions with others in the organization.

One advantage of multilevel marketing is that it helps some people discover a talent they didn't know they had, and they can then graduate to a true, full-time selling position. One thing you don't want to do is quit your regular job to join a multilevel organization. I've heard horror stories of people who've quit jobs only to find that either they weren't successful at selling or the multilevel organization left town and left them unemployed.

Cars

Too often when people ask me questions about cars, they are looking for remedies to problems. A new or used car turns out to be trouble-prone, a lease turns out to be a bad idea, or a minor accident turns out to be a major headache. I believe you're better off avoiding problems in the first place than trying to fix them later on.

With most purchases we know enough, or can quickly learn enough, to control the process. But when it comes to cars, many of us never gain control. Too few buyers do any research on their favorite model, even though learning about its poor repair record could save a lot of hardship later on.

When you're buying a car, whom can you trust? Contrary to what most people think, the vast majority of car dealers are decent, honest people. Unfortunately, a dishonest person can take your money in so many ways in a car transaction that it magnifies the harm you can suffer when you're not well informed.

Most of us simply cannot become experts in the complexities of car repair. Because of the diversity of car models and shortage of well-trained labor, it's difficult enough for mechanics

to do the work properly. The best way to handle an expensive car repair is by taking the time to get opinions and estimates from several repair shops.

In this chapter, I'll give you the information and resources you'll need to help you buy a new or used car, finance it, and get it fixed if something goes wrong.

BUYING A NEW CAR

The process of buying a new car — which most people have enjoyed about as much as a trip to the dentist — is at long last changing.

After years of treating people like dirt, manufacturers and dealers are changing the way they do business, and consumers are endorsing that move by flocking to these new alternatives. Happy car buyers are telling their friends about retailers like CarMax and AutoNation that have followed others, like Saturn, into the world of consumer-friendly, no-haggle selling.

There's no need to bring a professional negotiator with you when you buy a car at a true no-haggle dealership, or to brace yourself for hours of game-playing. The price of a car is listed on a sticker on the car, and that's the price you pay. There are no hours of negotiating while the salesperson goes back and forth to talk to the sales manager. It's just like buying a television set at an appliance store.

Dealerships are changing the way they do business because they're under pressure to raise their productivity. By selling more cars, they reduce the cost of their back-office operations per vehicle. The cost of getting cars to the consumer is simply too high in the car business.

A good example is Ford Motor Company's acquisition of a number of its dealerships in San Diego and Oklahoma. Ford replaced the dealerships with auto superstores and satellite service centers, making its distribution operation leaner and less costly so Ford could cope with competition from publicly owned dealer chains and superstore operators, such as Republic Industries, parent of AutoNation.

Saturn has kept its distribution costs lower by maintaining fewer dealerships, so the company is able to sell a Saturn for less than it could otherwise.

The gasoline retailing business went through the same change decades ago. When the dust has settled a few years from now, you're going to see far fewer car dealerships, and all of them will be offering better shopping experiences and better prices.

The cost may not be rock bottom at no-haggle dealerships, but buying there eliminates the risk of dramatically overpaying. When the whole industry goes to no-haggle, the price differences between dealers will be clear.

If You Want to Negotiate

I strongly recommend you seek out no-haggle dealerships when looking for a new car. But if you prefer the old-fashioned way, here are a few tips:

First, go to your bank or credit union and prequalify for a car loan. Once you prequalify, you'll know how much car you can afford and the monthly payment you will have to budget. And your purchase won't collapse because you can't get financing.

Once your financing is set up, decide what kind of car you want. This is the stage when you look at cars and test-drive them. One of the best times to look at cars is when a dealership is closed. If the dealership isn't open, there are no salespeople to pressure you. You're free to look around the lot at vehicles.

I recommend that people become familiar with the various versions of a car. The Honda Accord, for example, might come in a DX, LX, EX, and SE version. Each version comes with a different package of options and standard equipment. You'll find that the most expensive version will cost several thousand dollars more than the least expensive. It's to your advantage to buy the least expensive version of the model that meets your needs. That's because, over time, the values of those two vehicles will converge. An initial gap of $8,000 between the cheapest and most expensive versions can dwindle to $1,000 in the resale value of the two cars after a few years of ownership. If you buy the most expensive version, you pay a higher price both up front and at resale time.

I don't recommend test-driving a car at a dealership. You'll have only a short time to check out the car, and the salesperson will be right there. The best way to test-drive a car is to rent it for a day or two. Car rental companies make most of their money on business rentals, so they offer great specials on the weekends, when volume is light. I actually check out cars this way on business, since I travel so much. I've rented cars I thought I might want to buy and changed my mind after driving them for a few days. It's the ultimate test drive, and it's not expensive. After all, considering that you might spend $20,000 for a car, spending $25 to $40 to rent it is rather inexpensive.

If you do a test drive at the dealership, a representative may ask for your driver's license. If you turn it over, make sure the representative gives you a signed release saying the dealership will not pull a credit report on you. Dealerships like to check your credit while you're on a test drive, and if you visit several dealerships, the credit inquiries could damage your credit rating.

Start your car-shopping research with at least two different vehicles in mind. Then check out the price, reliability, and cost to insure each of the cars you're considering.

Everyone wants a car that will run dependably and stay out of the repair shop. The best way to improve your odds of getting a trouble-free car is to check out the repair records of the models you've selected. *Consumer Reports* magazine is the best place to find repair data. Each year, the magazine's April issue is devoted to car buying, and it contains detailed ratings and data on a variety of models for several model years. Consumers Union, which publishes *Consumer Reports,* also publishes a car-buying guide that is available year-round in bookstores.

Consumer Reports is available online for a monthly fee, or for free to America Online customers (keyword: Consumer Reports).

Of course, no repair data are available on newly introduced car models. I don't recommend buying a new or radically redesigned model, because if you do, you are the guinea pig for any problems the vehicle might have. After a few model years, you have a better idea if a car is well made and worth purchasing.

Cars today, both American- and foreign-made, are of a much higher quality than cars made 5 or 10 years ago. And there's such a broad selection that when a company makes a bad car, the marketplace eventually punishes the company by driving its sales down to nothing. When Hyundai Motor Corp. introduced its line of inexpensive cars in the 1980s, people were excited to see affordable cars that seemed to be good for basic transportation. But the cars didn't work, and Hyundai suffered terribly because of it. The company still is struggling to recover from the reputation it developed in its first 10 years in the United States. The marketplace works, but you don't want to be the guinea pig.

If you've narrowed your search to a couple of models, it's helpful to call your insurance agent to find out how much it would cost to insure those vehicles. There may be a significant difference between your choices, even between two versions of the same model. The size of the cars' engines, for example, could be one reason for such a difference.

The next task is to find out what the car actually costs, disregarding the make-believe list price printed on the window sticker at traditional dealerships. There are a number of ways to get this information. The best is go to the Edmund's Web site, www.edmunds.com, or ask a friend to look for you.

Edmund's and a competitor, Pace, also have books, which are available at most bookstores and libraries. If you're a member of a credit union, the dealer's cost of a car may be available to you there.

Price guides will give you a breakdown of the car's base cost and the cost of options such as automatic transmission and air conditioning. You'll get the dealer's actual cost and the suggested retail price. Ignore the suggested retail

TIPS ON BUYING A NEW CAR

- Buy new cars from no-haggle dealerships. In most cases, you'll save money and the process of buying will be faster and easier.

- If you choose to negotiate with a traditional car dealer, take your time in choosing and buying the car. A reasoned approach will save you a lot of money.

- First, go to your bank or credit union and prequalify for a car loan. That way you'll know how much car you can afford and the monthly payment you will have to budget.

- Look at cars when a dealership is closed, so there's no salesperson to pressure you.

- The best way to test-drive a car is to rent it for a day or two. It's the ultimate test drive, and it's not expensive.

- Start your car-shopping research with at least two different vehicles in mind. Then check out the price, reliability, and cost to insure each of the cars you're considering.

- Find out the dealer cost of the vehicle and options you want and begin negotiating from that cost, not the make-believe retail price.

- When you've narrowed the search to one or two vehicles and have the dealer cost for each, call a few dealers and ask for their best price on the vehicle. Do not go to the dealership; if you do, the balance of power will shift to the dealer.

- The success of a particular model in the marketplace is critical in determining how much you'll pay. If a vehicle is selling very poorly, a smart shopper may end up paying below dealer cost. You'll pay much more for a hot seller.

- When you go into the dealership to sign the paperwork, make sure that what is on the purchase agreement is what you agreed to previously by phone or fax. If it's not the same, do not agree to go through with the deal.

- The best way to protect yourself in a dealership is to be willing to walk out.

REFERENCE

Consumer Reports April auto Issue or *Car Buying Guide*
Edmund's car guides, by Edmund Publications Corp.

INTERNET

www.edmunds.com

price. Just add up the dealer's base price, the dealer cost of any options you want, and other necessary charges, such as transportation. In most states, you'll also have to pay sales tax.

When you negotiate to buy a car, you should work from the dealer's actual cost. Most dealers will sell a car for a few hundred dollars above that. In some very rare cases, you can buy a car for less than dealer cost. Yet buyers regularly pay sticker prices that contain mark-ups of several thousand dollars. What you ultimately pay is strictly a matter of supply and demand and your own ability to shop.

Edmunds tells you the dealer cost and retail price for the vehicle and options. The Web site tells you about holdback, which is under-the-table money the dealer receives from the manufacturer. It's more of a true reflection of the actual dealer cost. If you're buying a $20,000 car with a holdback of 5 percent, the dealer may get up to an additional $1,000 back. That's how dealers can afford to sell the vehicle at "invoice" or "below invoice" and still make a profit.

When you've narrowed the search to one or two vehicles and have the actual dealer cost for those vehicles, call a few dealers and ask for their best prices on the vehicles. Tell them what options you want and what colors you will accept. Do not go to any dealership. As soon as you do, the balance of power shifts to the dealer and you are in a weakened negotiating position.

Most dealers will be happy to quote you a price on the phone. Some dealers will offer to beat whatever deal you come up with, or give you a very low price, which they don't intend to honor later. Don't do business with anyone who won't play straight with you.

When you get quotes from dealers, make sure you have a full breakdown of the price, including all fees, services charges, and taxes for a total, final cost. I've heard from my callers that dealers will

quote a fair price for a vehicle, then add hundreds of dollars in various fees and charges, such as an advertising fee, a documentation fee, and a preparation fee. One caller said a dealer tried to charge her a $300 documentation fee — essentially to do the paperwork for her license plate. You should know up front about every single potential expense.

One method that eliminates any potential for misunderstanding is using a fax machine to exchange information with dealers. I've had calls from people who have used faxes very successfully to ensure a low-pressure, no-pain transaction. The idea here is not to prevent the dealer from making a profit. It's for you to get a deal you believe is fair, without being subjected to the high-pressure sales tactics some dealers employ.

There's no formula that says you should pay $300 or $500 above dealer cost. Some people like to buy at the end of the month, the end of a model year, or the end of the calendar year, when sales goals, the influx of new models, or inventory taxes may cause a dealer to be more motivated to negotiate. But there are drawbacks. If you buy a car at the end of a model year, you have a one-year-old car as soon as you drive it out of the dealership. You should consider an end-of-year closeout only if you keep a car a long time. The depreciation hit of that lost year doesn't matter once you have owned the car for several years. But it matters a great deal if you buy a car every few years.

More important than calendar cycles is the success of a particular model in the marketplace. If a vehicle is selling very poorly, a smart shopper may end up paying below dealer cost, because all the dealer is trying to do is move the vehicle. The dealer may be hurting because the vehicle is just sitting on the lot (that's called flooring), or the manufacturer may be offering incentives to sell slow-moving models.

When small cars aren't selling well, the manufacturers offer huge incentives to their dealers to move them. Because of the Corporate Average Fuel Economy (CAFE) standards, manufacturers have to sell a certain number of small cars to balance the number of large cars they sell, so that their average fuel economy will meet federal standards. If they don't meet the standards, manufacturers face huge fines. Usually your most aggressive negotiating tactics will work best with a domestic manufacturer, whatever that means now, for smaller, entry-level vehicles they must sell.

At the other end of the spectrum is the "hot" car, the one everyone wants to buy. In this case, the sky's the limit as far as price goes. Dealers sometimes can get $1,000 above sticker price for a trendy vehicle, such as the Ford Explorer or the Jeep Grand Cherokee, and customers will line up to buy. If you want to pay a premium for a hot car, that's fine — as long as you know the cost, both up front and at resale time, when the heavy demand probably will have waned. The size of the holdback, which you can see on the Edmunds Web site, reflects how well or poorly a vehicle is selling. The larger the holdback or rebate, the more bargaining power you'll have.

The demand for most cars is average, so the price you pay will depend mostly on your knowledge of actual dealer cost. The more you know and the less emotional you are about the purchase, the better off you'll be. As you contact dealer after dealer, you're quickly going to get a feel for the market. You may have one quote that's very high, but most will be in a narrow range and the marketplace will establish the fair value of the car. I recommend calling at least six dealers. Some people get obsessed with this process and call many more. Just call until you feel comfortable with the quotes.

When you go into the dealership to sign the paperwork, make sure that what is on the purchase agreement is what you've agreed to previously by phone or fax. If it's not the same, do not agree to go through with the deal. Remember, you've been shopping. If finalist A pulls a con job, you can go to finalist B. I've used this method for years, and only once has a dealer tried to cheat me. Every other time the dealers treated me with complete dignity and honesty.

There are car-shopping services on the Internet, such as Auto-buy-Tel, that are paid for by dealers and others that you join by paying a fee of perhaps $200 that enable you to bid in an auto auction. I would much prefer that you pay the $200 so that it's a true auction. The great thing about this is, because the dealer is actively bidding for your business, there's no give and take and none of the pressure that you normally have to deal with.

If you choose to buy a car by walking into a dealership and talking with a salesperson, be prepared for a difficult process. Some dealers still use a variety of tactics to snare you. They know you're excited about buying a new car and will use that to their advantage. One strategy they'll employ is delay. Dealers know that the longer they can keep you at the dealership, the more likely you are to buy a car. So they'll try to keep you there for several hours.

One common tactic to delay you is to make your car unavailable. When you show up at the dealership, a salesperson says the used-car manager needs to check out your car, to evaluate its trade-in value. While you're test-driving a new car, they send somebody to look over your car and make sure you don't get it back too quickly.

I recommend that you discuss any trade-in only after you've negotiated the purchase of the new car. I'll talk more about why in the next section. But if you keep the transactions separate and stay close to your car, you won't be kept in the dealership any longer than you want.

One of the most despicable practices in the industry is "roofing," in which used-car people literally throw the keys to your car onto the roof of the dealership, then report that they somehow can't find the keys. The purpose is to get you to drive home in the new car while they look for the keys. The best way to protect yourself in a dealership is to be willing to walk out. Only those who are willing to get up and leave are able negotiators.

One problem many Americans have in negotiations is they are too polite. We might think that it's rude, when a salesperson is being too aggressive, to say, "I'm sorry but I need to leave." But sometimes that is the only answer.

TRADE-INS, FINANCING, AND EXTENDED WARRANTIES

If you have a trade-in, the time to discuss it with the dealer is after you've completed the purchase transaction for your new car, particularly if you're not buying from a no-haggle dealership. Do the trade-in as a completely separate transaction from the purchase. If you do these transactions together, you'll never know whether a dealer is offering you a great price on your new car and making up for it by giving you a poor value for your trade-in.

Once you've shopped around and the dealers realize you're a good shopper, their prices will be similar. To help you decide which dealer to buy from, ask how much he'll give you for the trade-in. Take the car to each dealership for a trade-in quote, and use that as the decision maker.

I always skip the trade-in process and sell my cars myself. Many people sell privately, and they are able to get better prices. But most prefer to trade in their cars to the dealership because they don't want to deal with the hassles of a private sale — classified ads, phone calls, and test drives.

You can find out what your trade-in is worth by checking the Edmund's Web site, www.edmunds.com, or asking a friend to look for you. Edmund's also has books, available at most bookstores and libraries, that list the average retail prices of used vehicles, plus their average trade-in values. By selling the vehicle yourself, you'll get a price about halfway between the average trade-in and the average retail. A dealer will give you the trade-in price. Once you've measured that gap, you can figure out if selling the car yourself is worth the bother.

Financing the Car

It's critical to finance the purchase of a car in advance at a bank or credit union and not at the dealership. When you allow the dealer to arrange financing, all kinds of terrible things can happen. If you drive your new car home and give the dealer your trade-in, you're in trouble if, as happens more and more, the financing later collapses.

Here's what happens when the dealer calls you a few weeks later with the sad news that your loan didn't go through. Because the loan and purchase are done separately, you may not be able to undo the sale. But even if you can, your old car may be long gone. So you either have to come up with a lot more money for a down payment or pay an exorbitant rate of interest so that a lender will accept the loan. You can try to get the dealer to undo the sale and give you the value of your used car in cash. But depending on the laws in your state, you may have to fight to reverse the deal. When I get calls about these problems, it's like trying to fix a train wreck. The damage is already done.

You also can end up paying higher interest rates on dealer-arranged loans, because dealers will sell loans to customers at whatever rate the dealers can get customers to pay. A disgruntled

TIPS ON TRADE-INS, FINANCING, AND EXTENDED WARRANTIES

• If you have a trade-in, the time to discuss it with the dealer is after you've negotiated the purchase price of the new car.

• After you've negotiated a price for a new car, you can decide which dealer to buy from by asking how much it will give you for the trade-in.

• You can find out what your trade-in is worth by checking the Edmund's Web site, www.edmunds.com, or asking a friend to look for you. Edmunds also has books, available at most bookstores and libraries. By selling the vehicle yourself, you'll get a price about halfway between the average trade-in and the average retail. A dealer will give you the trade-in price.

• Finance a car for 48 months or less. With a 60-month loan, the value of the car declines much faster than the loan balance. So for much of the five-year period, you owe more than the vehicle is worth.

• Keep the financing separate from the car-price negotiations. When you allow the dealer to arrange financing, all kinds of terrible things can happen.

• Don't buy an extended service contract from an automobile dealer or from anyplace else until you've had time to think about it and check prices. You do not have to make this decision at the moment you buy your vehicle.

INTERNET

www.edmunds.com

finance manager told me that a dealership might get a loan at 8 percent and mark it up to 14 or 18 percent if it can get a customer to pay that much. The spreads are scary. The finance manager gets the car buyer to pay a higher rate by pointing out blemishes on the customer's credit report, scaring him into thinking he might not be approved. When the finance manager is done psyching out the customer, he's ecstatic to get the loan at the high rate.

Dealers want to do the financing, because that's where most of the profit is in car sales today. If you take the extra effort to prequalify with your bank or credit union, you will steer clear of a lot of financial danger.

Payment-oriented car buyers are more and more likely to opt for long loans, but you should finance a car for no more than 48 months. The 60-month loan is a poor financial choice because the value of the car declines much faster than the loan balance. So, for much of the five-year period, you're "upside down" in the loan — you owe more than the vehicle is worth.

Being "upside down" can be a major problem. Let's say you decide after a couple of years that you can't stand your car. Selling it won't generate nearly enough money to pay off the loan. Unless you can come up with several thousand dollars to pay off the balance, you're stuck with the vehicle. If it's totaled in an accident, you can end up owing the lender thousands of dollars. You have to cover the gap between the amount the insurance company pays and what you owe.

The beauty of a shorter loan, particularly 42 months or less, is that the loan amount tracks the value of the vehicle. For most people, 48 months is a good compromise. I know this sounds harsh, but if you go in for a car loan and the payments for a 48-month loan are too high, you're trying to buy too much car. Stretching it to 60 months is the wrong response.

Extended Warranties

I don't like service contracts or extended warranties. But if you're terribly afraid of having a car that does not work and want to buy an extended warranty, at least shop for the best price.

The price on extended warranties is highly negotiable. One manufacturer's contract that retails at $795 costs a dealer $180. The dealer may make little profit on the sale of a car, but, depending on the type of warranty you purchase, the markup may be 400 to 1,000 percent.

You can buy an extended warranty from three different sources: an extended warranty company, an insurance company, or an automobile manufacturer. Never buy a warranty that is not provided by the manufacturer or backed by an insurance company. I've heard case after case of extended warranty companies selling cheap contracts to dealers and then going out of business without paying claims.

These rip-off companies sell service contracts to dealers for $90, and the dealers resell them to car buyers for $1,100. The pitch is that the dealer makes a fortune even if it sells

the warranty for $600. After a few years, claims start coming in and there's not enough money in the pool to pay them. The company collapses or vanishes, and the consumer ends up with a worthless service contract.

If you buy an extended warranty, make sure you know who is behind it. If you buy a General Motors car, ask if the service contract is a General Motors branded product. If it's an insurance company product, ask what insurance company it is from and its rating from A. M. Best Co., a rating company. If the insurance company is not rated A++, do not buy the product. If the salesperson tells you it's rated A++, make sure the rating is stated in your purchase contract.

You can negotiate the price on a warranty with a dealer, but the best way to negotiate is to call an independent insurance company that writes service contracts and compare their costs and coverages with those offered under the dealer's contract. Another place to get a quote is the company that writes your auto insurance. Many times your agent will be able to give you a quote on an extended warranty.

It's important to give yourself time to think about whether to get an extended warranty from the dealer or anyplace else. This is not a decision that has to be made at the moment you buy your vehicle. In fact, that's the worst time to decide because you're not thinking clearly. You're excited about buying a new car and you want to be done with the paperwork.

Most extended warranty providers give you at least 12 months from the date you purchase the car to decide whether to purchase a warranty. One of the advantages to waiting is that if the car turns out to be a lemon and you're always having problems with it, you'll know you should buy an extended warranty. During the first year, the manufacturer's warranty protects you.

LEASING

It's almost impossible to talk to an auto salesperson today without hearing a pitch that you should lease, rather than buy, a vehicle. That's because leasing is very profitable for dealers.

Car buying can be complicated enough. Leasing is much more complicated, and that makes it very difficult for you to compare prices, even if you're a savvy consumer. With the sky-high financing costs built into most leases, you'll almost certainly end up with a bad deal.

One of the most popular tricks is for manufacturers and dealers to advertise incredibly low monthly lease payments — $169, $199 or $249 a month. What they don't tell you, except in the fine print, is that you'll have to pay a large, non-refundable fee up front. This fee, sometimes called a capital cost reduction, or a capital acquisition fee, often amounts to $2,000 to 4,000. Essentially, you're getting that low monthly payment by paying off part of the lease in advance. The idea is to sell based on low payments, because a lot of consumers buy a car today by figuring out if a particular payment will fit into their budget.

The low monthly payment makes it appear you're getting a good deal, but typically you're not. Let's say you pay a $3,000 up-front fee for a 36-month lease for which you'll pay $249 a month. If you spread the $3,000 over the 36 months, it amounts to more than $83 a month. So the actual cost of the deal is $332 a month, not to mention that you give up the use of the $3,000 right away. Clearly, not a good deal.

Some shoppers figure they can make the up-front payment by signing over their old car as a trade-in. That makes the loss invisible. But you could use the same trade-in money as a down payment on a car you buy.

TIPS ON LEASING

- It's harder to compare prices on a lease, and there are very high financing costs built in.

- It may seem cheaper to lease than to buy, but you're mortgaging your future when you lease. After four years of leasing a vehicle and making payments, you own nothing.

- Manufacturers and dealers like to use up-front fees to create ultra-low monthly payments that mask the actual cost of a lease.

- Most leases allow you to drive an average of 15,000 miles per year. If you exceed the limit, you have to pay a penalty of 8 to 15 cents per mile.

- A five-year lease is a recipe for disaster. Many customers end up married to a vehicle they hate or end up paying severe early-termination penalties.

- If you lease for five years and your car is totaled in an accident, you could be responsible for the gigantic difference between what the insurance company will pay and the residual stated in the lease.

Whenever you lease, you're giving away your future. If you buy a vehicle and pay it off in four years, you own a vehicle that still has value. You can keep it and avoid making payments for a while, or sell the car and use the money to help you buy a newer vehicle. But after four years of leasing a vehicle and making payments, you own nothing. When the lease is over, you're left with no car and no trade-in.

A lot of people use leasing to get more car than they can afford. The monthly payment for two similar cars will be cheaper for someone who leases than for someone who buys, so people will lease, foolishly, so they can have a more expensive car. Let's say you buy an $18,000 vehicle with no down payment. Over four years, you'll pay $18,000 plus interest, and your monthly payment will be based on the cost of financing $18,000. If you lease a vehicle, you may finance $8,000 and have a residual value of $10,000. Your monthly payments will be based on the $8,000 being financed, so the payments will be much lower. You'll have the option of paying $10,000 to buy that car at the end of the four-year lease.

You may also owe sizable mileage penalties at the end of a lease. Most leases allow you to drive an average of 15,000 miles per year. If you exceed the limit, you have to pay a penalty of 8 to 15 cents per mile. If you lease a car for four years and drive a total of 80,000 miles, you might owe as much as $3,000.

Too often, people are not realistic about how many miles they're going to drive. Or they end up changing jobs and driving much more than they originally intended. Before they know it, they're near the end of the lease and tens of thousands of miles over the limit. If you owe a big mileage penalty, the best thing to do is buy the vehicle at the predetermined price specified in the lease. Then you won't have to pay the penalty.

I had a call from one fellow who turned in his Mercedes-Benz at the end of his lease, not realizing he was way over the mileage limit. He wasn't asked to pay any penalty. But two years later, he was told that he owed $8,000 in excess mileage costs. It would have cost him just $2,000 more, a total of $10,000, to buy the car outright. But the car had been sold long before, and he no longer had the option to buy it.

If you're going to pay a mileage penalty or buy the car, you'd better have some cash on hand. If the car has lots of miles on it, a bank won't lend you the money to pay off its residual

value. You avoid all these problems if you just buy a vehicle in the first place.

Short-term leases can be bad enough but five-year leases are recipes for disaster. Many customers end up married to a vehicle they hate. Even if they like the car, most don't keep it the full five years. Instead, they frequently end up paying severe early-termination penalties.

If you lease for five years and your car is totaled in an accident, you may have really big problems. You could be responsible for the difference between the amount the insurance company will pay and the stated residual in the lease — and this difference could be gigantic. It's not at all unusual in these cases for the gap to be as much as $8,000. Some leases contain an automatic gap clause, which states that if the vehicle is totaled in an accident, the manufacturer's financing arm accepts the insurance company payment and releases you from further responsibilities. Be certain any lease you sign includes this gap provision. Some car dealers, if you raise this issue, will offer you a separate insurance product called gap insurance. You should require them to provide it for free as part of the deal.

There are two circumstances in which leasing a vehicle makes sense. The first is if you like to have a new car every two to three years. If that's your goal, to always have a new car and get rid of it before the warranty is up, you're a candidate for a short-term lease. You won't have to deal with getting rid of the car.

The other circumstance in which leasing can be okay is when the financing on the lease is factory-subsidized . If the manufacturer offers no-interest financing, your total cost to lease for four years and then buy the vehicle might be lower than if you bought it outright. But you have to have the discipline to put aside your savings each month so that you have the money to buy the vehicle at the end of the lease. If you're not a disciplined saver, buy a car, even with the prospect of factory-subsidized leasing.

If the manufacturer subsidizes the lease by stating an unrealistically high residual value on the vehicle, you can lease for three or four years at a great price, but then you should walk away. In any case, don't lease for more than four years. My preference is for no more than three. You can tell if the lease is factory-subsidized because the ad will be from the manufacturer, not the dealer.

BUYING A USED CAR

As little as a few years ago, you were completely on your own when you bought a used car. Warranties were rare, and consumers were justifiably afraid of buying someone else's headache. In some states, once you signed the papers, the car engine could fall out and there was nothing you could do about it.

The emergence of used-car mega-dealers, such as CarMax and AutoNation, has changed the picture completely, creating one of the largest shifts in used-car selling since before World War II.

The trend is significant because Americans now buy three used cars for every new one. A generation ago, we bought one used car for every one new car. So the practices of used-car dealers control how 75 percent of us feel about the car-buying experience.

It's really smart to buy a used car because of the tremendous savings you get. The value of a new car depreciates so much in the first two years that a nearly new two-year-old car is quite a bargain. And because leasing has become so common, there is a tremendous oversupply of high-quality two- and three-year-old used cars available for purchase. This has depressed prices even further and provided a great selection, making buying a used car a marvelous deal.

I recently priced a brand-new Ford Taurus at $18,345 retail. A two-year-old version of the same model would have cost as little as $12,000. That's a savings of $6,345, or nearly 35 percent, for buying a two-year-old car. Prices change, but the discount will always be sizable.

CarMax, the brainchild of Circuit City, has revolutionized the car business. The company was started from scratch and came up with the best way to sell cars. People hated the pressure and the game-playing, so CarMax threw all that stuff out and created a pleasant, easy car-buying experience.

In spite of my advice that people should arrange their car loans through a bank or credit union, most people still get loans through dealerships. CarMax finances 90 percent of the cars it sells, and makes its profit that way, so the company doesn't need to make a penny on the sale of the cars. And since the salespeople aren't paid a commission for writing loans, they don't care if you finance at CarMax or not.

CarMax's success has led to several imitators, including AutoNation USA and Driver's Mart. At all three, the price you pay for the car is on the window. There's no negotiating. It's up to you to check the national pricing guides and the Internet (www.edmunds.com) to see if the price is fair. Look at the classifieds in your local newspaper, too, because used-car prices vary by region. But keep in mind that many people overvalue their car's worth.

With a new car, you negotiate from dealer cost. With a used car, the best price is the one closest to the average trade-in.

Some people think you pay more at an auto superstore, and there's anecdotal evidence both ways. But CarMax and the others do such a high volume that their cost of doing business is indisputably lower than that of a traditional dealer. Even if the price is the same as at a traditional dealership, the superstores can offer you very expensive

TIPS ON BUYING A USED CAR

- The price, selection, reliability, and ease of purchasing a used car has never been better.

- Your best bet is to buy from a used-car superstore, such as CarMax, AutoNation USA, or Driver's Mart. The price you'll pay for the car is on the window, and you're given the right to return the car for seven days for any reason for a refund, plus a 90-day warranty. In addition, there often will be some of the manufacturer's warranty left on the vehicle.

- If you like the car, have it inspected within seven days by a diagnostic mechanic.

- With any used car, knowing the repair record is important. Check *Consumer Reports'* listings of car models that have performed well.

- Before you buy a used car, find out what the vehicle is worth. Go to the Edmund's Web site, www.edmunds.com, or ask a friend to look for you. Edmund's also has books that are available at most bookstores and libraries.

options at no extra cost — including the right to return the car for seven days for any reason for a refund, plus a 90-day warranty. In addition, with a newer used car, there often will be some time left on the manufacturer's warranty.

The superstores say that they verify that the cars they sell haven't been in significant accidents, and they also put them through their own service checks. I still recommend that you have the car evaluated by a diagnostic mechanic during the seven-day grace period. The advantage you have over the traditional safeguard — making the purchase of a used car contingent on the car passing an inspection — is that you can drive the car for a few days first. If you hate it, return the car and save the money you would have spent on the inspection.

The average car sale today still takes six hours, spread over two days. I bought a van at CarMax in 70 minutes — from when we walked in the door until we left with the car. That's pretty quick.

People are voting for this no-pressure way of buying cars in huge numbers, and it is putting pressure on traditional dealerships to adopt the

philosophy of the used-car superstores. Just be careful the dealership isn't just pretending to have adopted no-haggle selling. If there's a problem, walk out.

When buying any used car, it's important to know the repair record, and you should consider only car models that have performed well. *Consumer Reports* publishes a list every year in its April issue of recommended used cars, price ranges, and used cars to avoid. Don't buy a car if it's on the latter list. Buying a used car always will be riskier than buying a new one, and you don't want to do anything that worsens your odds.

The Traditional Method

If you choose to buy a used car from a traditional dealership or a private individual, or if there's no used-car superstore where you live, make the deal contingent upon having the vehicle inspected by an independent mechanic.

Only a handful of states provide any legal protection for used-car buyers. New York State has one of the best laws. Its Used Car Lemon

Law allows buyers to get a refund or replacement if a used car is defect-ridden or unsafe. Further, it requires dealerships to provide minimum warranties of 30 to 90 days, depending on the vehicle's mileage. In many other states, you own the car as soon as you sign the papers.

Some dealers still sell worthless cars salvaged from wrecks. I once got a call from a couple who spent $2,800 on a used Honda Civic, only to find that they couldn't get a title for it. The car had been wrecked in another state and shabbily repaired. The frame was bent in the crash, and a plate was welded to the undercarriage in a half-hearted attempt to fix it. When my staff and I interceded, the dealership offered to buy back the car, but it wanted a $600 fee for eight months of use.

There are businesses that do nothing but diagnostic inspections of cars and trucks. For $70 to $100, they will do a full test on the vehicle, often right on the dealer's lot. In most areas, you can find services like these listed in the *Yellow Pages* under the heading "Diagnostic Services." If a seller refuses to allow the vehicle to be inspected, don't buy it. That's a deal killer.

Having a car inspected isn't foolproof, but it improves your odds of avoiding a lemon tremendously. It's funny, but when a buyer insists on having a car inspected, the seller often remembers some defect or repair work that was done recently. Suddenly, his memory returns, because he knows he's going to be caught.

It's important to have nearly new cars inspected, even though they're still under warranty, because quite often such cars have been in accidents. A wreck can cause tremendous operating problems, as well as huge losses in value. The only way to know whether a car has been in an accident is to have it inspected by a diagnostic service.

Diagnostic tests aren't pass or fail. Sometimes the mechanic will report that a part is worn and you'll have to decide whether to buy the car. You can also use the disclosure of certain problems as leverage to lower the price. Then you can use the savings to pay for repairs.

The hardest calls I take on my radio show involve cars. Typically, someone has recently purchased a used car, sometimes for several thousand dollars, only to discover that it is ridden with problems. He or she is faced with impossible choices. Often, the vehicle can't be repaired properly, and the dealer won't take it back. That could mean scrapping it, absorbing an expensive loss, and trying again. It's even worse if the buyer is making car payments. These situations are very sad, because in many cases nothing can be done to help the caller. Most people who find themselves in these situations have been ripped off by an unethical used-car dealer.

To protect yourself, buy a used car from a superstore. If you can't do that, buy from a private citizen, or at the used-car lot of a new-car dealership. Do not buy vehicles from old-style dealers who sell only used cars. When a new-car dealer takes a trade or a return from a rental company, it keeps the best vehicles on its lot and sells the rest through auction. The most problem-ridden cars end up at used-car lots.

The worst used-car lots are the "Buy Here, Pay Here" lots. Almost always, the cars are incidental to the purpose of these places. They make their money on the loans they extend. They're in the loan business, not the car business.

CAR REPAIRS

Cars have become a lot more reliable over the years, but they've also become far more complex. The proliferation of car models, technological advancements, and the lack of properly trained repair people have made getting satisfactory car repairs much more difficult.

So often when I hear complaints about car repairs, the problem isn't that a repair shop is trying to rip someone off — it's the mechanic's lack of competence. We fear the crook, but the reality often is that the mechanic doesn't know enough about your car to fix a problem.

One of the best safeguards you can use when you take your car in for service — and especially if you have to take the car back for the same problem — is to control what is written on the work ticket. Don't let the mechanic list a cure on the ticket, but rather write a description of the symptoms. If the car is stalling out at 30 miles per hour, that is what should be written on the ticket. You don't want the ticket to say, "Do a tune-up." If the problem isn't corrected, the mechanic will correctly be able to say that he did what was promised.

How the service ticket is prepared is key if you want to assert your rights under your state's Lemon Law (see also the Lemon Law section). To claim benefits under most of these laws, you have to produce service tickets that show you attempted to repair the vehicle. Make sure the shop writes a service ticket, and make sure you keep a copy. If the service tickets you receive do not show clearly that the vehicle was brought in several times to repair the same problem, you may not be able to provide the proper documentation to force the manufacturer to buy back or exchange your vehicle.

If you're having an estimate done on your car, make sure the work ticket says that you have authorized only work related to doing an estimate. If you're authorizing specific work, write down the exact dollar limit you are authorizing, and don't permit any work to be done beyond that limit.

If the estimate is high, don't accept it as the final word. Even if your car is not driveable, it would be wise to have it towed to another repair shop for another estimate of what is wrong and how much it would cost to repair. If the repair is $2,000 or more, it would not be overkill to bring it to three places for estimates.

Obviously the best circumstance is when the vehicle is still driveable. You'll feel like the worst kind of sitting duck when the car isn't driveable and you think you're married to the first repair shop to which it is towed. But a $50 tow charge is money well spent when the alternative might be hundreds of dollars in unneeded repairs.

Many times estimates vary because two different mechanics can come up with two different explanations for what is wrong, or different ways to fix a problem. One summer, my air conditioner went out when a $550 computer module failed. I could have paid for a new module, but my car was four years old at the time and had 60,000 miles on it and that sounded like an expensive answer. But the mechanic had a great idea. The module's job was to temporarily turn off the air-conditioning compressor when the car was started. The mechanic suggested a simple rewiring of the air-conditioning system to bypass the module. I just had to remember to turn off the air conditioner before I started the car. Getting a second opinion in that case saved me hundreds of dollars.

If your car is towed to a mechanic, don't allow the tow-truck driver to choose the repair shop. Quite often, he or she is paid to steer your vehicle to a particular shop. You have no way of knowing if that shop is legitimate, honest, or competent. Make your own decision about where to take the car.

Don't rely on nationally famous names when you go for a car repair. Too often at a franchise location, the parent company fails to accept responsibility for a problem. A common response is, "We're not responsible, but we'll see if we can talk to the company about an accommodation." That doesn't mean the national company is behind you. Make sure you know who backs the warranty. If the warranty is good only at that location, then taking your car to a chain or franchise means nothing.

Over the years, I've received a lot of complaints from people who've had their cars repaired at Goodyear and Firestone service centers. The regional offices for these companies have become infamous for backing away from anything their independent dealers do. Go to these centers only if you're confident in the work of the individual dealer, because the company isn't likely to help you if there's a problem.

No matter which repair shop you use, always ask the mechanic to return parts to you that are replaced. That's one of the best ways to prove that a repair shop didn't make a repair it was supposed to make. At the very least, it gives you peace of mind that the shop made the promised repair. There's always the risk it can dig out some old parts. If you're dealing with true crooks, these precautions don't really matter. That's why word of mouth is so important in car repair. If you know someone who has been thrilled with a certain service facility, you may want to consider taking your car there.

I've taken my cars to an independent shop that works on nothing but my brand of car. They've seen all the problems hundreds of times, so it's easier for them to make the correct diagnosis. Even if a specialty shop charges more, it's valuable to know the repairs are done right. My mechanics knew about a potential engine failure on my car that could be avoided by replacing a belt. They recommended this preventive maintenance to make sure there was no catastrophe.

That's a real benefit of using an independent shop. A dealer knows your make and model of car but may side with the manufacturer and not disclose the kinds of problems my mechanic

TIPS ON CAR REPAIRS

- Every time you take a car to a mechanic — and especially if you have to take the car back for the same problem — you should control what is written on the work ticket.

- If you're having an estimate done on your car, make sure the work ticket says you have authorized only work related to doing an estimate. If you're authorizing specific work, write down the exact dollar limit you are authorizing and don't permit any work to be done beyond that limit.

- If the estimate is high, don't accept it as the final word. If your car is not driveable, have it towed to another repair shop for a second estimate.

- If your car is towed to a mechanic, don't allow the tow-truck driver to choose the repair shop. Quite often, he or she will be paid to steer your vehicle to a particular shop.

- Don't rely on nationally famous names when you go for a car repair. Too often, the parent company will fail to accept responsibility for a problem at a franchise location.

- No matter which repair shop you use, always ask the mechanic to return parts that are replaced.

points out. However, using an independent mechanic is not fail-safe. You still have to make sure you're happy with the work the shop does.

Another problem with dealer repairs is that often you don't get to speak with the mechanic who works on your car. You speak to a service writer who writes a note to the mechanic that describes the problem. If you need to go to the dealership because your car is under warranty, or if you like going to that particular dealership, insist on speaking personally to the mechanic if a repair is unsatisfactory. If you can talk to him directly, you can often explain the problem more completely.

I once had a Chevy Nova that was stalling out at any speed and the dealership couldn't repair it after two tries. On the third trip, I demanded to speak to the mechanic and explained what was wrong. He hadn't been able to understand the scope of the problem from a few perfunctory notes on the service ticket. But after I explained it to him, he realized what was wrong and fixed it in 15 minutes.

There are two schools of thought on the shops that specialize in vehicle components. Some like to go to a quick-lube place for oil changes, a tune-up shop for tune-ups, or a brake-repair place for brake work. Others like to go to one mechanic for all repairs. I tend to have routine servicing like oil changes done at a place that does just those but have anything significant done by a shop that specializes in my brand of vehicle. The most important thing about oil changes is that they're done regularly, not where they're done.

I have a built-in skepticism about general repair centers that claim to be able to repair all the components of all vehicles. You're asking a lot from a mechanic if you throw any number of different vehicles at him or her and say, "Fix this." I don't think that's possible; specializing by component or by vehicle are the two wisest methods.

Whichever kind of place you choose, try to find a reputable, qualified service center before your car is in trouble. Then you'll know where to go when repairs are needed. Ask people who have the same brand of car as you where they go and whether they're happy.

Most car owners have only rare encounters with auto body shops, so they have no idea what to expect when they need body work. First, get an estimate of the cost to repair the vehicle. Many insurers require two estimates, so they can be sure the estimate is accurate. Some use their own adjusters.

Most insurers figure the cost of new, brand-name parts in their estimates. Unless you insist on new parts, some body shops will sneak in a used or generic door panel or fender and charge you as if it were new. If you have an older car, you may not mind used parts. But if you're paying for new parts, you ought to get them.

The insurance company check may be sent to you or to the body shop you select. If you have a collision deductible, usually $250 or $500, you may have to pay that as well. Some body shops will agree to do the repairs for the amount paid by the insurer, so you won't have to pay the deductible. Check with a few body shops and see what kind of deal you can cut. If you don't mind generic or used parts, you can agree to let the body shop install used parts to reduce the cost.

You can have repairs done by any body shop you choose, even if the other driver's insurer is paying for them. Ask friends or your insurer for a referral, or try a new-car dealer's body shop. Since the dealer is likely to be a stable business, you know its body shop won't be a fly-by-night operation.

RECALLS

If your brakes don't work or your ignition system fails, it's possible the trouble is due to a design or manufacturing error. Other car owners may have had the same trouble, perhaps prompting the manufacturer to issue a general recall or send a service bulletin to dealers detailing the defect. Unfortunately, the public usually receives no such notification.

In many cases, the dealer either won't know if a service bulletin has been issued or won't disclose it to you. That's when the Center for Auto Safety, a nonprofit consumer organization, becomes a great resource. Write to the center and list the make, model, and year of your car and the exact symptoms you've been having. If you enclose a self-addressed, stamped envelope, you will be notified if there are any known defects in your vehicle. Another great resource is www.alldata.com, a Web site that allows you to see instantly all the service bulletins that relate to your vehicle. Once you are aware of a defect, you can have your vehicle serviced to prevent serious damage. Even after a repair has been made, information about a recall or a service bulletin can help you get a full or partial refund from the dealer or manufacturer. It is more difficult to get a refund if the work was done at an independent repair shop, but you can get one if you're persistent.

Even if a manufacturer does its job well, many consumers are going to be unhappy. After all, things do break and need to be repaired. The manufacturer's representative talks to unhappy people all day long. To get satisfaction, you have to stand out from the pack and justify what you want. You don't want to be viewed as just another complainer who doesn't like having to spend money.

You also help others by letting the Center for Auto Safety know about your car's problem, because the data on your vehicle can help establish trends. If you have trouble with your brakes and other car owners have the same complaint, the center knows there may be a broad failure in the brake system of that vehicle.

Callers have told me for years about a tendency for the paint to flake on several car models. If you know the paint has flaked in certain paint colors on specific vehicles, you'll have a lot more leverage if your car's paint also starts to flake. You might be able to convince the dealer to repaint

TIPS ON RECALLS

- A breakdown in your vehicle may indicate a defect in the model that is affecting other car owners. You may be able to negotiate a lower repair price or receive a reimbursement for repair work if the vehicle has been cited in a recall or in a service bulletin.

- The Center for Auto Safety, can tell you of any known defects in your vehicle. Or check www.alldata.com

- You can't count on the government or the manufacturer to disclose defects.

CONTACT

Center for Auto Safety
2001 S Street NW
Suite 410
Washington, DC 20009
202-328-7700
www.essential.org/cas

National Highway Traffic Safety Administration
DOT Auto Safety Hotline
1-800-424-9393
www.nhtsa.dot.gov/

the car for free, or for less than $100. If you don't know about the paint defect, you may have to pay the full cost of a paint job, more than $1,000. Or you may be able to negotiate a cost-splitting deal with the manufacturer. Knowledge here is so important. If you know a particular vehicle has had a problem, you're going to win.

The only way vehicle defects become widely known is because consumers are willing to stand up and complain, by contacting the Center for Auto Safety and the National Highway Traffic Safety Administration.

THE LEMON LAW

A lemon is a new car that breaks down repeatedly for the same reason and cannot be repaired. Lemons are not nearly as common as they once were, but getting one is still a major headache.

Every state except South Dakota has enacted a Lemon Law to protect consumers by allowing the car buyer to exchange the flawed vehicle for a new one or have the manufacturer buy it back.

Lemon Laws vary widely by state but, in most, if the defect involves the major safety systems of steering and braking, the dealer will have one chance to fix the vehicle. If the dealer cannot fix it, the manufacturer will have one chance to make the needed repairs. In the case of other safety-related systems, the laws allow two repair attempts for the dealer and one for the manufacturer. With any other component of the vehicle, it will be three repair attempts for the dealer, one for the manufacturer.

In most states, the Lemon Law applies to problems that arise during the first year or 12,000 miles of ownership. If you have a new vehicle with a serious problem, your best bet is to document everything. Keep records of every phone call and every repair attempt. That's why it's so important that repair work tickets be written correctly. If they don't show a persistent defect, you may have a hard time invoking your rights under your state's Lemon Law.

You must follow other specific procedures to make a Lemon Law claim. For example, you might have to notify the manufacturer by certified mail. You can obtain the specific procedure in your state by calling the administrator of the state's Lemon Law. Ask for a copy of the rules governing the law.

Under the Lemon Laws in most states, the manufacturer figures out how much to pay to buy back your car by assuming it has a useful life of 100,000 miles. The manufacturer divides your purchase price by 100,000 miles to come up with how much money it will charge you for each mile you've driven the car. Let's say you buy a typical $18,000 car and drive 20,000 miles on it by the time the manufacturer agrees to buy it back. The manufacturer will charge you 18 cents a mile for each mile, or $3,600, for the miles you've driven, and give you $14,400 for your car. While that seems like a big hit financially, it isn't because of how much value your car loses in the first year of ownership. The manufacturer's deal is better than you'd get by trying to sell it. In some states, you may be able to negotiate the mileage charge with the car maker.

TIPS ON THE LEMON LAW

• Every state except South Dakota has enacted a Lemon Law to protect consumers. It allows the car buyer to exchange the flawed vehicle for a new one or have the manufacturer buy it back.

• In most states, the Lemon Law applies to problems that arise during the first year or 12,000 miles of ownership.

• You can obtain the rules and procedures to make a claim under the Lemon Law in your state by calling the administrator of the state's Lemon Law.

• Once you've established that the manufacturer is going to buy back your car, the battle will be over the vehicle's value. You want the per-mile charge to be as little as possible.

• The best way to guard against getting a lemon is to buy a car that has a good repair record.

You'll have to pay the manufacturer to exchange your lemon for a newer model of your car. To figure a fair amount, subtract the dealer cost for the model you have from the dealer cost for the new model. Generally, the manufacturer will ask for the difference between the suggested retail price of each vehicle, which will be a larger sum.

If you follow the steps under your state's Lemon Law and keep good records, the manufacturer often will offer to buy back your vehicle before you go all the way through the arbitration process. And the sooner you execute the buy-back, the less of a mileage charge you'll incur.

The best way to guard against getting a lemon is to buy a car that has a good repair record. This strategy won't always work, but it will certainly improve your odds.

ARBITRATION

If you are unable to resolve a dispute with a car manufacturer, arbitration may be a better option than filing a lawsuit. Most manufacturers agree to participate in arbitration to help resolve disputes over cars still under warranty. The arbitration programs may be independent of state-sponsored Lemon Law programs or a provision of the law.

Call the Council of Better Business Bureaus' Autoline for details on how to file for arbitration in your area.

In most cases, arbitration is binding on the car manufacturer but not the consumer. You still have the right to sue if you are unhappy with the arbitration decision. But you don't want to sue. You want to solve the problem either through negotiations with the manufacturer or through arbitration.

Interestingly, just filing for arbitration often is enough to get the manufacturer to make a settlement offer.

TIPS ON ARBITRATION

- If you are unable to resolve a dispute with a car manufacturer, arbitration may be an option. Most manufacturers agree to participate in arbitration to help resolve disputes over cars still under warranty.

- In most cases, arbitration is binding on the car manufacturer but not the consumer. You still have the right to sue if you are unhappy with the arbitration decision.

- Just filing for arbitration often is enough to get the manufacturer to make a settlement offer.

- *Lemon Law: A Manual for Consumers* is the guidebook for documenting claims both under state Lemon Laws and in arbitration cases not covered by the Lemon Law.

CONTACT

Council of Better Business Bureaus
Autoline
4200 Wilson Boulevard
Suite 800
Arlington, VA   22203
1-800-955-5100
www.bbb.org (online complaint form)

Ford Consumer Assistance Center
300 Renaissance Center
P.O. Box 43360
Detroit, MI 48243
1-800-392-3673

For a time, General Motors was fighting every arbitration claim filed against the company in the state of Massachusetts. The state started publishing statistics on arbitration, which showed that GM was the only manufacturer making no attempts to settle. Ever since those statistics became public, General Motors has shifted gears, both in Massachusetts and around the nation, and now it attempts to negotiate with the consumer rather than fight to the last inch in arbitration.

As a consumer, you have to weigh what you might gain in arbitration versus what you might lose by not settling. If you believe your case is well documented, you might want to take your chances with the arbitration panel. If you think your case could go either way, the best approach might be to file for arbitration, then cut the best deal you can before your case is heard. That's really no different from what lawyers do. *Lemon Law: A Manual for Consumers* is the guidebook for documenting claims both under state Lemon Laws and in arbitration cases not covered under Lemon Laws.

Even if you go through with arbitration, you will not appear before the arbitrators. They will decide the case based on written arguments submitted by both you and the manufacturer. So you want to provide a short, clear, and detailed explanation of what has gone wrong with your vehicle, what efforts you and the manufacturer have made to repair the problem, why you believe the problem has not been solved, and what remedy you believe is fair. You want to have strong documentation and appear to be eminently reasonable. It's a good idea to organize your presentation carefully and make it easy to read. Include a short summary and then an index, with tabs that guide the reader to each area of specific documentation, such as your work tickets. It's very frustrating to get a car problem fixed, but writing a novel won't get you anywhere with an arbitration panel.

ACCIDENTS

I hope you're never in a car accident. But if you are, don't just drive away, even if it seems to be the most minor fender bender. Taking a few simple steps can save you from big headaches later.

First, wait for a police officer to write an accident report. It will be vital to you in case any claims are filed.

Second, exchange information with the other driver about yourselves and your insurance companies. There's about a two-thirds chance that the other person will be insured. If the person is not, you'll file the claim with your insurer.

Third, as soon as possible after the accident, report it to your insurance company, even if you don't plan to make a claim. I realize this sounds like strange advice, particularly if the amount of damage is too small to make a claim. People rarely want to tell their insurance company about minor accidents, but you have to guard against the possibility of a lawsuit, even if the accident was only a fender bender. Many times drivers will consider an auto accident a chance to get rich. They'll see a TV commercial for a lawyer who claims he can get accident victims a lot of money. A lawsuit may seem absurd, but that doesn't make it less serious. Normally, your insurer will defend you in a lawsuit. But if you failed to notify the company, it may not have to defend you or pay a claim if you lose.

On the other hand, if you have soreness or any injury following an accident, do not negotiate with an insurance company on your own, unless you're sure your complaints are very minor and temporary. While I make fun of personal injury lawyers, if you've been injured, it's very risky, both financially and legally, to try to negotiate without a lawyer.

Most commonly, accidents cause damage to a vehicle but no injuries. When that happens, getting your car fixed and being reimbursed properly is a real trick. In most cases, insurers will maintain that their driver was not at fault and try to force you to make a claim against your own insurance company. The best way to avoid being

TIPS ON ACCIDENTS

- Don't just drive away from an accident, even if it's a minor fender bender. Wait for a police officer to write an accident report.

- Exchange information with the other driver. Get the names and telephone numbers of as many witnesses as you can.

- As soon as possible after the accident, report it to your insurance company, even if you don't plan to make a claim. If you believe the other driver was at fault, contact his or her insurance company also.

- If there's a dispute about who's at fault, file the claim with your own company. The two companies will duke it out later over the amount each will pay.

- If your vehicle is going to require some repair, insist on being supplied with a rental car or reimbursement for a rental car.

- Don't agree to release the body shop or the insurer of final responsibility until you're comfortable that the repairs are complete and the vehicle operates properly.

- If your vehicle is totaled, don't accept your insurance company's first settlement offer. Check on the Internet (www.edmunds.com), or look at a used-car price guide to see what your car was worth.

- If you have a five-year lease or loan and owe more than the car is worth, ask for "substitution of vehicle." The loan or lease will remain in force, and the insurer will find a similar vehicle for you as a replacement.

wrongly blamed for an accident is to get the names and telephone numbers of as many witnesses as you can at the time of the accident. That's very difficult to do in a highway accident. However, most accidents occur on surface streets, and in many cases witnesses will be blocked temporarily by the accident and unable to scatter. While the accident is fresh in your mind and you're waiting for the police, draw a sketch of the accident scene. If you think it was the other guy's fault, it's essential to have a police report. If the officer gives the other driver a ticket, it's a very strong piece of evidence in proving fault.

Establishing fault is even more important if you have an older vehicle and no longer find it

worthwhile to carry collision coverage. If you're ruled at fault, you will have to pay for the repairs to your vehicle. Sadly, some insurers try to take advantage of drivers who don't have collision protection. Be prepared to document every single phone conversation you have with your insurance company. Write down the date and time, whom you talked with, and what was said. Be prepared to sue the company in small claims court, if necessary.

If you have no collision coverage and the other driver has no insurance at all, your only recourse is to sue the driver. But the odds are if the person doesn't have any insurance, he or she probably doesn't have anything worth getting.

When you choose not to carry collision coverage, you agree to live with the risk.

Contact both your insurance company and the other driver's insurance company after an accident. Even in situations when there isn't a shadow of a doubt about who was at fault, some unethical insurance companies will attempt to avoid you or avoid responsibility for the accident. Be persistent and use your state insurance department as a resource if an insurer fails to act in good faith. The state insurance department may not want to get involved in questions of fact, but it can help push an insurer to discuss the accident and try to reach some accommodation. If there's a dispute about who is at fault, file a claim with your own company. The two companies will duke it out later over the amount each will pay.

I heard about one case in which someone's car was damaged in a collision, and the other driver's insurance company initially accepted responsibility for the claim. The car was fixed, but poorly, and the insurance company tried to duck out of its responsibility to pay for additional repairs. The victim was worried that she would have to pay for thousands of dollars in repairs herself. But there was no reason at all to do that. Instead, she made a claim against her own insurance company and paid her deductible. Finally, her company went after the other company for the bill.

You pay premiums to your insurance company so that you will have protection when you have a problem. When you buy insurance, it's important to see if your state insurance department can tell you which insurers do the best job of handling claims. You should expect your insurance company to provide speedy service and fair treatment, to make sure the body shop does the job correctly, to track down the other insurer if the company is eluding you, and to defend you if you are sued. You are the customer.

I'm always disappointed when I hear callers say their insurer is treating them like the enemy, rather than as a valued customer.

In its most recent study, *Consumer Reports* rated Amica Mutual Insurance, USAA, and Cincinnati Insurance as the best at providing service. For $12, the magazine will send you a report on the lowest-cost auto insurers in your area.

If your vehicle is going to require some repair, insist on being supplied with a rental car or reimbursement for a rental car. If it will take 10 days to repair the vehicle, make sure the rental car is authorized for at least that long. Don't agree to release the body shop or the insurer of final responsibility until you're comfortable that the repairs are complete and the vehicle operates properly. Typically with major body work, the first repair isn't the final one and more work is required to finish the job.

I receive a lot of questions about how much the insurance company is required to pay for a vehicle that has been totaled in an accident. No matter which insurance company you're dealing with, this is an area of great frustration. Insurers tend to offer approximately 70 percent of the amount it would cost to buy your vehicle on the used-car market. But the initial offer is negotiable. To improve your odds of getting the best price, check on the Internet (www.edmunds.com), or look at a used-car price guide to see what your car was worth.

If you don't know any better, you'll take too little money for your car. Once the company realizes you've done your research, the negotiating usually gets to be more fair and honest. If the insurance company won't budge, then accuse it of failing to act in good faith and request a face-to-face meeting with the adjuster and the adjuster's supervisor. Your state insurance department won't get involved in determining the fair market value of your car, but it will push the insurer to meet with you if the insurer refuses.

In many states, you also have the option of hiring a public adjuster to be your advocate. This is usually someone who has worked for an insurance company adjusting claims and who knows how to talk the insurance company's language. Public adjusters are listed in the *Yellow Pages* under "Insurance Adjusters" or "Public Adjusters." If you're arguing about enough money, it's worth the several hundred dollars to hire somebody.

If the insurer still won't budge, talk to him about arranging a "substitution of vehicle," under which your car loan or lease remains in force and the insurer finds you a similar vehicle as a replacement. If the insurer thinks the car is worth so little, let him find a replacement vehicle for you for that price.

Substitution of vehicle is critical for people who have long-term leases or loans. It may be the only way to keep a lease in force without being subject to extremely large termination penalties. With a loan, it may prevent you from being left with a sizable loan balance and no car, because you owed more than the vehicle was worth. It's very common for drivers with five-year loans to be "upside down" in a loan, because, with relatively small monthly payments, the car's value drops much faster than the loan balance.

Rip-offs

You really have to be on your toes these days to avoid rip-off artists. They're all around and looking to take your money. Many of the calls I get each week on my radio show are from people who have been ripped off by a phony loan company or telemarketer, or who are suspicious that something they've heard about is not legitimate.

Most scams appeal to your dreams or your vanity. The common cons operate on the premise that you will make a decision quickly and emotionally, instead of doing the legwork to verify information or to develop your own basic knowledge. If you rely exclusively on what someone else tells you, you become a sitting duck. Often when you are taken, you have no recourse, because the rip-off artists are clever enough to avoid committing a crime.

I especially hope that you beware of a sales technique called the "No Be Back," which is often used in high-pressure sales schemes. It turns up in health clubs, buying clubs, time-shares, and whenever else a salesperson wants you to buy something that isn't a good value. In the "No Be Back," the salesperson forces you to buy right then, because if you're able to leave the high-pressure sales environment, go home, and think about what you are buying, odds are you'll realize it's not a smart decision and you won't waste your money. The sales-person would rather have you say no than leave as a maybe.

There's a much greater danger of someone stealing your credit card number when you use your card at a store or a restaurant and you're dealing strictly with people than when you're buying a book or a sweater via the Internet. In one case, there's an electronic barrier that a hacker has to pierce. In the other, there is no barrier. There are plenty of opportunities for crooked clerks to steal your credit card number and use it for fraudulent purposes.

There's so much at stake for online retailers to get it right that I'm not that worried about online credit card transactions going wrong. Just take a look at your credit card bill each month when you pay it. If an unauthorized transaction appears, notify the credit card issuer right away.

In this chapter, I'll tell you about many of the most common rip-offs and help you to avoid being taken.

HEALTH CLUBS

Most health clubs are interested more in your checkbook than in your health. And signing a long-term contract with one can really hurt your financial fitness.

When you go into a high-pressure health club, you're greeted by a commissioned salesperson, not a health expert. Her job is to strong-arm you into signing a long-term membership contract, typically for three years.

Callers have told me that you're not even shown the facilities during many sales presentations. If you do see the facility, it's a very limited tour. The salesperson concentrates on making oral promises that are not in the contract and doesn't bother to show you the contract until very late in the presentation.

Salespeople use all kinds of "closer" techniques — words and phrases designed to pressure you into signing. For example, a salesperson might say, "Don't you think today is the day you should start building a healthier body?"

People usually go to a health club with the best of intentions. Sometimes they go to get healthier or, more often than not, to slim down. People often sign a health club contract because they believe they're doing something to improve themselves. But signing the contract doesn't do anything except obligate you to a long-term commitment to pay a lot of money, usually with hefty finance charges attached.

The enthusiasm of a new health club member often wanes quickly. For the first few weeks after you join, you'll probably visit the club several times. Then you start going twice a week and then once a week. Suddenly, you're going every other week and, before you know it, usually within three months, you're not even setting foot there. You're feeling so guilty that you're driving a different route home so you don't have to see the place.

At that point, the deal starts to look very unfair. You're getting a bill every month from a health club you're not visiting, and you don't want to pay anymore. But if you don't pay, the club will come after you, either with its own collectors or with a third-party collection agency. I often get calls from people who can't qualify for a mortgage because of something on their credit report. A major reason — number one as far as my callers are concerned — is a past-due bill for a health club.

Once you enter into a health club membership, you own it — with one exception. Most states give you three business days from the day you sign the contract to cancel your membership with no consequences. You must follow the exact procedure in the contract for canceling. Don't telephone and tell the club you're canceling. Don't drop by and hand them a note. Usually you'll have to send a letter by certified mail, return receipt requested. Keep a copy of that letter and your certified mail slip forever. You never know when someone's going to get amnesia about the fact that you properly canceled. One day you may need to provide proof.

If you've waited beyond the allowed number of days to cancel, you have little choice but to keep paying. If you stop paying, the club will ruin your credit, making it difficult for you to buy a car or a house or to obtain a credit card. Normally you'll get a notice from the club or its finance company. Later the claim will be turned over to a collection agency. The collection efforts will continue, often sporadically, through the years. Eventually, when you try to establish new credit, the delinquent membership will jump off your credit report to bite you. At that point, you will have to come to an accommodation with the health club.

Rip-off health clubs often operate right on the edge of the law, and their goal is to get

TIPS ON HEALTH CLUBS

• Don't sign long-term contracts for health club membership or pay for more than 30 days in advance. Month-to-month deals are much safer.

• Don't fall for "free membership" contests that are really sales pitches.

• Take the contract home with you and read it thoroughly. Don't sign the contract at the club.

• Get any promises the salesperson makes included in the contract, or they won't mean a thing.

• In most states, you have three days from the day you sign a health club contract to cancel with no consequences.

• If you finance your membership and the club closes, you have no further obligation to pay.

• If you think a particular club may suit you, call the appropriate consumer agency in your state to check whether there are outstanding complaints against the club. Tour the facility and ask questions.

money out of you no matter what. I had one case involving a 17-year-old boy who signed a health club contract, then went home and realized that he was pressured into it by a salesperson. In his state, a contract signed by a 17 year old is voidable, but it's not automatically void. He tried for months to cancel his contract, but the health club kept stalling. He called the day before his 18th birthday. Once he turned 18, he could no longer void the contract. So I had to walk his father through the steps to make sure the boy didn't get taken at midnight that night. It would have been an unfriendly birthday present.

Another thing to watch out for with health clubs is "free membership" contests. Health clubs offer free memberships to gather names and addresses of possible new members. When you sign up at the yogurt store to win the one-year membership and win a free 30-day membership instead, you know you're just being taken in for a sales presentation. Normally the clubs won't give you your membership card until you've been

on the sales presentation, and by then, they expect to have sold you a membership. Every single person who enters the contest at the yogurt store wins the 30-day membership. By winning, you're actually losing.

Reputable health clubs do exist, and if you're looking to join one, here's what I recommend. First, look for a club that allows you to pay as you go. Very few health clubs will tell you outright that you can sign up on a month-to-month basis, but if you're persistent and are willing to pay a little more per month, several clubs probably will cut you that kind of deal.

I heard of one club that charges $10 a month more for month-to-month memberships, and it requires that you authorize a monthly draft from your checking or credit card account. That's not a great offer, but it's better than a three-year contract.

Another had a no-pressure approach and a membership that included a $150 initiation fee and a $40-per-month charge with a two-month minimum. A third asked for a $150 down payment and charged $37.98 per month. That was actually $4 a month less than their one-year contract. These are just some examples. Health clubs come and go, and offers change. But you can find acceptable deals out there if you look.

It's okay to sign a three-year agreement with a health club if the agreement has a buyout clause, and as long as you don't pay in advance. With a buyout clause, you're protected if you move to a different area. A fair buyout is two months of membership fees. At least it gives you a way to get out early.

In some states, membership money isn't held in escrow or by bond. So if the club closes its doors and you've paid for a full year in advance, you lose all your money. It's a real danger because health clubs close all the time.

I remember one club that was offering very inexpensive one- and two-year memberships. The club kept collecting cash from members right up to the day it closed its doors. All those people got stuck without a membership and without refunds. When you pay in advance for a health club, you do so at your own risk.

Some states do provide greater protection. New York, for example, requires each health club to post a bond of up to $150,000 if it signs members to long-term contracts. The money is used to reimburse the club's members in the event the club closes.

If you finance your membership contract and the club closes, you no longer have to make any payments to the finance company. If your club has closed, send the finance company a certified letter saying that the club has closed and that you owe no more money on the contract. However, some states may require you to attend another location of the club that remains open.

If your club does close, competing clubs nearby may take you as a member at little or no cost.

They do it for goodwill, and they figure you may sign up with them when your original membership expires.

If you think a particular health club may suit you, call the local consumer agency in your state to see if there are any unsatisfied complaints against the club. If the club passes that test, take a look. Visit during the busiest time of the week — usually early in the week in the evening. Ask for a tour, and look at the condition of the equipment and how crowded the facility is. If you wanted to use a stair step machine, is one available, or would you have to wait in line? Go into the locker room to see how clean it is. Watch an aerobics or other fitness class and see whether the instructor seems knowledgeable. Talk to some of the participants after the class. Interview a fitness trainer. Ask him how long he has been with the club and what his training recommendations are for you. This will tell you how interested he is in you and how knowledgeable he is. Nobody can tell you exactly what your weight program will be in just a brief conversation, but you'll be able to tell how much he knows.

If you like the club, ask for a copy of its contract that you can take home. Do not sign the contract while you're at the health club; ask for time to read it carefully. If there's anything you don't understand, put a question mark next to it. Then call the club — don't go back in — and get answers to those questions. The reason you don't go back in is you may not get any answers, or you may get false answers, and you'll feel pressure to sign when you're back in the club's environment. If you're calling, you maintain the balance of power.

Don't agree to anything you don't understand. If there's anything a club salesperson can't explain to you, put a slash through the item, put your initials by it, and sign the contract without that clause included.

If the health club does not allow you to leave with a copy of the contract, do not sign and do not join that health club. Any reputable business will give you an unsigned contract for you to review. I don't care what you're buying.

Don't listen to what the salesperson says unless she includes it in writing. I had one caller who was thinking about moving to another state and wondered what would happen to his membership if he moved. He was told that it would be no problem, that all he had to do was provide documentation — say, a copy of his new lease — and the club would let him out of the membership. That wasn't true at all. The agreement he signed keeps him obligated no matter where he lives.

Another fellow was told he could either use his local health club or transfer his membership to another place. That was wonderful because he loves to play racquetball. But the membership was not truly transferable, because although he could play racquetball at facility number 1, at facility number 2, the membership was good only for general health club use. The racquetball portion was an extra $500 a year. He was obligated to a membership that was useless for what he wanted.

Any promises that are made about facilities, terms and conditions of the agreement, or potential termination promises must be included in the language of the contract.

TIMESHARES

Most people would love to own a vacation home or cabin, a place to get away for a week when life gets hectic. The trouble is, many of us can't afford a mountain or beach home.

Rip-off artists who sell timeshares are able to make a killing by promising to put a vacation paradise within reach.

When you buy a timeshare, you get the right to use a vacation property at a particular time each year, usually for one week. It sounds like a decent idea, but timeshares turn out to be very poor deals. In addition to the cost of buying a timeshare, usually $8,000 to $10,000, you have to pay an annual association fee of about $400 for each week you get to use the timeshare. I could stay somewhere for seven days for roughly the same amount that a timeshare owner has to pay for maintenance, about $60 a night. That's a lot of money for a place you already own. And you can't simply decide later that you don't want it anymore, because nobody else will take it off your hands.

A timeshare is virtually impossible to sell because it has no real value. Even if the up-front cost were zero, the burden of paying the annual fee makes owning a timeshare a bad idea. I get calls every week from people who would gladly give their timeshares away. Nobody will take them, because they don't want the obligation, either. Once you own a timeshare, you have it forever.

Purchasing a timeshare seems like buying real estate, but it isn't. When you buy a house, you know that in a few years you can sell that house, often for a profit. You also can give up ownership through foreclosure. You can't do either with a timeshare. Developers won't take timeshares back because they know they ripped you off by selling them to you. If you don't pay, they'll send you to a collection agency and eventually sue you. Your obligation continues no matter what.

In fact, if you ever inherit a timeshare, I recommend that you disavow your inheritance of it. Otherwise, the obligations of the deceased become yours. Generally, things you inherit are to your benefit. A timeshare is to your detriment.

People are so desperate to sell timeshares that they get conned by timeshare brokers, people who say they can successfully market your timeshare for you. These folks will charge a listing fee of about $300. Once you write the check for the fee, you can kiss it goodbye. I have never heard from any caller who was able to sell a timeshare through a broker.

Sometimes, you buy a timeshare and don't even get to use it. One of my callers bought a houseboat timeshare for $5,500. He purchased the right to use the houseboat for vacations one week a year. Then the operator went bust and none of the buyers were able to use their time- share. But their obligations continued. My staff and I were able to help several of the timeshare owners form an organization to fight their case. Eventually, the place was fixed up and the buyers were able to use the houseboat again.

Even though you pay a maintenance and asso- ciation fee, you don't have control over what hap- pens if a timeshare is not well maintained. You don't have the rights you would have with a con- dominium complex, where the owners of the condominium units run the association that takes care of maintenance. Timeshare agreements are always done so the timeshare operator has the power even when you have the ownership.

Timeshare presentations are very elaborate con games. First, you'll be called by a telemar- keter, whose job is to convince you to come to the presentation. That person is paid based on how many people show up for the presentations, so he'll tell you anything to get you in the door.

The biggest lie he'll tell you is that it's a short presentation; in reality, it will last about three hours. The idea is to immerse you completely in a carefully orchestrated event. A timeshare pre- sentation is theater.

The prizes you're offered as an incentive to attend a presentation are almost always overly glorified. For example, you'll be told you're going to receive two free tickets to Hawaii, with a retail value of $1,200. Later, it turns out that you've

TIPS ON TIMESHARES

- Timeshares are worthless and cannot be resold.

- Don't attend timeshare presentations because you might be tempted to make a huge mistake and buy.

- The prizes that are promised by timeshare salespeople are usually overblown and of little value.

won a certificate allowing you to purchase a trip to Hawaii. You get the free tickets only if you agree to buy 10 nights at a specific hotel. Before you know it, the hotel and free tickets cost more than it would have cost if you'd bought the airline tickets and arranged for a hotel room yourself.

Such certificate programs are a common tac- tic in high-pressure sales schemes. The timeshare operator can obtain these "free airfare" certificates for $5 each. If a company is selling these certifi- cates for $5, it's obviously not going to redeem them for free airline tickets to Hawaii.

When you show up for the timeshare presen- tation, the first thing someone will do is check to see if you're qualified to be a timeshare owner. If you have good credit but aren't wealthy enough to buy your own beach house, you're probably a good target.

If you qualify, you're brought into a very impressive-looking reception area. A salesperson will then take you through an elaborate presenta- tion, normally followed by a film. Next you'll be shown a model of the timeshare unit, fully built and beautifully decorated.

This is another "No Be Back" sale. The time- share isn't a sensible purchase, and the salespeo- ple know that once you leave their high-pressure environment, you'll never buy.

During the film segment of the presentation, there will be a product endorsement of the time-share by someone who appeals to the potential buyers. I went to a timeshare presentation for a property in Myrtle Beach, South Carolina, in which a stockcar driver made the pitch. The endorser can be any of a number of people, depending on what market segment the time-share is targeting.

The message is seductive. "Just imagine your-self once a year with us on this beautiful stretch of sand." They're selling an illusion, a piece of the American dream. A lot of people figure they can't afford to have the whole dream but that they can have this for seven days each year.

Most people have to stretch to come up with $8,000 to $10,000, and generally they have to finance it. Even with financing, people just don't have an extra $100 or more to throw away each month.

After the presentation and film, you're brought into another room, usually with a lot of tables and chairs, and all kinds of psychological tricks are used to get you to buy. For example, every time somebody buys, someone pops a champagne bottle. The sales reps stand up in unison and start applauding. There's a festive atmosphere. The buyers smile, their picture is taken, and champagne is poured. Then the sales rep will say something to you like, "Do you see the joy in their face? Don't you want to be able to experience that joy of ownership yourself?"

If you don't agree to buy, a closer is brought to your table, a professional who knows how to hit people where they're weakest. At the presen-tation I went to, the closer alternately tried to humiliate me, tried to be charming, and tried to be threatening. He'll frighten you into thinking you're letting a wonderful opportunity get away. Or he'll put you down by saying you don't have the money to make the deal. The idea is to get you to prove you do have the money by signing a contract. Many people do buy the timeshare after the closer comes to the table.

If you don't buy, just wait until you try to get your prizes. It's not easy. I had a call from some-one who didn't buy and was told to walk down a hallway to get his prize. The fellow and his wife opened the door and started walking down the corridor, then realized it was the fire exit. They were locked out, and the only way to head was for the parking lot. They could have gone back in the entrance, but they didn't. They never got their prizes.

Whether or not you get a prize, I recommend you avoid going to timeshare presentations. There's too much of a chance that you will be tempted or intimidated into buying something that will turn out to be a very big mistake.

Don't underestimate how persuasive timeshare salespeople can be, even if their targets are highly educated. I have a friend who called from a resort area where she and her husband, both lawyers, had been looking at a timeshare. At the high end of the market, the units are sold by giving prospective buyers a free weekend at the resort. My friends had been immersed in this weekend and had gone to see the sales presentation. They called me and asked if they should buy the timeshare and I said absolutely not. I went through all the reasons they shouldn't buy, but they bought anyway. It doesn't matter what your income level is or what your level of education, you can fall for false pitches.

BUYING CLUBS

Nobody enjoys a bargain more than I do. I buy soft drinks by the case and keep them in a little refrigerator in my office because I won't pay 50 cents a can at the office vending machine. But the desire to save money can also get you into trouble.

One way to get burned is to join an illegitimate buying club, an organization that charges a big membership fee and promises to allow you to buy merchandise at wholesale prices. The initiation fee typically is $900 to $1,500, plus an annual membership fee of $50 to $100.

These buying clubs are nothing but catalog distributors. They have a showroom, where they display a variety of merchandise, but they don't actually have merchandise in inventory.

Not having the merchandise on hand is one way these clubs differ from legitimate warehouse clubs, such as Costco, Sam's Club, and B.J.'s. In the legitimate clubs, you pay a membership fee of up to $40 a year and the merchandise is right there on the shelves for you to purchase.

At the very least, the illegitimate buying clubs depend on an antiquated method of retailing. Nobody wants to have to get into a car and drive to a buying club for the privilege of looking through a catalog. People who buy via mail order like it because it's convenient to look through the catalog at home and order through an 800 number.

These clubs claim their merchandise is sold at cost and therefore is extremely cheap. But you have no way of knowing if that's true unless you comparison shop.

Even if these buying clubs did have decent prices, you would have to buy quite a bit of merchandise to make back the initiation fee of $1,500 and annual fees of $50 to $100.

In the last few years, illegitimate buying clubs have started selling franchises. But the clubs are being sued by franchisees, who allege that the merchandise prices are so high they can't sell any memberships. Even the people who operate these clubs — the franchisees — are saying they're a rip-off.

In all the years I've been attacking illegitimate buying clubs on the air, I've had only one consumer

TIPS ON BUYING CLUBS

• Legitimate warehouse clubs such as Costco, Sam's Club, and B.J.'s often can provide excellent savings on merchandise.

• In the legitimate clubs, you pay a membership fee of up to $40 a year, and the merchandise is right there on the shelves for you to purchase.

• Illegitimate buying clubs are nothing but catalog distributors. They have a showroom, but it's just a front, because they don't actually have merchandise in inventory.

• Illegitimate buying clubs typically charge an initiation fee of $900 to $1,500, plus an annual membership fee of $50 to $100.

• The rip-off clubs don't care if you ever buy anything from them, but they'll force you to pay the fees, to the point of suing you.

call and say a club saved him money. He had just bought a house, then joined a club, and then bought every piece of furniture for his house through it. The caller believed he had saved money.

Buying clubs use mailings and telemarketers to lure you in to hear their presentation on "a great new way to buy products." Just for coming in, they promise to give you one or more great prizes.

One caller to my show was offered eight sirloin steaks, a weekend at Epcot Center, and a car alarm to get him to listen to a buying club presentation. When you get there, a high-pressure salesperson will try to convince you to sign up for a lifetime membership.

Joining these clubs is a foolish decision that people regret the second they do it. Most people who join never walk in the place again, and the club doesn't care either way, as long as members pay the fees. If a member goes into default, the buying club goes to court and seeks a judgment against him.

Judges don't like to rule in favor of the clubs, but there's not much they can do. One caller told a judge the buying club had promised she could simply stop paying if she no longer wanted to be a member. But that's not what the contract said and she had signed it. The judge had no choice but to rule against her.

Most states give you three days after you sign to back out of a buying club membership. Unfortunately, most buyers don't cancel within that time. If they try, the club often will lie to them to keep them from canceling on time.

Any time you walk into a high-pressure sales presentation, whether it's for a buying club or a timeshare, and you're told you must make a decision right then, just say no and walk out the door.

EXTENDED WARRANTIES

One of the things people worry about most when they buy a new TV or VCR is what to do if it breaks. Repairs can be costly, and manufacturers' warranties are notoriously short. That's why service contracts, or extended warranties, have been such a successful rip-off.

Extended warranties are a bad deal for the consumer because they rarely pay off. Only 12 to 20 percent of the money paid for the warranties is ever used to pay for repairs or claims, making the warranties a remarkably profitable product. By contrast, a typical insurance product pays out 70 cents of every premium dollar in claims.

There are several reasons the claims rate is so low on service contracts. People often lose the contracts, or they move, or they forget they purchased the contract in the first place. The usage rate is even lower than the breakdown rate of the appliance.

In any case, you are better off taking the money you would have spent on service contracts and putting it into a repair fund, although admittedly this takes quite a bit of discipline. However, over time you'll come out way ahead by not buying service contracts and self-insuring appliances in this way.

Better yet, make a point of buying inexpensive TVs and VCRs, and when one breaks, throw it out and buy a replacement. The prices for many new electronic items have come down so much that spending money on repairs doesn't make sense.

TIPS ON EXTENDED WARRANTIES

• Extended warranties often are the most profitable part of the sale of a TV, VCR, or stereo for an appliance dealer.

• Extended warranties are a bad deal for the consumer because they rarely pay off. Only 12 to 20 percent of the money paid for them is ever used to pay for repairs or claims.

• People often lose the contracts, move, or forget they purchased the contract in the first place. The usage rate is even lower than the breakdown rate of the appliance.

• You're better off taking the money you would have spent on a service contract and putting it into a repair fund.

When you make a purchase, the salesperson may heap on a lot of pressure to buy the extended warranty. Extended warranties are very profitable — often the most profitable part of the sale — and salespeople risk being fired if they fail to sell enough of them. In fact, the warranty is often the *only* profit on the sale, because of the razor-thin margins in appliance retailing and the fact that consumers do a lot of comparison shopping.

Best Buy, one of the few retailers that doesn't push extended warranties, has improved its financial performance simply by asking customers if they want one.

Consumers are hit with extended warranties most often when they buy appliances, rather than cars, because they purchase appliances more frequently. But in the case of a car, the decision represents a far greater amount of money. Actually, it's more important to check out the reliability record of the car you're considering than to decide on whether to buy an extended service contract. For more on cars and extended warranties, read the section on trade-ins, financing, and extended warranties in the Cars chapter of this book.

INVENTION SERVICES

There's been an explosion of interest in the United States in inventing. People are tinkering in their basements and garages, hoping to strike it rich with a new, commercially successful product. They want to create the next big hit, as the founders of Apple Computer did.

Enthusiastic would-be inventors have become perfect prey for a group of rip-off artists who promise to help take these inventions to the marketplace. Instead, they steal hundreds of dollars from each inventor, without ever providing any help.

The rip-off "invention services" attract folks by offering to evaluate inventions for free. Inventors call an 800 number, send in some application forms, and inevitably receive a call from a salesperson who raves about the invention and its potential. But the salesperson says that in order to do further research, the organization needs $500. Many people quickly send a check.

After a few more weeks, the company will start the second phase of the scam. It'll send a second, more complete information kit and tell the inventor that his idea is now ready to be prepared for the marketplace. The company will ask for a larger amount, usually $5,000 or $6,000, "to conduct a thorough market analysis." Many inventors send in a second check, only to learn weeks or months later that the rip-off invention service did nothing but take their money.

One of these companies, Invention Submission Corporation, entered into a consent agreement with the federal government in which the company agreed to disclose that less than 1 percent of the ideas people submit ever make it to market. These companies are not in the business of bringing ideas to life but of getting rich off their victims.

The reason these phony organizations continue to operate is that it's very hard for law enforcement authorities to prove that the companies' actions are criminal. So authorities have taken civil action to try to win restitution for victims and, through greater disclosure, to warn others to stay away. Unfortunately, con artists who have little fear of going to jail will continue what they're doing.

The Federal Trade Commission has information about invention promotion firms at its Web site (www.ftc.gov). You can also access the U.S. Patent and Trademark Office online at www.uspto.gov.

TIPS ON INVENTION SERVICES

- Most rip-off invention services use a three-step program to steal money. They offer a free evaluation of the inventor's product through an 800 number, take $500 or so to fund "research," and later request another $5,000 to $6,000 for more extensive "market research."

- One such company was forced to disclose that less than 1 percent of the ideas people submit ever make it to market.

- Local bookstores and libraries have publications with legitimate advice on how to bring inventions to market.

- It's important to create a working prototype of your idea, because companies won't buy ideas from sketches.

- Your best bet is to find an invention broker to propose your idea to a company.

- Nonprofit inventors clubs, which are found in many cities, also are excellent for sharing ideas and providing encouragement.

REFERENCE

Patent It Yourself
by Nolo Press

The Inventing and Patenting Sourcebook: Desktop Companion
by Richard Levy

INTERNET

www.ftc.gov
www.uspto.gov

If you believe you have a good idea for an invention, there's legitimate help at the local bookstore or library. I like two books in particular, *Patent It Yourself,* by Nolo Press, and *The Inventing and Patenting Sourcebook: Desktop Companion,* by Richard Levy. Not surprisingly, *Patent It Yourself* describes the process of patent-ing an idea. The Levy book addresses how companies select products to market and how inventors can increase their chances of getting an audience for their ideas.

To have any chance of success, inventors must have a working prototype, Levy says. Companies won't buy sketches; they have to see a working model of the product. So if you've tinkered and drawn, finish tinkering and start building.

Inventions fall into three basic categories: weak ideas that don't have a chance, ideas that are good but can't generate enough demand for them to make money, and a small number of good ideas with potential for profit. So inventors have to be both good and lucky.

One of the most helpful parts of Levy's guide is his explanation of the role played by brokers in bringing inventors' ideas to large corporations. The job of these brokers is to help separate the good ideas from the weak ones. Most large companies prefer to deal with established brokers, rather than speaking directly with inventors.

Another alternative, available in many medium-sized and large cities, is to join a nonprofit inventors club. Their members share information that can be very helpful. If it's a real non-profit inventors club, you won't be asked to sign any licensing agreements. It's a shared self-help organization, in which people encourage and advise you along the way, and you share your information and success stories with others.

Inventors as a group are unusually paranoid that everybody is going to steal their ideas. There is some justification for that fear, and deciding whom to trust can be difficult. My advice is to seek a patent to protect your concept before you present your idea to a corporation.

Employment Scams

The extraordinary number of corporate layoffs in recent years has provided fertile ground for the growth of rip-off employment recruiters. Particularly vulnerable are people who worked at one company for a long time and thought they were going to work for that company for a lifetime. Suddenly, they are unemployed and suffering a dramatic loss of confidence.

Because of this sense of loss and hopelessness, they are easy prey for organizations that promise to find jobs for them. The organizations claim to have special contacts or special influence. In fact, they're just taking advantage of the unemployed.

Nobody can guarantee he'll find a job for you, and, unless you have a very special skill, none of these recruiters has special influence with employers.

I urge you not to do business with any employment organization that requires you to pay an up-front fee. If you are really timid about your job search and want to use a placement service, it should be one whose fee is paid after you are hired. Your preference should be that the employer pays the fee or that the fee is split between you and the employer. It's obviously less desirable for you to pay the full fee.

If you do have an unusual skill that is highly desirable to employers, you may benefit by turning to a recruiter with expertise in your field. People who might be helped by a specialized recruiter have skills in engineering, medicine, or the sciences. But such areas are by far the exception, and for these job candidates the employer would pay the fee and the recruiters would never have any up-front charges.

Work-at-home offers continue to be a very popular employment rip-off. They almost always are scams. You can steer clear of these with a little common sense. After all, if you have had a lot of trouble finding a job, why would you suddenly be able to earn several hundred or several thousand dollars a week doing a job in your home? In most cases, someone is supposedly willing to set you up in business without having interviewed or screened you.

TIPS ON EMPLOYMENT SCAMS

• Placement offices can't guarantee that they'll find you a job, and — unless you have a very special skill — none has special influence with employers.

• Don't do business with any employment organization that requires you to pay an up-front fee.

• Work-at-home offers almost always are scams. If you have had trouble finding a job, it's unlikely you will suddenly be able to earn several hundred or several thousand dollars a week doing a job in your home.

• If you think you need help looking for a job, try an informal networking group, or find a group on the Internet.

I had a call from a woman who heard about a work-at-home scheme in which she would pay $7,000 for lesson books and software that would enable her to process medical claims for doctors by hooking up her computer to a computer in another state. This business was supposed to make her filthy rich. A medical consultant told me this was complete baloney. According to the expert, most doctors use their own employees to process their claims, or they use independent processing companies.

One of the best ways to check out a scheme like this is to call someone in the profession it involves. In this case, I suggested the woman call doctors' offices and ask the office managers if they were interested in this service and, if they were, what fees they would be willing to pay to have claims processed. She compared her research against the claims being made by the work-at-home company and found out that this was not a legitimate way for her to make money.

Another employment rip-off I've spoken with callers about concerns the sale of vending machines. One company promised a fellow he could work for four hours a week, on his own routes, and earn $400 a week in supplemental income. That's simply not true.

It's extremely difficult to place vending machines because the high-traffic locations are already taken up by large national vending machine companies or by small businesses that own their own machines. To get business, you have to contact the owners of the businesses and offer either to supply machines or to service their machines. Going up against the big guys isn't easy; you don't have the leverage to get your machines into the places you need to make money. The sad thing is you'll end up with $5,000 to $7,000 worth of vending equipment sitting in your garage, because these rip-off artists require you to buy several machines. You also have no way of knowing if the equipment will be of decent quality.

Ironically, the warehouse clubs sell vending machines, so you can walk right in and buy your own soft-drink or candy-dispensing machine. They're really good quality and sell for a lot less than the machines vending machine companies will try to sell you. If you're really interested in developing vending routes, you could buy a single soft-drink machine for about $1,500, try placing it in a store, and see if you're any good at this business. If your machine does well, you could buy a second. Why buy $5,000 worth of machines in advance?

Sometimes people can work at home successfully. You might start making something as a hobby and, because you're good at it, create a natural demand for what you produce and expand it into a business. The most famous example of that is Apple Computer. There's another possibility if you already have a skill.

Because of the technology that exists today, people can communicate with an office almost as if they were on site.

I know a paralegal who's been running a business out of her home for several years. She loves it. She gets up in the morning and goes over to her computer and there are instructions waiting for her on the screen. It's as if she's in the office. That's how I communicate with the *Atlanta Journal and Constitution* for my travel columns. I write my columns on my computer and transmit them to the newspaper's mainframe computer. I also have a link, through a travel agency, with an airline reservation system. I do research for my travel columns, my TV travel stories, and my radio show right in my home. You can work out of your home, but generally it will be by using a technical skill.

If you believe you need help looking for a job, I have several recommendations. A number of informal networking organizations exist that don't charge fees and meet in local churches. I heard about one group that meets once a week at a cafeteria. These groups gather people who are looking for jobs to share ideas, leads, and contacts.

Almost all jobs in America are found as a result of direct contact with employers or through friends and relatives. The number of jobs found through classified ads or any form of advertising is less than 15 percent of the total openings. Because most people are passive in their job searches, the overwhelming majority of people end up competing for the very limited number of advertised jobs. Very few people are out there looking for the vast majority of jobs through informal and formal networking.

More people are prospecting for jobs and networking through the Internet. They're E-mailing resumes and applications for jobs and using the Internet to find people with common interests. Ask people in your trade or profession for ideas. Use whatever method you can to become familiar with people who might be making hiring decisions.

If you've lost a job, you may become passive and even have trouble getting started in the morning. One of the ways to pick yourself up, build confidence, and move toward getting a job is by treating the job search as a job. Give yourself specific assignments every day: people you're going to see and things you're going to do. One of the first things you should do is list every single person you know on three-by-five-inch index cards or in a computer. It may sound like busywork, but actually it's not because there are many people you know or knew in the past who may be able to help you in your job search. By going through the mental exercise of making this list, you give yourself a very helpful tool with which to start your job search.

One major word of caution: when you start contacting people who are potential job leads, don't call and ask if they know about work, because people hate that. Ask for advice or information, not for a job. People love to be asked for their advice. They hate to be asked for a job.

MODELING SCHOOLS

This rip-off appeals not only to a person's vanity and dreams, but to parents' dreams for their children. Modeling scams give individuals and families false hope of a brilliant new career and then shatter those dreams by just taking their money.

Modeling schools tend to target parents with young children, but they're willing to take anybody's money. Other common victims are young men and women in their late teens and early 20s.

I call these scams modeling road shows because they take the con on the road. The con artists come into a city and advertise their model-

TIPS ON MODELING SCHOOLS

- Do business only with legitimate, in-town modeling agencies, and never pay up-front fees. Stay away from traveling modeling recruiters.

- If you think you or your child has modeling potential, seek an evaluation by a legitimate agency.

- Get a photo portfolio done by a professional photographer, but only if a legitimate modeling agency advises you to take that step.

ing tryouts or seminars. If you think you or your child has what it takes to be a model, they want you to come to their show — usually in a hotel ballroom. By showing up, you're prequalifying yourself to be taken.

When you arrive at one of their shows, there will be a large presentation, kind of like a pep rally. Then they'll meet with each person individually or in small groups.

Let's say a parent goes in with three children. To increase the credibility of the modeling road show, they'll take only one child. It'll sound something like, "We think your daughter Letitia has great talent and we'd like to see her some more, but the other two children aren't ready yet." Or, "We like Mark, but Sara is too young. Maybe in another year or two." They pretend they're eliminating people when all they're really doing is setting you up for a squeeze play. The squeeze usually will come in some type of listing fee, modeling fee, lessons charge, or photography charge. They also have something they call a placement fee. Typically, they'll take a victim for $200 to $300.

A real modeling agency makes its money off the bookings it gets for you. It's paid a commission for placing you in an ad. Only fake modeling agencies take these road shows all around America. Any time you're hit for money up front from a modeling organization, you should know something is not right.

One of my callers agreed to pay $180 to one modeling company, including a $50 application fee, $25 for an orientation program, and $105 for a photo session. Interestingly, the contract mandated a $200 penalty for rescheduling the photo session, certainly an exorbitant charge.

She had regrets almost immediately and called me for help. A road-show contract would have had a three-day cancellation option, but because it was a local company, a three-day option wasn't required. The company did agree to let her out of the deal and return her money after my staff and I interceded. She was lucky; the company could have kept the money and she would have had no recourse.

One legitimate charge you will have to pay if you want to become a model is for a photo portfolio. To get one, you'll have to go to a professional photographer and pay a fair amount of money. You shouldn't get a portfolio unless a legitimate modeling agency, one that is looking for actual talent, gives you an encouraging evaluation.

I've seen pictures that phony modeling agencies have supplied to my listeners, and there wasn't a chance at all that the kids in the pictures were going to be models. The problem is the parents absolutely believed their children were the most gorgeous creatures who ever walked. Parents should believe their children are gorgeous, but, by that definition, every child is gorgeous. Granted, there are certain "real-people" looks that modeling agencies want, but, for the most part, they want people who have a special look.

Once the modeling road shows have collected their cash, they leave town. It's impossible to go after them because they generally deliver what they promise, usually modeling lessons. They never promise any modeling work, so they haven't done anything illegal. Breaking hearts isn't against the law.

TELEMARKETING

How many times have you sat down for dinner with your family and been interrupted by a telephone sales call?

Telemarketing has become a truly intrusive industry. If I get a piece of junk mail, I can choose to throw it away without even opening the envelope. But if a human being has me on the phone, I'll probably listen to the pitch to avoid being rude.

For many marketers, it's actually cheaper and more effective to have a human being call you than it is to send you a piece of junk mail. Since the postal service was cut loose from the federal budget and forced to balance its own budget, the cost of direct mail has skyrocketed. At the same time, because of deregulation, long-distance telephone costs have steadily decreased. That's why the nation's 300,000 telemarketers make 18 million calls each day, according to the American Telemarketing Association.

Telemarketing has divided itself into two categories — legitimate businesses and charities, whose calls are annoying but not otherwise worrisome, and rip-off telemarketers, who are out to steal your money.

You can avoid both groups by using an answering machine to screen your calls, particularly around the dinner hour, when telemarketers are most bothersome. With an answering machine, you can hear who's calling and pick up the receiver if it's a call you want to take. You can even tailor your message so friends and family will know what you're doing and telemarketers will know you're not interested.

Another excellent defense against telemarketers' phone calls is Caller ID, a widely available telephone service that allows you to see the name and number of the caller before you pick up the receiver. Many telemarketers block Caller ID, so although you may not know exactly who's calling, you'll get a message such as "Out of area" or "Private call." You'll avoid a lot of telemarketers by electing to let those calls go unanswered. If the caller turns out to be a friend, he or she can leave a message and you can call back.

The other side of the coin is that, when you call a person or business, there's the possibility that he will use Caller ID to see who you are and learn your telephone number. If you don't want that, ask your phone company how to block someone else's Caller ID.

Dishonest telemarketers are more than just annoying. They are also dangerous. Because mail and telephone lists are so easily obtained, illegitimate businesses have no trouble getting your name and number. Con artists have found boiler-room operations (the name comes from the cheap office space they rent) to be the most efficient way to steal money. They call you from these boiler rooms and try to get you to buy a product or service. If anyone attempts to sell you something on the telephone and says you must make a decision right then, don't have anything to do with the company. Ask phone solicitors to mail you information; otherwise, don't do business with them.

In the worst cases, the con artists get you to provide your checking account number or credit card number over the telephone and use it to steal from your account. The most ironclad rule I can give you is never give out your credit card number or your checking account number on the telephone, unless you make the phone call, because you will live to regret it.

I got a call from a fellow who was solicited on the telephone for an $800 vacation trip and, somewhat reluctantly, agreed to give out his credit card number. As soon as the call was over, he changed his mind and called back to say he wasn't interested. The telemarketer told him the $800 charge had already been posted to his account.

It's okay to use your credit card if you're calling a mail order company like Spiegel or Land's End and you know it has an outstanding reputation. In fact, in that instance, using a credit card is preferable to sending a check. That way, if something goes wrong, you can get a refund from your credit card company under the chargeback process.

I especially urge you not to give out your checking account number, because that's all criminal telemarketers need to withdraw money from your account. The hoodlums simply present your bank with a draft from your account, and within 24 hours they have your money. It's unbelievable what they do in their boiler rooms. They'll have a check encoding machine right there, and as soon as you give one of them your checking account number, he'll walk over to this machine and create a very professional-looking bank draft.

These schemes work in two ways. Sometimes they get your credit card or checking account number and immediately draw money out of your account. At other times, they sell you a product or service and get your account number for the purchase. You may receive the merchandise or you may not. But while you're distracted, they tap your account. By the time you realize what happened, they've left town.

Money can be taken from your account without your knowledge or consent because of the banking system's failure to have any meaningful safeguards. Banks are supposed to pay a draft only when you have authorized it in writing. But most banks have no internal security system in place to verify the accuracy of a draft. The bank is fully liable for any money it pays out in unauthorized bank drafts. But why should you have to sue your bank to force it to live up to the law? It's better for you to help prevent a crime by not giving out your checking account number.

Banks are failing miserably in their responsibility to prevent fraud. Often when you call the customer service center to report a fraud, you're told that your rights to do a chargeback are explained on the back of your bank or credit card statement. Here's what's wrong with that. Let's say the charge posts on your next statement. You then write the bank and protest the charge. From the date of your original complaint, as many as 60 days pass before the bureaucrats at the bank send your protest through to the criminals' bank. By that time, the criminals have stolen a bunch of money. The banks look at this fraud as a cost of doing business. That's wrong and foolish. It's an open invitation to the hoodlums.

The banks' security departments should consider it their responsibility to limit losses. The security departments should be notified whenever a consumer believes he or she has been hoodwinked by a criminal enterprise. In the case of credit card issuers, they generally don't care because the criminals' bank, not the consumer's, ends up being stuck with the chargeback. Instead of realizing that these losses hurt the whole industry, the banks tend to blame the customer for not being more careful and try to find some reason not to honor the chargeback.

TIPS ON TELEMARKETING

- Use an answering machine or a Caller ID device to screen your calls, particularly around the dinner hour.

- If anyone attempts to sell you something on the telephone and says you must make a decision right then, don't fall for the pressure.

- Never give out your credit card number or your checking account number on the telephone, unless you make the call. With these numbers, con artists can steal from your accounts.

I had a caller whose credit card was sent to someone else and used fraudulently to purchase $1,200 worth of goods. It seemed clear that this was part of a larger scheme to create phony credit cards. The bank agreed to remove the fraudulent charges from the caller's account but didn't want to be bothered to look into the scheme.

With the popularity of E-mail, telemarketers have found a new way to intrude on our lives: junk E-mail, also known as spam. Spam has been a massive problem for the 10 million members of America Online, and a lesser problem for people who have traditional Internet service providers. America Online has put a lot of effort into eliminating unsolicited E-mail, so far with limited success. The good news is that it is quick and easy to delete unsolicited E-mail, and it doesn't increase the trash in our nation's waste dumps.

One more thing about telemarketing. If you work for a telemarketer, getting paid could be a problem. I've heard case after case of people who showed up for work to discover that the telemarketer they worked for had packed up and left, without paying them for their final week. If you work for a telemarketer that doesn't seem legitimate, or you're thinking about such a job, understand that you, too, may lose.

CONTESTS

We've all read stories about people who won state lotteries and whose lives were changed dramatically. Who wouldn't want to win a huge sum of money or some valuable prize?

Direct-mail contests play upon your desire to win, a rip-off that makes you think you've won when in reality the contest companies simply want to take your money.

When you receive a piece of mail saying you've won a prize, run the other way — you're being set up for a rip-off. Almost always, a letter that talks about prizes or promotions is an attempt to get you to purchase some overpriced product in return for what appears to be a valuable prize but is actually worthless.

One caller sent me a contest notice he got that proclaimed, "You have won the American Travelers Sweepstakes Giveaway!!" What he had actually won was the right to call a 900 telephone number and pay $3.95 per minute to get a "Hawaiian Dream Vacation for Two" that wasn't worth anything.

In the typical prize offer, the postcard or letter will say you are guaranteed to win one of five prizes. A car is always on the list. Usually the list also includes $10,000 in cash, a stereo system, a piece of jewelry, and a vacation. If it says you

TIPS ON CONTESTS

• When you receive a piece of mail saying you have won a prize, run the other way. You're being set up for a rip-off.

• Almost always, these "contests" are an attempt to get you to purchase some over-priced product in return for what appears to be a valuable prize but is actually worthless.

• People always want to believe there's something legitimate about illegitimate contests, even when common sense tells them something isn't right.

• The rule of thumb is, don't participate if you have to pay to do so. If you can enter for free, then it's okay to enter.

have definitely won one of these prizes, it will be the vacation. If it says you've won two prizes, it will be the vacation and the jewelry, both of which are absolutely worthless.

As in timeshare rip-offs, the vacation will be a certificate offer that has no value. What you usually get is a coupon good for "free" plane tickets — provided you also buy nights at an expensive hotel from the same company. The jewelry tends to be costume jewelry of minimal value.

Rip-offs don't have to come with big price tags. In fact, when the rip-off is for less than $20, the company knows nobody is going to report the rip-off to law-enforcement authorities. Although we hear more about rip-offs that cost the victims several hundred dollars, more people get taken for about $20 or less.

One of my callers got a notice that said photographic equipment was being held in his name and that he could pick it up for $13.78. Supposedly, it

was a 35mm camera with "50mm optical lens, lens cap, tripod mount, film counter, and hot shoe synchronized for electronic flash." Actually, it was a flimsy, worthless piece of junk.

Sometimes the prize offers include the odds of winning each prize. For the two least valuable prizes on the list, the chances of winning are 1 in 1 or 1 in 2. For the other prizes, such as the Lincoln-Continental Town Car, the odds will be 1 in 1,000,000 or 1 in 100,000.

At other times, the companies get around the odds with careful wording. One of my favorites was in a letter a caller got from a firm called O'Brian & O'Brian saying it had decided "to consider giving" her a new Cadillac. There was an order form she was supposed to use to select a style, upholstery, and color. All the company wanted was an "optional" $38 check or money order. Not bad for a car, but in truth an absolute rip-off.

The purpose of these "contests" can be to take your money directly or to get you to buy a product. I had a call from a gentleman who received just such an offer and was asked to buy pens for his business. The pens were priced at 10 times their market value, and if he had bought them, he would have thrown away thousands of dollars. Still, he was ready to buy. That's what's so interesting. When we put someone on the air who has received a postcard for one of these "contests," he is dying for me to tell him his offer is different from all the others he's heard about. He insists this one is different. People want to believe the contest is legitimate, even when common sense tells them it isn't.

The rule of thumb here is to use what I call zero tolerance. If you receive a postcard or a telephone call saying you have won a prize, the only answer you can give is that you are not interested. I guarantee that if you participate, you will be taken 100 percent of the time.

Let's take the example of Publisher's Clearinghouse, which is a legitimate sweepstakes sponsor. If you fill out all the sweepstakes certificates, you might end up being independently wealthy. But one of the things that separates Publisher's Clearinghouse from illegitimate companies is that the latter require you to make a purchase to participate. You can enter the Publisher's Clearinghouse sweepstakes without subscribing to any magazines, and subscribing does not improve your chances of winning. I think people probably assume that buying a magazine will help, or that their name won't be put in the drawing if they don't subscribe. But that doesn't happen. In fact, one winner of the company's $10 million sweepstakes said in a radio interview that she didn't order any magazines. Publisher's Clearinghouse has to play this one straight, and it does.

All you need to know is if you have to pay to enter the contest. If you do, you know it's a con. If you can enter for free, it's okay.

CHARITIES

How do you know when you're donating money to a legitimate charity? A lot of folks collect money for fake charities, and because criminals have become more clever and technology has improved, it's become a lot harder to tell a true charity from a fake one. What makes the problem especially frustrating for consumers and small businesses is that many of these fake groups have names that are very similar to those of real charities.

A good approach is to pick a cause you're involved in, such as helping the homeless or fighting cancer. That way you'll know the cause is something you believe in and whether your money is being spent efficiently. If you're not actually involved in a cause but still want to give money to charity, request literature from the organization before giving a donation. That's a good idea whether you're solicited in person or on the phone.

Even better, don't make decisions about giving to charity in a haphazard manner. Instead, make all your charitable-giving decisions at one time each year. Some people do this at the end of the year when they have a snapshot of their income tax picture. Then they can make charitable donations with an eye toward their personal finances. When you know how much you can give and make all your donations at one time, you're able to figure out exactly where you want your money to go. If you avoid just pulling out your checkbook or wallet, and instead plan your donations, you'll be much wiser in giving to worthwhile causes. You'll be giving your money from the heart by using your head first.

This approach works very well for small businesses. If you have your own small business, you no doubt get solicitation calls frequently from charities and quasi-charities such as civic organizations. If you explain that you review requests at a set time each year, and then require that they make a written request, you will never hear from many of those companies again. Those that actually do write will be patient and realize you'll consider them during the time of year when you make donations. I recommend that small companies have a committee of three employees who decide how money should be distributed to charity. You as the owner of the business decide how much money is going to charity each year. Then empower the employees to hand it out.

A friend of mine did this in his business, and he said it was the greatest suggestion I ever made. He used to get bogged down with calls from people trying to convince him their causes were worthwhile. Now that requests have to be submitted in

TIPS ON CHARITIES

• If possible, pick a cause you're familiar with personally so you know your money will be spent efficiently.

• To help verify that a charity is legitimate, always request literature from the organization.

• Plan your charitable giving, making all decisions at one time each year.

• If you own a small business, decide how much to give and have a committee of employees hand out the money.

• Never give any money to door-to-door solicitors.

• Watch out for phony charities that telephone and ask you to buy products at inflated prices.

• Never allow anyone to pressure you into giving to a charity.

CONTACT

National Charities Information Bureau
19 Union Square West
New York, NY 10003
212-929-6300

INTERNET

National Charities Information Bureau
www.give.org

Better Business Bureau
www.bbb.org

writing and they're considered only one week of the year, he has eliminated most of the hassle.

My advice on door-to-door solicitors is to never give them one cent. There's no way to know whether they are with legitimate organizations or not. If you want to give money to their causes later on, that's fine. Ask the solicitor for literature, but do not give one penny at the door. You need an opportunity for perspective, to think about whether this is a cause you really want to support.

When you're asked for contributions that amount to pocket change, 25 or 50 cents for the Shriners or the Salvation Army, for example, just make your own best decision. Do what you feel like doing at the moment — you're not going to miss the quarter. I'm not as worried about people being taken in that way as I am about contributions of $5, $10, or more that con artists try to get you to give on impulse.

I did a series for local television on how much money rip-off artists can make through fake charities. I put on a Santa Claus suit and stood near a highway off-ramp with a collection bucket labeled with the name of a fictional charity, "Homeless Families Fund." I never asked anybody for money, but people just gave it to me, one after another. People in one out of every nine cars gave me money. If I'd kept it, I would have made $27 an hour tax free. Instead, the station donated it to a legitimate charity, Habitat for Humanity. Although you may feel better giving money to a roadside fundraiser, more often than not the money will be going to a scammer.

Charities that solicit by telephone are definitely something to avoid. Often with these pseudo-charities, you're asked to make a purchase rather than a contribution. Such groups will have someone call and say he's with the "Handicapped Veterans of America." He'll tell you they don't want charity but would like you to consider buying their "long-life light bulbs," which supposedly last eight times longer than normal bulbs. If you buy, he'll tell you you're helping veterans stay off welfare. These pitches are thinly disguised con games. This is not the way to give to a cause. If you're interested in helping the disabled find employment, then give to a vocational or educational training program. Don't buy overpriced light bulbs.

I've noticed an increased aggressiveness recently among solicitors for charities that pretend to work on behalf of police officers, firefighters, and other public safety organizations. These groups are not charities, and almost without exception hire professional fundraisers. They're so aggressive that if you agree to make a "contribution," they'll send a courier to your house or business to pick up your check. Unfortunately, the chance that your money will go to a real charity is near zero.

There are organizations that report on the performance of charities and can tell you exactly what portion of your money actually goes to those in need. The National Charities Information Bureau publishes a list that rates charities. You can also get great information at its Web site, www.give.org. The Better Business Bureau also has a Web site, www.bbb.org, that provides information on charities.

If you follow my system for determining how much to give each year to charity and use your list to help decide which charities will get your money, you'll feel really good about the money you do give. You'll be confident that you've served society well with your dollars.

Interestingly, I don't get a lot of calls from people complaining that they've been ripped off by charities. Perhaps people just write their losses off to experience. But what these rip-offs do is prevent people from giving to worthwhile charities. If someone has been burned by a phony charity, he or she is reluctant to give the next time to a legitimate cause.

In any case, never allow anyone — a solicitor, your employer — to pressure you to give to a charity. The money you give to charity should come from your heart.

CREDIT LIFE INSURANCE

Credit life and disability — also known as croak-and-choke insurance — is a terrible buy for you but a big moneymaker for those who sell it. Not surprisingly, then, people trying to get you to buy credit life are almost everywhere you turn.

Your bank or mortgage company will try to rip you off with credit life and disability, as will the lender that finances your automobile. When you buy a major appliance, the store will also attempt to sell you croak and choke.

This is the most worthless product that has ever been dreamed up by the insurance industry. Croak and choke pays off your loan balance if you die or become disabled. But it protects the lender, not you. By buying it, you are paying to protect the lender.

People agree to buy credit life under the mistaken notion that they're protecting their loved ones from inheriting debts. Let's say you have an outstanding mortgage balance of $50,000 and you're concerned that your family will lose the house if you die. The better thing to do is to buy a term life insurance policy that pays your loved ones directly. Then they can decide how to use the money. It may be better for them to keep the mortgage and use the insurance proceeds to pay for living expenses. But if you have this rip-off credit life and disability, your family has no choice in the matter; all the insurance pays for is the loan on the home or car.

Credit life insurance is far more expensive than legitimate life insurance. By buying term life instead of credit life, you pay a lot less for the same amount of coverage. Or, if you spent the same amount on insurance, term life would provide a much larger death benefit.

For example, a 40 year old could buy $100,000 worth of term life insurance for as little as $150 per year, or $1.50 per $1,000 of coverage. By contrast,

TIPS ON CREDIT LIFE INSURANCE

• Credit life and disability insurance, also known as croak and choke, is worthless.

• It protects the lender if you die or are disabled. It doesn't protect you.

• If you're concerned that your family will lose your house if you die, buy a term life insurance policy that pays your loved ones directly. They can decide how to use the money.

• Credit life insurance is far more expensive than term life insurance.

I received a quote for credit life insurance of $660 a year (or $55 a month) to cover a mortgage of just $66,000. That's $10 per $1,000 of coverage, or nearly seven times the cost of term life.

To make matters worse, the balance of any installment loan declines as the consumer makes payments, but the cost of credit life doesn't decline, making credit life even more expensive. If you pay $9 a month for credit life on a $15,000 car loan, you'll pay the same $9 a month a few years later, when you owe just $5,000 on the loan. You pay the same amount for less coverage.

Even after rate cuts in many states, Americans who purchase credit life insurance are being overcharged by more than $500 million each year, according to a study by the National Insurance Consumer Organization and the Consumer Federation of America. Further, insurers have paid an average of just 44 cents for every dollar collected in premiums, the study showed.

In only three states — New York, Maine, and Vermont — are consumers getting a respectable 60 cents in benefits for each premium dollar. The cost, including finance charges, to insure a $10,000 12 percent loan in those states would be $155 over 48 months. In Louisiana, the worst offender in the study, the cost to insure the same loan would be an astronomical $673.

You may not even need to protect your family from a car note or similar debt. If you die and have a car note under your signature alone, then responsibility for that car goes to your estate, not your family. It will be up to the executor or the executrix of the estate to decide what to do. He or she can either give the vehicle back to the lender or make arrangements to continue payments on the loan and decide how to distribute the vehicle. If the vehicle were worth less than the amount still owed, the lender would have a right to make a claim on the estate for the difference. Turning the vehicle in could not hurt the credit rating of any member of your family.

Some people believe that they will not be approved for a loan unless they agree to buy credit life and disability, and lenders will lie to loan applicants to make them believe it. But legally that cannot be a determining factor in whether you get the loan.

Insurance

Insurance is one of life's obligations. None of us wants to buy it, but we do because it's necessary. Because of our reluctance to deal with insurance, we tend to buy it hurriedly. We buy too little of some insurance and too much of other kinds. This chapter is designed to guide you painlessly through what you need to know.

One piece of advice applies to all your insurance problems. Most states have a consumer help line in the state's insurance department to provide assistance. These folks are overwhelmed with calls, so get the name of the person you speak with and follow up with the same person so you're not forgotten. They're busy, but with a little effort they can get results. When dealing with an insurance claim of any kind, keep every letter and document every phone call and promise that the insurer makes.

LIFE INSURANCE

We've probably all heard at least one awful joke about life insurance salespeople, usually about not wanting to get near one. I think people make fun of life insurance agents because we don't like to think about anything connected with death, be it wills, funerals, or insurance.

But many of us need to have life insurance to protect our loved ones from financial chaos in the event we die unexpectedly. Consider your own situation to see if life insurance makes sense for you, how much you need, and which type would be best.

If your family would be unable to make the mortgage payments without your income, you need life insurance. But if you're single or married with no children, you might not. Some married people without children don't buy life insurance, believing their spouse could make due without their income. That's really a personal family decision.

I've seen lots of formulas that help people calculate how much life insurance to buy, but none supplies a definitive answer. My rule of thumb is to buy insurance equal to six times your annual salary, before taxes. So if you make $30,000 a year, get $180,000 of life insurance, to replace your income for six years. If both spouses work, both should have life insurance to replace their incomes. If either works at home, consider insurance to cover the cost of child care if the homemaker dies. Don't buy insurance on your children. A three year old doesn't earn a salary, so there's no need to replace his income.

There are two main types of life insurance: term life and whole life. Term life provides a payment only if you die. Whole life builds cash value and serves as a savings vehicle.

Term life is like automobile insurance in the sense that you buy it year after year and the coverage stops if you stop paying. Although term life premiums rise as you get older, the annual cost is far less than for whole life. For example, a 35-year-old woman who doesn't smoke could get $250,000 worth of term life insurance for about $180 a year. The same $250,000 death benefit would cost more than $2,600 a year on a whole life policy.

Whole life not only provides a death benefit, it also serves as a kind of savings account. Part of each premium payment you make is set aside and accumulates value, and eventually it can amount to a sizable sum. In addition, you can set up a whole life plan so that you pay premiums for 10 years, then stop, but maintain coverage for the rest of your life. Because life insurance gets more expensive as you get older, having lifetime coverage has some appeal. On the other hand, whole life premiums are high and the policies contain high commissions, making it a favorite of insurance salespeople.

A 25-year-old man who doesn't smoke could buy $250,000 worth of term life insurance for about $200 a year, versus $2,000 a year for a whole life policy. But after 15 years, it's likely the whole life policy would be worth more than if he'd paid $200 a year for term life and invested the difference in the premiums, $1,800 a year, in mutual funds.

If you can afford the premiums and can dedicate yourself to making the payments for at least 15 years — no small feat — whole life is a better deal. Most of us don't fit either of those circumstances and are far better off with term life insurance.

If you decide to get term life insurance, the best way to buy is by calling an independent shopping service or using one on the Internet. There are an increasing number of Internet services, including www.quotesmith.com. Just plug in your age, sex, state, how much insurance you want to buy, and your medical condition for an instant quote. It's unbelievable. You get a long list of companies and the premiums almost instantly.

Be realistic about your health, because you will have to pass a medical exam. If you smoke or have health problems, you'll have to pay a higher rate. But you'll still get a far better deal by shopping.

I recommend you buy 20-year level term coverage, which simply means the premium is guaranteed to stay the same for 20 years. There's so much competition now in insurance that you can get a very good price and know what you'll be paying well into the future.

I don't recommend buying the cheapest policy but the least expensive one with a financially stable company. Choose a company that is rated at least A+ or A++ by the A. M. Best Co., which means it is top rated for financial stability and strength, or AAA by Moody's Investor Service, Standard and Poor's, or Duff & Phelps. The death benefit is of little use if the insurance company goes out of business. The company I bought from charged 30 percent more than the cheapest company.

This was a touchy family issue, because my brother sells life insurance, and he was very upset with me that I would buy my insurance on the Internet, instead of through him. But he was shocked that he could not match the rate I had gotten.

TIPS ON LIFE INSURANCE

• Consider your own situation to determine if life insurance makes sense for you, how much you need, and which type would be best. If your family would be unable to make mortgage payments without your income, you need life insurance.

• Life insurance is meant to replace your income. My rule of thumb is to buy an amount equal to six times your annual salary.

• If both spouses work, both should have life insurance to replace their incomes. Don't buy insurance on your children.

• There are two primary types of life insurance. Term life coverage provides a payment only if you die. Whole life builds a cash value and serves as a savings vehicle.

• Buy whole life insurance only if you can afford it and can dedicate yourself to making the premium payments for at least 15 years.

• If you decide to get term life insurance, the best way to buy is by contacting an independent shopping service to get some quotes, either by phone or on the Internet.

• Don't cancel a whole life policy. Once you've purchased it, it's best to keep it.

• Avoid buying more than one policy for any person. Every insurance policy you buy has hidden fees in it. So two $50,000 policies would cost more than one $100,000 policy.

CONTACT

U.S. Office of Consumer Affairs
202-634-4310
(For consumer and insurance questions and to ask for
a free copy of the *Consumer's Resource Handbook*)

USAA Life Insurance Company
USAA Building San Antonio, TX   78288
1-800-531-8000

INTERNET/PHONE

www.accuquote.com (1-800-442-9899)
www.iquote.com (1-800-972-1104)
www.quotesmith.com (1-800-556-9393)
www.instantquote.com (1-888-223-2220)
www.masterquote.com (1-800-627-Life)
www.quick-quote.com (1-800-867-2404)
www.rcinet.com/term-quote (1-800-444-8376)

If you don't have Internet access, ask a friend for help, or pick up any issue of *Money Magazine* and check the ads for insurance quotation services. Most have both 800 numbers and Web sites.

If you don't use an online service to get a life insurance quote, make at least one call to USAA Life Insurance. USAA Life is a financially strong company that offers exceptional pricing on both term and whole life insurance. Normally, you have to be a member of the military, a military retiree, or a dependent to do business with USAA, but you don't to purchase life insurance.

Most people who buy life insurance still do so through an insurance agent. Otherwise, they generally wouldn't buy insurance, even if they knew they needed it, because doing so forces them to deal with death. Agents earn their commissions by getting you to do what you need to do but wouldn't otherwise.

When you deal with an agent, remember that the financial strength of the company the agent represents should be your first priority. Insurance agents have a number of increasingly complicated products they can offer you. If an agent tries to sell you an insurance product you don't understand, don't buy it. If what you want is to insure your life and someone presents you with a policy that has seven different riders and 12 different payout formulas, none of which you understand, that's a policy you don't want.

If you buy a whole life policy, don't cancel it and convert to term insurance or you'll lose a lot of money. Almost all of the premiums you pay in the first year of a whole life policy go to pay commissions and other expenses, including underwriting and setup fees. A 50-year-old woman who pays $4,644 in premiums ($387 a month) in the first year of a whole life policy would lose most of that money to fees. Her policy would have a cash value of just $189 after one year. So canceling the policy after a year or a few years, before the policy started working for her, would be a terrible mistake. It takes 15 or more years, depending on the circumstances, before a whole life policy starts to produce returns equal to what you could earn if you bought term life insurance and invested the rest of your money. Few people have the discipline to pay premiums for 15 years or more. That's a long time.

Older readers have to weigh a few other factors. Often they buy insurance through the age of 65, then drop their coverage. If that's your situation, it's okay to buy term life insurance. But if your survivors would need replacement income in addition to what they would inherit, shop for insurance based on your needing it into your 70s or beyond. In many cases, that would mean buying whole life, rather than term, while in your 50s. The cost of $200,000 worth of term life coverage for a 50-year-old nonsmoker would be quite high, at least $340 a year for a man, $300 a year for a woman. At age 70, the cost would be more than $2,300 annually for a man, $1,200 annually for a woman. In those cases, it might make sense, at age 50, to buy a whole life policy for $5,000 to $7,000. The policy would build cash value, and the premiums would never increase.

Whichever insurance you prefer, avoid buying more than one policy for any person. Every insurance policy you buy has hidden fees in it. So two $50,000 policies cost more than one $100,000 policy. Some of the worst abuses I've seen concern poor people who've ended up with a dozen or more small life insurance policies when they could have bought one large policy for the same amount of money.

DISABILITY INSURANCE

Your odds of being disabled are far greater than your odds of dying during your working years, yet few people buy disability insurance. People have an aversion to the idea that they might be partially or completely disabled, so they don't protect themselves financially.

Imagine the powerlessness you would feel as the breadwinner for your family if you were disabled, could not work, and had no source of income. Your family wouldn't have any money to live on. With disability insurance, you're buying a financial safety net for your family.

The cost of disability insurance is affected dramatically by the purchase decisions you make. Disability insurance that kicks in 30 or 60 days after you are disabled costs a lot more than coverage that takes effect after six months. I recommend the coverage that kicks in after six months. The premium will be more reasonable, and you'll still get good coverage. It's wise to have enough in savings so that you can survive for six months if you lose your job, or in case of any other emergency. If you don't have enough savings to cover a six-month loss of income, consider a disability policy that pays benefits after 90 days.

At the other end, people sometimes buy disability coverage that stays in effect for too short a period. Don't get a policy that will pay for only three or five years. Get a policy that covers you through age 65.

The next question is how much coverage to buy. I recommend you get an amount equal to 60 percent of your gross pay. That will give you about what you take home after taxes.

Look very closely at how these policies define a disability. Because the Social Security Administration has such a strict definition of a disability, it pays benefits on just a third of its claims. If your policy uses the same definition, you could lose twice. Social Security might determine that you're not disabled under its guidelines, and your insurer would make the same determination. The top insurers use this definition: "The insured is totally disabled when he

TIPS ON DISABILITY INSURANCE

- Your odds of being disabled are far greater than your odds of dying during your working years, so disability insurance is more important than life insurance.

- It's best to get a disability policy that begins making payments three or six months after you are disabled and continues until retirement.

- Buy coverage equal to 60 percent of your current pay before taxes.

- Get a policy that uses a more liberal definition of disability than the one used by the Social Security Administration.

(or she) is unable to perform the principal duties of his (or her) occupation."

The Social Security Administration pays Americans up to $1,300 a month if it accepts their claim of total disability. Private insurers offer disability policies that pay $2,000 a month in benefits, tax free, for a cost of about $670 a year (with benefits taking effect after 90 days). The insurance costs more if you're older or have a high-risk job or if cost-of-living adjustments are built into the benefits.

I don't recommend buying either life or disability insurance through your employer. The coverage may cost more, and it won't go with you if you change jobs. Worse, if you develop a health condition that makes you unable to buy these types of insurance, you will have squandered the opportunity you had to buy them while you were healthy.

HEALTH INSURANCE

One of the most difficult areas I deal with is health insurance. Callers to my show have every imaginable problem with the nation's health care system: not being able to get coverage, not being able to get the insurer to pay what they believe is a fair amount, poor treatment, not being able to get referrals to specialists they want to see, and finding access to good care when they are ill.

The nation's health care system is still a work in progress, and the brightest people in the country continue to disagree about how to make the system work on behalf of consumers. One of the biggest problems consumers face in health care is that they are not actually the system's customers. Health care insurance is generally provided by employers, which pay the lion's share of the premiums. And their interests are very different from yours. The primary goal of employers is to hold down their costs; way down the list is the quality of the health care provider.

You have to hope your employer offers a choice of plans, rather than one take-it-or-leave-it possibility. If there is a choice, it will likely be either a traditional plan, a health maintenance organization (HMO), or a preferred provider organization (PPO).

The traditional plan is rapidly disappearing. That's the kind in which you choose your doctor and the insurer pays its share of the cost of a visit, usually 80 percent, after you've paid a yearly deductible. But it isn't a true 80 percent. The insurer pays 80 percent of what it says is a reasonable charge. The problem with these "fee-for-service" plans is that costs have increased so much that most employers no longer will pay them.

The high costs have pushed us into managed care, which includes both the HMO and PPO. In the HMO, there's a closed system of doctors and medical facilities. You may receive treatment only from the HMO's doctors at their facilities. In return for that rather severe limitation, you get a great financial deal. Your out-of-pocket costs, regardless of how serious the illness, are minimal.

My wife, who is an HMO member, was in the hospital with a serious illness and received intensive medical care for three days. She recovered fully, and her entire medical bill was $25.

So the HMO offers the starkest of choices. You give up a great deal of freedom and mobility in selecting your medical care providers, but you have virtually no financial risk.

The real movement in the country has been not to HMOs but to other managed care choices, such as the preferred provider organization. PPOs don't force you to go to a closed system of doctors, as HMOs do. Instead, PPOs provide incentives to choose specific doctors and facilities, and disincentives for you to choose others. For example, you might have a $15 co-pay to visit a PPO doctor, with no annual deductible, and get a 90 percent reimbursement for other costs. If you go outside the plan to a non-PPO doctor, you might have a $250 annual deductible, and get an 80 percent reimbursement for your costs after you meet the deductible.

The biggest complaint I get about PPOs is that you have to be absolutely certain before you go to a medical practice that the individual physician you see is on the plan. If the doctor says you have to go to the hospital, you have to make sure the hospital is in your plan. If you need surgery, unless it's emergency surgery, you have to make sure that the attending physicians and anesthesiologists are in your plan. If you don't, you could be exposed to enormous out-of-pocket costs.

We had a case in which my caller thought she had done all her homework before undergoing a hysterectomy but wound up responsible for a $3,500 bill, instead of the $200 she thought she would pay. Her doctor was in her medical plan, but the hospital the doctor recommended was not. You almost need to complete a checklist to avoid financial disaster.

TIPS ON HEALTH INSURANCE

• Many employer-paid health care plans include a traditional fee-for-service plan, a health maintenance organization, and a preferred provider organization. Choose the plan you find least objectionable.

• HMOs protect you from financial risk, but you have no freedom to choose your own doctor, and many consumers complain about the lack of access to quality care.

• PPOs give you a choice of doctors in or outside the plan and use a carrot-and-stick approach to encourage you to choose plan doctors.

• If you're not getting the care you expect from an HMO, send a letter to the HMO's medical director, by certified and regular mail, go through the HMO's appeal process, and consider paying for a second opinion from a doctor outside the HMO.

• If you're in a PPO, make sure every doctor you see and every hospital you go to are in the plan.

• If you don't have coverage and are healthy, consider opening a medical savings account, which combines a catastrophic insurance plan with a tax-advantaged savings account.

These are the consequences when we aren't the customers and the provider doesn't have any financial incentive to make sure we are happy. The result is that the customer is forced to decide between receiving quality care and ensuring financial safety. When you're sick and in pain, you want relief and it's even more difficult to make the right choices. That's the reality of the marketplace.

The biggest problem with HMOs has been what to do if you're sick and don't believe you're receiving proper care. Until better consumer protections are enacted, the first thing I recommend is to complain and complain loudly to your state's insurance department. Most states regulate HMOs. Second, send a letter directly to the medical director of your HMO, both by regular and certified mail. If you're not well enough to do this, have a family member send the letter for you. State your condition, why you believe you're not receiving proper treatment, and what you want the HMO to do. If necessary, see a specialist out-

side the HMO, pay for his or her opinion, and attach that information to the complaint you file with your insurance department and the medical director of the HMO. In addition, go through the appeal process at the HMO. If you're really sick, go directly to the medical director also. The HMO may hope that you die or get better before your appeal is heard.

Many Americans are having trouble getting health care coverage or are worried that they can't afford the cost. If you aren't insured but are in very good health, get quotes on Medical Savings Account (MSA) plans. An MSA is a combination plan that includes a health insurance policy with a very high deductible and a tax-advantaged savings account, the MSA. The policy protects you if you have a catastrophic illness or injury, but because the annual deductible is usually $2,500, it's useless for minor medical expenses. The policy also has a very low premium. The money you don't pay in ultra-high premiums goes into the savings account, free of income tax. When you have medical expenses, you draw money from the MSA until you meet the deductible.

Being in good health is important if you have an MSA because you need some time to build up the amount of money in your account before you are faced with medical bills. If you need surgery 30 days after you open an MSA, you'll bear the cost of the first $2,500 in bills.

Essentially, an MSA gives you a tax break to self-insure your health, and, over time, for most people an MSA will work out well. In the short term, MSAs are a smart financial risk mostly for people who could not afford to have coverage otherwise, or for people who have a good deal of money in savings that they could draw from if they had an unexpected illness or accident.

MSAs are a great choice if you rarely get sick, because you roll over the money in the account from year to year and eventually get it, tax free. MSAs also are a good choice if you're under age 30 and are active and in good health. People under age 30 generally call on the health insurance system only if they have a major illness or accident, so they're great candidates for MSAs or other catastrophic health care policies.

MSAs have done poorly so far in the market, possibly because insurers are charging fees that are so high that they wipe out the benefits of having one. Also, because you have an individual insurance policy, you have no negotiating power with doctors and hospitals to get discounts. So you pay full list price for medical care, which almost nobody does anymore. Finally, I think people have shied away from MSAs because insurance is confusing enough for most people without having both an insurance policy and a savings account.

Many employers offer a benefit called a cafeteria plan or a flexible spending plan, which employees can use to help pay medical or child care costs. They work a little like medical savings accounts in that you ask your employer to take a specified amount of money out of each paycheck, and you use that money to pay for deductibles, co-payments, and other medical costs that aren't paid by the company health plan. The advantage is that you can pay those costs out of gross dollars, not net. Since $200 off your gross pay will often equal $140 or less of your net pay, you get a substantial discount.

However, you can't tell your employer to take out more or less money during the year, and you lose any money that's left in the account at the end of the year. So if you have $1,000 taken out and draw only $600 from the account, you lose $400. That's the reason I don't favor using flexible spending accounts for medical care, unless you have known expenses like prescription medicines you must have that aren't covered by insurance. If you don't budget well, you could lose. For child care, you'll know the cost in advance, so putting money into a "dependent care account" is a great idea.

In some markets around the country, individuals or small groups can join an HMO. I strongly advise that for people who are looking to keep their out-of-pocket costs minimal if they become ill. If that's you, contact the HMOs in your area and see if they accept individuals. You'll have to pass medical screening, which generally means you cannot smoke or have any serious medical history.

Another option is to call the agent who handles your homeowner's or auto insurance and ask for a referral to a health insurance broker. He or she can advise you on what options are available for individuals in your part of the country.

CAR INSURANCE

The most important thing to know about auto insurance is that you should carry it. It's been estimated that a third of all motorists in America don't have any auto insurance, even though carrying it is required by law.

People don't carry auto insurance because of the cost. Premiums are high, and many people can't, or won't, pay. But not carrying insurance is a false savings. If you have no insurance and are involved in an accident, you could end up with no car and no money.

Worse yet, if you have a car loan and don't get insurance, the lender has the right to force-place insurance and may not tell you what it's done until the end of your loan. That means the lender buys insurance for your car, at a cost five or six times what you would normally pay. This is a giant profit center for lenders and a rude surprise for many borrowers. I heard of one case in which the borrower thought he'd made his last car payment when a bank officer told him he still owed $2,600, plus interest, for not carrying insurance.

There are several types of auto insurance, and you should think about how much of each you need. Collision coverage takes care of damage to your car in the event of an accident that is at least partially your fault. Normally you'll be responsible for a deductible of $250 or $500 and your insurer will pay the rest. You should maintain collision coverage in almost all circumstances.

If you have an older car that's worth very little, it may not make sense to carry collision coverage. The other exception is if you have substantial assets. In this case, you may prefer to self-insure an older car worth $6,000 or less. I had a car that was six years old and maintaining collision coverage was a borderline decision. I was paying $262 a year for collision. If the car had been totaled in an accident, I would have received about $2,700 from my insurance company. It really wasn't worthwhile to keep the coverage.

TIPS ON CAR INSURANCE

- It's very foolish not to carry auto insurance, yet perhaps a third of all motorists don't have any.

- If you have a car loan and don't carry insurance, the lender may buy insurance for you at five or six times what you would normally pay.

- Collision coverage takes care of damage to your car from an accident that is all or partially your fault. Normally you'll be responsible for a deductible of $250 or $500 and your insurer will pay the rest.

- Comprehensive coverage takes care of noncollision calamities, such as damage from a break-in, theft, or windshield cracking.

- Liability is the most important component of auto insurance and the one to which people pay the least amount of attention. It pays for damage to property and physical injury from an accident that is your fault.

- Medical coverage riders, available in some states, often duplicate health insurance coverage. If you don't have health insurance, consider getting it rather than adding medical coverage to your automobile insurance.

If your annual premiums for collision and comprehensive coverage exceed 10 percent of the value of your car, consider dropping them.

One way to limit the cost of collision coverage is to carry a higher deductible. If you can afford to pay the first $500 in damages, you can save $50 to $100 a year by carrying a $500 deductible instead of a $250 deductible. Over 5 to 10 years, that's a substantial savings. Plus, you don't want to make a lot of small claims, because insurers tend to count the number of claims against you, and you could be canceled if you make too many claims. But don't carry a high deductible if you can't afford to pay that amount if you have an accident.

Comprehensive coverage takes care of non-collision calamities, such as damage from a break-in, theft of the car, a windshield cracking, or damage from natural disasters such as floods or hurricanes. Use the same rules of thumb to decide your deductible as you would for collision coverage.

Liability is the most important component of auto insurance and the one to which people pay the least amount of attention. This is the type of insurance many states require you to carry, because it pays for damage to property and physical injury from an accident that is your fault. Most people try to save money by buying the absolute minimum liability coverage, often $15,000 per person up to a maximum of $30,000 per accident. That's okay if you don't own anything. But if you have personal assets, you need to protect them against the threat of personal injury lawsuits. If you injure somebody in an accident, that person's medical bills will exceed the minimum liability coverage very quickly. I recommend you carry coverage of $300,000 per accident, which sometimes has a limit of $100,000 per person. Better to have too much liability coverage than too little. It won't cost you much more.

If you are very wealthy, get an umbrella policy. It shields you from liability in almost every phase of your life. Umbrella coverage, which is sold in amounts of $1 million, $2 million, and higher, supplements your auto and homeowner's liability coverage. You can buy umbrella coverage around the country for $100 to $350 a year, not a big cost because the potential risk of a catastrophic liability claim against you is very small.

The last decision to make about insurance is whether to have a medical coverage rider, which is available in some states. I'm opposed to such riders, because they often duplicate your own health insurance. If you don't have health insurance, I would consider getting it rather than adding medical coverage to your automobile insurance. Agents will try to sell these riders by saying they will protect a passenger in your car. But here's my answer to that. If the passenger is a friend, he or she will claim against his or her health insurance. If it's not a friend, he or she will sue you against your liability. You're covered in either case.

There are two important considerations in picking an auto insurer. One is the cost of the premium. The other is the quality of the service. First decide what coverages you want in the three major areas — collision, comprehensive, and liability. Then it's a fairly easy matter to call insurers and get quotes. The quotes vary tremendously from company to company, so don't take the first offer.

There's an even larger difference in customer service, from the best insurers to the worst. Ask friends, relatives, and co-workers which they use and how they've handled claims. Another good source is *Consumer Reports* magazine, which occasionally surveys customers to determine service quality. In the Cars chapter of this book, the section on auto accidents lists the top insurers as rated by *Consumer Reports*. They're ranked by service quality.

For $12, *Consumer Reports* (1-800-808-4912) will shop for the lowest-cost auto insurance in your state. This service is offered in a number of states around the country, and I think it's well worth the cost. The difference between insurers is incredible. One sometimes will charge up to six times more than another company for the same driver.

HOMEOWNER'S INSURANCE

Shop for homeowner's insurance the same way you do for other kinds of insurance. Figure out what limits you want and what value you need to insure, then call several insurers for quotes. Sometimes you'll get a better deal if you buy your homeowner's and auto insurance from the same company. If you're happy with your auto insurer, get a quote from your agent and ask about a multi-line discount.

Make sure the quote you get is for insurance that would pay to replace your belongings, rather than pay you based on their depreciated value. There's a big difference. If your television is stolen, replacement coverage would allow you to buy another, instead of giving you half of what you paid for it three years ago.

I recommend that you get a homeowner's policy with a high deductible. The premiums are cheaper, and it will prevent you from making a lot of small claims. I'm getting more and more calls from people whose insurers have canceled their coverage, even after they've been with the company for many years, because they've had a couple of small claims in the last few years. Insurers are notoriously inefficient, and it's hugely expensive for them to process the paperwork for a claim and pay an adjuster. So they now grade you on the number of claims you make, rather than simply on the amount of money you might cost them in a claim.

If you have a relatively small loss, say $750, you're better off absorbing the loss than filing a claim. If you have a $500 deductible, the insurer would pay you $250, but you would risk losing your coverage. If your insurer cancels you for making too many claims, finding replacement coverage will be enormously expensive. Other insurers will ask you if you were canceled and why and then will place you in a high-risk category. You can avoid that by raising your deductible to $1,000 or $2,500. My preference is $2,500, but if that's just too high for you to go, choose a $1,000 deductible.

I raised my homeowner's insurance deductible to $2,500 and saved 38 percent on my coverage. If you do that, you'll save so much on premiums over the years that it will more than make up for any lost benefits on smaller claims. If someone breaks into your house and steals a couple of televisions and a VCR, it's going to kill you to have to spend $1,000 to replace the stolen items. But over the long term, you'll benefit more from having a higher deductible. If you don't believe me, check with your insurer to see how much money you would save each year by going with a higher deductible. And think how many years it's been since you've actually had to make a claim with your insurer. Multiply the savings by the number of years and you'll understand my reasoning.

If you ever do have to make a claim due to a theft or a fire, ask your agent what documentation you need to substantiate it. The insurer makes big money over the years from you in premium payments. You want to make sure that if you have a major claim, you will be compensated for your loss. My favorite method of documenting what you own is to use a video camera. If you don't have one, borrow one from a friend. Walk through your house, room by room, and shoot a video of your possessions. As you're taping, talk about each item, when you bought it and, if you remember, how much you paid. Make sure to tape the electronic equipment, furniture, and anything else you consider valuable. If you have an expensive wardrobe, pan your closet and talk about how many suits or dresses you have. If you have a fire or other loss, you'll be reimbursed for each item. So you'll need to indicate that you have eight suits and 15 pairs of underwear. There are limits in some basic policies on jewelry. If you have an individual piece worth more than $2,000, or several pieces worth more than $5,000 collectively, you may need to purchase additional coverage.

TIPS ON HOMEOWNER'S INSURANCE

• Figure out what limits you want on your homeowner's insurance and what value you need to insure, and then call several insurers for quotes.

• Sometimes you'll get a better deal if you buy your homeowner's and auto insurance from the same company.

• Make sure you get a quote for insurance that would pay to replace your belongings, rather than pay you based on their depreciated value.

* Update coverage for the value of your home and its contents, if needed, every five years.

• Raise your deductible to $1,000 or $2,500. You'll pay less in premiums but, more important, you'll reduce the risk that your insurer will cancel your coverage because you made too many claims.

• Ask your agent what documentation you need to substantiate a claim, in case of a theft or a fire. I think it's easiest to videotape your house and describe your possessions. Don't store the tape in your house.

• Carry enough liability coverage to protect you against a lawsuit if someone gets hurt on your property.

If you don't like the idea of using video, use a still camera and take pictures of each room and each item of value. Put the pictures in a photo album with a written description of everything, or, if you're lazy like I am, take a cassette recorder and make an audio description to go with the pictures. Keeping receipts of your purchases is ideal, but the number of us who keep receipts is minuscule.

It's helpful to make a new video or take new pictures once a year, because you may buy new items. When you're done, store the tape or photos somewhere safe — not in your house. If there's a fire, a melted tape or burned album won't do you any good.

It's also important to update the amount of your coverage every few years, because your house may have increased in value. If you bought a $125,000 policy a few years ago and your house is now worth $150,000, you may not have enough coverage to protect yourself from a catastrophic loss. Even if you have replacement value coverage to rebuild your home, you may not have enough insurance. When you've been in your home for five years, check to see that the coverage you have is adequate to replace it if the house were destroyed. Check the coverage on your possessions, too. You may have accumulated so many things over the years that you don't have enough coverage to protect the contents. Also check your coverage if you refinance your mortgage. The additional cost in your premiums is tiny, but the risk is great. If you raise your deductible and increase your coverage at the same time, you'll pay less and be better protected.

As with auto insurance, liability coverage is an important consideration in your homeowner's policy. You need to have enough liability coverage to protect your assets in case someone gets hurt on your property, or if your dog bites someone.

Many policies offer minimum liability coverage of $100,000, but it costs only about $20 more per year for $300,000 in coverage.

If someone is injured on your property, it's a good idea to express your concern and to say you're sorry that the accident happened. Just be careful not to admit fault. Sometimes people are sued just because they've hurt the injured person's feelings. A lot of lawsuits could be prevented if people just expressed that simple act of human decency.

I have a nephew in Washington, D.C., who lived next door to a police officer who had a police dog. The dog got loose one day and badly bit my nephew. He needed stitches and minor plastic surgery, which ran up a few thousand dollars in medical bills. His mother never would have sued if someone with the police department had shown some common courtesy. When nobody did, she sued and won $17,000.

Travel

The travel business has changed more in the last few years than at any time I've ever witnessed, and the change has been brought about by the Internet. Travel already was democratized by the deregulation that occurred in 1979. It used to be that traveling was something people did for business, or because they were rich enough to visit exotic places. Today, most people see travel as a possibility in their lives.

I was in the travel business for six years and was fortunate to do very well in it. I ended up with a chain of travel agencies, which I sold in 1987. Since I got into the business, I've traveled constantly. I've visited every continent in the world, except Antarctica. My visit to the Arctic Circle, the flip side, will easily suffice.

Traveling around the world is incredible fun, I've found, but it has also taught me something — the importance of saving money. Many of the people I've observed in my travels make things last; they don't have to have the latest of everything, unlike many in our consumption-oriented society. I've also met a lot of people in poor countries who were very happy despite their lack of material possessions.

In this chapter I'll tell you about how to travel for less, what hazards to avoid, how to save on hotels and car rentals, and some great places to visit.

SAVING MONEY ON TRAVEL

It's one of the ironies of the travel industry that vacationers get the best deals and business travelers, who travel far more often, get the worst. The Internet has only accelerated that trend. An airline, cruise line, or hotel can now post last-minute discounts on the Internet, and people who act quickly can get amazing savings.

There are certain strategies that will save you the most money when you travel. The number-one way to save is to be ready to buy when there's a great deal available, then figure out a reason you want to go. My wife and I were planning to take a trip to Japan, using frequent-flier miles. Three weeks before we were supposed to leave, there was a sale from my home city of Atlanta to Rome, Italy, for $318 round-trip. I didn't even have to think about taking advantage of that good a deal. We immediately bought a pair of tickets to Rome and cashed in the frequent-flier miles, paying a $50 penalty to use the miles at a later date.

I go on incredibly cheap trips, none of which are to places I planned to go in advance. When a deal pops up, I go. I've traveled from Atlanta to San Francisco for $79 round-trip. I've been to Tucson, Arizona, for $99; Portland, Oregon, for $100; Salt Lake City, Utah, for $110, all round-trip. And many of my listeners joined me on a special from Atlanta to Honolulu, Hawaii, a journey of nearly 5,000 miles, for as little as $182 round-trip. I paid $320 for a trip that included a free stop in San Francisco.

Now, I recognize that a lot of people don't have the travel flexibility that I do, but many of us are able to wait for a special bargain instead of planning a trip months ahead to a specific place. For the technologically savvy, finding the deals that happen along actually is pretty easy. The most popular Internet site to get information is www.bestfares.com. People must be looking, because Best Fares claims to get 6 million visits a week. There's a section called news desk that gives the best deals on airfares, hotels, and cruises that are available for minutes to days at a time.

There are a number of reasons why extra-cheap airfares pop up so often these days. One reason is that a certain airline may be trying to send a signal to another. One day, Northwest Airlines was mad at Continental Airlines, so Northwest published extra-cheap fares out of Newark, New Jersey, Cleveland, Ohio, and Houston, Texas. Newark, Cleveland, and Houston happen to be Continental's three main flight centers. Northwest probably was retaliating because Continental had run some fare specials out of Detroit, Minneapolis, or Memphis, which are Northwest's main flight centers. Sometimes we benefit from these competitive scuffles.

I share a vacation home near Salt Lake City, Utah, with several members of my family (it's not a timeshare), and I got three incredibly cheap fares in one year from Atlanta to Salt Lake — $110 round-trip, $134 round-trip, and $172 round-trip — and all three times it was because of airlines dueling with each other. Delta has hubs in Atlanta and in Salt Lake City, and the other airlines were mad at Delta for cutting fares to their hubs.

The second-most common reason an airline will offer an unusually cheap fare is because somebody just makes a mistake. There are so many hundreds of thousands of fare changes a day that sometimes somebody just enters the wrong price. The fare is still perfectly good, although it may not be available for more than a few hours or a day.

Finally, airlines run specials when seats on a particular route aren't selling well, so the carriers dump these "bottom-bucket" tickets. Because of the economic turmoil in Asia in 1998, airlines were heavily discounting seats from the U.S. to cities all over Asia. Fares dropped as low as $399 round-trip. And every time there's unrest in the Middle East the same type of thing happens, and airfares to Israel and Egypt also drop precipitously.

If you enjoy fare-shopping, check Internet sites such as www.bestfares.com once a day. Word of mouth is another great way to find specials. But you have to be able to act. This is one of those times when he who hesitates loses.

My in-laws have totally changed their thinking about air travel. They used to think it was too expensive and took most of their trips by car. But I've got them going everywhere, because I'll call them at 10 P.M. and tell them about some great special they have to try. I have them going to Anchorage, Alaska, for $205 round-trip, to Italy for $388 round-trip, and to Paris for $365 round-trip. I like people to use travel agents to book their trips, but if you find a hot special at night, you're stuck calling the airline to buy your ticket.

TIPS ON SAVING MONEY ON TRAVEL

- Be ready to buy tickets when there's a great deal available, then figure out a reason you want to go to the destination.

- Check the Internet for special fares, but don't use it to shop for the best fare to a particular destination.

- Do the reverse of what other travelers do. Buy airfare and hotel rooms during off-peak seasons, when rates are lower.

- Plan vacations so you can take advantage of weekend specials in urban areas and mid-week specials in resort areas.

- Be flexible about the dates you travel and the airports you fly out of or into.

- Consider taking trips that involve changing planes. They're cheaper and often don't take that much longer.

- Be flexible about the airline you use, and don't be fixated on using frequent-flier miles. A thousand frequent-flier miles is worth only about $10 in free travel.

- Join every airline's frequent-flier program, even if you fly infrequently. Joining is easy, costs nothing, and allows you to receive mailings advertising private sale fares.

- Register at each airline's Web site to receive E-mail about special savings.

INTERNET

www.bestfares.com
www.travelocity.com
www.expedia.com
www.180096hotel.com or call 1-800-96Hotel

I recommend that you use the Internet for research and not to book your ticket, unless there's a deal you must book on the Internet to get it. Don't play travel agent, because the Internet works best when you can sit back and cherry-pick specials. If you need to travel to New York or Chicago, or to any city, on a particular date, a travel agent will do a much better job than the Internet in helping you find the best fare. If you shop yourself, you'll pay too much.

Another place to find airfare specials online is at the airlines' own Web sites. You register at each site by giving them your E-mail address, and every week, often Sunday through Wednesday, the airline sends you a message with deals that are available only for the next weekend. TWA recently had a one-weekend sale between Atlanta and St. Louis in either direction for $99 round-trip and between Lincoln, Nebraska, and Atlanta for $129 round-trip. You buy the ticket during the week and, in the case of TWA, you leave on Saturday and return two or three days later, on Monday or Tuesday.

Foreign airlines, such as British Airways, typically offer special deals on their Web sites that are good for several months. Cathay Pacific has done special online fare sales and online auctions in which travelers submit bids for tickets. The airline did an auction in which it took bids for tickets to Hong Kong, where the minimum bid was $300 round-trip. The 1,000 highest bidders got tickets. The fare was good from all the cities Cathay Pacific flies from. As with all such deals, you're on your own in getting to the departure city. But the savings are tremendous.

A great strategy to save money on travel is to do the reverse of what everyone else does. Obviously, if you go to the beach over Christmas week, you will pay the highest possible prices of the year. But, believe it or not, if you go from December 1 to December 15, you'll pay a fraction of the cost, even though you're still aiming for a warm-weather getaway. One of the key secrets to unlocking savings in travel is to know the calendar. Ideally, you go to a place at a time when the weather is right and the rates, because of a quirk of the calendar, are especially low. If you're willing to live with less-than-ideal conditions, you'll go during the opposite season, such as to south Florida in the summer.

Europe is a perfect example of a travel destination where the price gaps have gotten even larger. From November 1 through March 31, the very lowest rates are offered. On the other hand, summertime is very expensive. It would not be unusual for a summertime ticket to Europe to cost several times the winter equivalent for the same seat. In the winter of 1998, European fares dropped below $200 from the northeast United States and below $300 from everywhere except the Far West. That's cheap.

Prices to the Caribbean work similarly, although the swings in price are not as extreme.

Rates from April 15 through December 15 usually are about 30 percent below the prices from December 15 through April 15. I love going to the Caribbean or Florida during the off-season or summer. Some people worry about hurricanes, but the chances of being in the wrong place at the wrong time are very slim, even during hurricane season. With modern forecasting technology, seldom would you be in any danger. The greater threat is of having your vacation cut short or canceled by a hurricane.

You can also use the calendar to save on your hotel bill. I've taken combined vacations to San Francisco and Lake Tahoe, and paid bargain rates at hotels in both cities. In an urban area such as San Francisco, hotel rates are lowest on weekends, when volume from business travelers is minimal. In a resort area, it's just the opposite, with the best deals available during the week. So I visit both cities during the same trip and spend the weekend in San Francisco and the rest of the week skiing in the mountains.

Off-season travel to Florida isn't as cheap as it used to be, however, because Florida has become so urbanized that a lot of Floridians are filling rooms at resorts in the off-season that might have gone empty before. Resorts that used to offer fantastic deals are now offering more modest discounts.

You can save a lot of money if you're willing to be flexible about the dates you travel and the airports you fly out of or into. Be willing to travel on a Saturday rather than a Friday, for example. Fly into Newark airport in New Jersey instead of LaGuardia in New York, or vice versa. If you're going to Los Angeles, think about what else is nearby. There are five metro-area airports, and the fares are different to all five. San Francisco has three metro-area airports.

If a discount airline serves the airport you want to fly into, you're in great shape. But even if it doesn't, you may still be in luck. A nearby airport or city may be served by a discounter, and that could make a massive difference in what you pay. If you are going to Boston, for example, you should always check fares to Providence, Rhode Island, because Providence is served by Southwest Airlines, the nation's premier low-cost carrier. If you're going to Washington, D.C., check Baltimore, another Southwest Airlines city. This strategy applies with any of the lower-profile discount airlines as well.

A bonus for business travelers is that Southwest Airlines and its imitators do not charge higher fares to business people.

One thing that has always amused me is how desperately people want nonstop flights. So often you'll find a moderate to huge discount by taking a connecting flight. I think it's worthwhile to spend two hours of your time to get a much better deal on a connecting flight.

And don't be fixated on using frequent-flier miles. A thousand frequent-flier miles is worth about $10 in free travel. If you're going on a 2,000-mile round trip, that's $20 in frequent-flier value. If you can get a fare that is $30 cheaper by flying on a different airline, do it.

While I don't think you should overvalue frequent-flier miles, I do recommend that you join every airline's frequent-flier program, even if you fly infrequently. There's no cost to do so, and it takes no more than three minutes. All you do is call the airline's reservations office in your city and someone can immediately enroll you. By joining the frequent-flier programs, you can take advantage of off-the-books discounts, a great way to save money on air travel.

Hotel Bargains Online

Radisson and Hilton hotels have been the most innovative in offering special bargains on the Internet. They have specials for specific hotels on specific dates. They might have a conference center hotel that doesn't have any major bookings for a few days, so they'll heavily discount the rooms on the Web site. I've used the Internet, and the savings are fantastic. I took my staff to Santa Fe, New Mexico, and we booked the Radisson Sante Fe for $59 a night — a wonderful deal. I've seen deals for Scottsdale, Arizona, during the peak season for $105 a night, which is nothing for that area. When I went to Norway in 1997, I looked at the Radisson site and it had a special for Oslo that I thought was expensive until I got to Norway. Then I realized it was a great deal.

With these hotel specials, you can book the rooms yourself right online. Rooms tend to be available from one to four weeks in advance.

I used to use 50 percent-off coupon books a lot to save on hotels, but they've been harder to use as hotel occupancies have increased. They still work if you apply the contrarian strategy, doing the reverse of what others do. Use them if you're going to a nice airport hotel on a weekend, when there won't be many business travelers there, or, Sunday through Thursday nights at resort hotels.

For the budget and mid-priced hotels, look for coupons.

OPPORTUNITIES AND HAZARDS

Airlines routinely overbook flights, because of the frequency of no-shows. This creates a great opportunity for people who are flexible. Every time I show up at a gate and I see a big crowd, I go straight to the podium and volunteer to give up my seat if the flight is overbooked. It works like a charm, because volunteers are placed on the list in the order they give their names. If you're picked, ask to fly out on your airline's next flight or the next flight on any other airline, whichever is sooner. Always remember to ask when the next flight is, so you'll know if you can live with the delay.

TIPS ON OPPORTUNITIES AND HAZARDS

- By volunteering to give up your seat on an overbooked flight, you usually get a free ticket for travel anywhere in the continental United States.

- If you miss a connecting flight and are stranded, ask the airline to provide a free meal and long-distance calling. If you're stranded overnight, ask for a free hotel room, meals, and long-distance calls.

- If your bags are lost, file a claim at the airline's baggage service desk before you leave the airport.

- Be careful what you put in checked baggage. On domestic flights, the airlines have a maximum liability of $1,250 per passenger for lost bags. On international flights, you get just $9.07 per pound of checked baggage.

- If a hotel sends you away when you have a reservation, the hotel should pay for a free night at an equivalent property and move you back the next night.

- If you check into a hotel and it's dirty or dumpy, or you feel unsafe, go back to the desk immediately and ask for your money back.

- Remember that photos you see on the Internet are no different from the photos in glossy brochures you get in the mail. A hotel room or property that looks great on your computer screen may be worn or dirty when you get there.

- To check on the quality of a hotel, ask a travel agent or get the *Mobil Travel Guide*. Certain brands of hotels are consistently outstanding, including Courtyard by Marriott, La Quinta, Fairfield Inn, Sleep Inn, and Hampton Inn.

For your trouble, you usually will get a voucher for a free airline ticket, good for one year to anywhere in the continental United States. With some airlines, the voucher is good for a free flight anywhere in North America. I earn about three free tickets a year and use them during holiday periods, when airfares may be extra high or seats may be hard to find.

Sometimes a flight will be oversold and there will not be enough volunteers. That triggers a game of musical chairs that leaves someone without a seat. There are very specific rules governing what you get for being involuntarily denied a seat. For details, go to the airline's ticket counter and ask to see the contract of carriage.

If you're changing planes and the airline causes you to miss your connection, don't panic and don't allow it to ruin your day or your trip. If I get stranded, I take the free shuttle to an airport hotel and eat there, or check my bag in a locker and go jogging.

In addition to putting you on the next flight, the airline usually will compensate you if you're stranded — but don't take just any offer. If you get stranded overnight, don't accept anything less than an airline-provided hotel room, plus meal vouchers and long-distance calls to alert others where you are. For a minor delay, up to four hours, ask for a free meal and free long-distance calling at the airport terminal. Be nice to the gate agent, even if you don't feel like it; he or she has a lot of power.

If your bags are lost, file a claim immediately with the airline baggage service desk. Don't leave the airport without filing a claim. Many airlines have extremely hostile policies about lost baggage claims. While it's still fresh in your mind, try to detail every item that was in your bag and keep a copy of the claim. Better yet, keep a list in your wallet or carry-on luggage of what's in your checked bag.

On a domestic flight, the airlines have a maximum liability of $1,250 per passenger for lost bags. Do not put any jewelry, electronics, rare manuscripts, breakable items, cash, or prescription medicines in checked baggage. The airlines don't have to reimburse you fully for their loss, plus you're inviting theft. Put these items in your carry-on baggage. International rules are even more restrictive. Payments made for lost or stolen items are minimal, based on a rate of $9.07 per pound of checked baggage.

You can purchase excess valuation insurance, which costs about $1 per $100 of declared value. But I follow the simplest rule of all: I don't trust the airlines with my luggage. I have a carry-on bag on wheels and if I can't carry it on, I don't take it. That goes even for long trips. If they have laundries here, they have laundries where I'm headed.

Hotel overbookings are another big travel hazard. Even if you have a reservation, it's possible the hotel won't have any rooms. In industry lingo, that makes you a "walk." If a hotel walks you, it should pay for a free night's stay for you at an equivalent property and move you back the next night. If you arrive by cab, the hotel should transport you to the alternate hotel or pay for your cab ride there. The hotel also should allow you to call business associates or family, at no charge, to tell them your new location.

You have a right to be happy with the hotel, even if your reservation is guaranteed prepaid. If you check into a hotel and it's dirty or dumpy, or you feel unsafe, go back to the desk immediately and tell the clerk the hotel is unacceptable to you and you're going to leave. It's traditional in the hotel industry to release you from your obligation if you are unhappy or afraid.

Several hotel chains now offer a 100 percent satisfaction guarantee, promising that if you're not happy, you don't pay. Unfortunately, I got a couple of calls on my radio show from people who were not happy, and the hotels did not honor their money-back guarantees. One caller checked into a Comfort Inn with a young child, only to find the room reeked of marijuana. She went back to the desk and was told it was the only room available. She tried to exercise her right to not pay, but the hotel made her pay. Even after my staff and I raised a ruckus with officials at the company's headquarters, management only reluctantly honored the guarantee. So be aware that the guarantee is only as good as the location and the chain. In order to protect yourself, put something in writing before you leave the hotel, and speak to the highest-level management person on site at the time.

Another hazard of staying at a hotel is paying in cash or traveler's checks. When you check into any hotel, a clerk takes an imprint of your credit card. When you check out, you're free to pay in any way you wish. A lot of times, people prefer not to charge the cost to their credit card, so they hand over cash. Unfortunately, I've heard of at least half a dozen cases in which a customer paid by cash, only to find out later that the charge showed up on his or her credit card bill. Unless you keep a receipt, and people rarely do, there's no proof you paid by cash, and the clerk who stole your money is long gone. So you end up paying twice. If you provide a credit card imprint for a hotel room or car rental, pay by credit card.

If you're shopping for a hotel or resort on the Internet, remember that photos you see online are no different from the glossy photos in brochures you get in the mail. A hotel room or property may look great on your computer screen but be worn or dirty when you get there. My wife and I stayed at a place in Kauai, Hawaii, that looked spectacular in the photos on the Internet and very ordinary when we got there. The beach was much smaller than we expected, and the hotel was right in the middle of a construction zone.

People are more likely to be unhappy with hotels when they choose based on brand names alone. There are certain brand name chains that don't maintain consistent quality. One hotel might be nice, but another old and in disrepair. All you need to do to find out if a particular hotel is good is have your travel agent check it out in the *Travel Planner*, a publication that rates hotels from one to five stars. Consumers can also buy the *Mobil Travel Guide*, which uses the same rating system. Members of the Automobile Association of America (AAA) should rely on the recommendations of the company's tour books. I prefer to stay at hotels that rate two stars or above in the *Mobil Travel Guide* or three diamonds or better in the AAA books. Hotels in all price ranges are rated, so the guides are useful for car trips as well as resort vacations.

There are certain brand names of hotels that deserve mention for the consistent quality of their product from city to city. Among them are Courtyard by Marriott, La Quinta, Fairfield Inn, Sleep Inn, and Hampton Inn.

Some hotels have affinity programs that can be useful. You pay a nominal fee to join and in return get discounts and sometimes amenities packages, such as free local phone calls or free faxes. These programs are worthwhile only if you travel several times a year.

CONSOLIDATOR FARES

One of the best ways to save on international airfares is to buy tickets from a group of entrepreneurs called consolidators. When tickets on an international flight aren't selling well at the official price, the airlines sell them at a discount to consolidators, who then resell them, through travel agents, to bargain hunters. Consolidators are high-volume ticket brokers who act as intermediaries between the airlines and travel agents, although some consolidators also sell directly to the public.

Consolidators promise in advance to sell a percentage of the airlines' tickets, in exchange for lower prices. The more tickets they sell, the better prices they can negotiate from the airlines. So they want to move as many tickets as possible.

If ticket sales are soft, airlines may lower their prices to consolidators as the departure date approaches. So if you're flying to England in November, a consolidator will likely quote you a higher price in July than if you wait until October to buy your ticket. A few weeks before takeoff, the airline has a better feel for how many tickets it is going to have to dump. Although airlines normally advertise a sale to perk up slow-selling domestic tickets, they discount international fares privately through consolidators.

Consolidators started out serving the ethnic market, offering deals to immigrants who came to this country from nations such as India. Airfares between the U.S. and India were very high, so Indian entrepreneurs saw an opportunity to make money by selling off-price tickets to Indians. Korean consolidators emerged to serve growing Korean communities in areas such as Los Angeles. And other consolidators have followed the growth of large ethnic communities throughout America.

Consolidators vary widely in quality and professional ethics, so it's important to follow some

TIPS ON CONSOLIDATOR FARES

• Consolidators are high-volume ticket brokers who sell international airline tickets for an average of 20 percent less than the regular price.

• Often the best consolidator fares are available a few weeks before your departure date and on less well-known airlines.

• Always buy consolidator tickets from a travel agent or a consolidator in your city, and always use a credit card to pay for your tickets.

• Ask your travel agent to check the published fare for your destination, as well as the consolidator fares that she can find. You can also check the travel section of your Sunday newspaper for consolidator advertisements.

• Tell your travel agent if you would prefer not to fly on certain airlines. Sometimes the best consolidator rates will be on obscure airlines.

INTERNET

www.travelocity.com
www.expedia.com

key steps when you buy consolidator tickets. First, have your travel agent check the published fare for your destination. Sometimes the consolidator fare isn't that great a deal. Next, ask the travel agent to check with her preferred consolidators to see what's available. If you don't like the quote the travel agent gives you on a consolidator ticket, buy a Sunday newspaper and look for advertisements from consolidators in the travel section. Point the ads out to your travel agent and see if she can find you a better deal than she first quoted. Ads can be misleading, however.

It's very important to buy consolidator tickets from a travel agent or a consolidator in your city. Always pay by credit card, so you are protected in case the consolidator doesn't deliver the ticket. If you pay by check or cash to an out-of-town consolidator, you're in the worst possible position if

the company takes your money and doesn't send you a ticket. My radio show got a call once from a consumer who sent $5,300 to a consolidator a thousand miles away and never got his tickets. If you use a credit card and that happens, you can get a refund easily from your credit card company. If you don't, you could lose your money.

Make sure to tell your travel agent if you would prefer not to fly on certain airlines. Sometimes the very best consolidator rates will be on airlines you've never heard of, from countries you don't know much about. I'm not kidding. You'll find the best deals from New York to London on Third World airlines. Quite often, the cheapest tickets to Asia will be on the airline of a Third World Asian country, rather than on one of the first-tier Asian airlines. The irony is that Asia has two of the world's best airlines, Singapore

Airlines and Cathay Pacific, as well as some of the most unreliable airlines in the world. You need to know the airline as well as the price.

Despite some potential hazards, everybody who flies internationally should at least compare the cost of consolidator tickets to published airfares. When my family took a vacation to Asia in 1994, six of us used free tickets from frequent-flier miles. But my brother Neal used a consolidator ticket. He flew with us on the same plane; the only difference was that he saved 30 percent on the cost of his fare.

Depending on how flexible you are about the airline and the schedule, you'll normally save about 20 percent on the cost of an international ticket by buying it from a consolidator. Sometimes the savings can be as much as 55 percent, but at other times the savings are meaningless. Check the price and recheck the price. These tickets, like almost all airline tickets, are nonrefundable.

You can check consolidator rates at various Internet sites, such as www.travelocity.com or www.expedia.com, but consolidators still send out most of their fare deals by fax to travel agents.

CAR RENTALS

I get more complaints about car rentals than about any other aspect of travel. People don't rent cars that often, and the transaction at the car rental counter can be confusing and unpleasant.

I think car rental practices will improve eventually, because, over the last few years, most of the major car rental companies have been sold to owners that are more professional managers. But until change has clearly occurred, be cautious.

Most upsetting is the array of choices car renters are hit with for insurance-type products. When you rent a car, you'll often get a very heavy-handed pitch for a collision damage waiver, or CDW, also known by the codes LDW or PDW. This is a rip-off fee with the sole purpose of building profits for the car rental company. By paying it, you supposedly waive your responsibility in the event the car is damaged or destroyed in an accident. Nationwide, the fee averages $12 a day. On an annual basis, that's more than $4,000 per car, a lot more than you pay for total coverage on your personal automobile. Some states have banned collision damage waivers, while other states have put caps on the amount a company may charge in order to end the abuses.

My advice is to reject collision damage waiver, which is your option, under almost all circumstances. Check with your auto insurer before you go on a trip, because many times your own policy will cover you for temporary use of a rental car. Another way to avoid CDW is to use a credit card, such as Visa Gold or Gold MasterCard, Diners Club, certain American Express cards, or the premium Discover Card. They will provide collision coverage if you use their card to rent the car. If you've dropped collision coverage on your personal automobile, you should use one of these premium credit cards or see if you can purchase a short-term rider from your insurer. The regular Discover Card has an option that allows you to buy coverage for $6.95 per rental. Just contact Discover before you rent and the charge will automatically be added to your bill. For a one-week rental, paying $6.95 for CDW is a much better deal than paying $84.

Whether you take the collision damage waiver or not, check the rental car carefully before you leave the lot. Quite often I'll find a dented fender or a broken tail light after looking closely at a rental car. At night, I pull the car up underneath a light to check it. If you find any damage on your rental car, have an official of the company note it on the rental contract before you leave. If you don't, you'll probably have to pay for the repair.

TIPS ON CAR RENTALS

• When you rent a car, don't accept the insurance options the company wants you to buy. Check with your own auto insurance agent to see if you're covered under your policy, or use a premium credit card that offers travel insurance.

• Check the rental car carefully before you leave the lot. If you see any damage, have an official of the company note it on the rental contract before you leave.

• For the best deals, look for newspaper coupons, and give your travel agent the special code printed on the coupon. If you can't find a coupon, ask your travel agent for the best deal she knows about.

• Rent the smallest car available at the cheapest rate. Four out of five times, the rental company won't have the small car you ordered and will have to give you a larger car at the small-car price.

• Always take the car out with a full tank of gasoline and return it with a full tank.

• If you're renting for five days or more, a weekly rental will provide a large discount.

I had a caller whose car rental company claimed his wife had broken an outside mirror and wanted him to pay $371 for it, an outrageous price even if she had broken it. My staff called the company and got the matter dropped.

The second type of insurance you'll normally be offered is excess liability coverage. Again, check with your own automobile or homeowner's insurance provider, because either or both may provide you with such coverage, making it unnecessary to purchase it from the car rental company. The cost is about $7 a day.

There are two other optional insurance coverages you'll see quite often on car rental contracts. Personal effects coverage, or PEC, covers you against theft of your possessions from the rental car. Normally your homeowner's, or renter's, insurance will cover that. Personal injury protection covers some of your medical bills if you're injured in an accident. This coverage is completely unnecessary if you already have health insurance.

Car rental companies have started to use newspaper advertising as the principal way of providing special deals on car rentals. You used to get the best deals through travel agents, but now you have to find the newspaper coupon and give a travel agent the fare code that's printed in the ad. That's also true of the deals on the rental companies' Web sites. Without the code, your travel agent can't get you the special rate. If you ask your travel agent or the car rental company for its cheapest rate in Philadelphia, you might be told it's $36.99 a day. If you ask for the rate with a coupon code, say "2GL," you might be told it's $24.99. So it pays to know the code.

Rental companies are forcing the price-conscious car renter to do extra legwork in order to get special deals. If you don't do the extra legwork, you're simply going to pay more money.

Another change in the car rental business is that most of the inexpensive rates require you to keep the car for a Saturday night. The car companies have taken a lesson from the airline industry and found out how to keep business travelers from getting the best rates.

A great trick for saving on a car rental is to rent the smallest car available at the cheapest rate. I always ask for the smallest car, but 80 percent of the time I get a larger car for the same price. Car rental companies load their fleets with larger cars, so they rarely have the smaller car you ordered when you show up.

When you book a small car, the rental company may try to rent you a larger one, at a higher cost, when you get to the counter. Just remember that four out of five times you'll get the larger car without paying for it. So don't give in.

The only time I ever received the subcompact, ironically enough, was on the day of my wedding. And my mother-in-law is probably never going to forgive me. The wedding was very posh, and as we left the reception hall, we got into this two-door econo-box, probably the cheapest car sold in America. It just killed my wife's mom. But believe me, this will almost never happen.

Some rental companies will offer you fuel options. You can pick the car up with a full tank and drop it off with a full tank. Or you can pick it up full and bring it back empty. The only option to choose is taking it out full and bringing it back full. Just stop at a service station on your way back to the rental lot and fill the tank. If you forget, the company will charge you two to four times the normal retail price for gas.

Don't fool with any of the other options that require a calculator and a mathematics degree. Any of the plans that require you to bring the car back with an empty tank are dangerous. With crime so prevalent, it's not smart to play it cute and run out of gas trying to coast in on fumes.

If I rent on a weekend, I usually find the best rates with one of the major on-airport rental companies, such as Hertz, Avis, National, or Budget, which rely almost exclusively on business travelers. There's little business travel on weekends, and these companies have huge fleets they need to push into the marketplace, so they discount heavily.

If your rental is for weekdays, you'll usually pay a high price per day with on-airport rental companies and get much better prices with "second-tier" companies. The largest second-tier renters are Thrifty and Alamo. There is a substantial number of third-tier renters in major markets, but the quality of service varies tremendously.

If you're renting for five days or more, a weekly rental will provide a large discount. A seven-day rental usually costs less than a three-day rental. That's because car rental companies have high costs for processing rentals. With a short-term rental, you're paying mostly for the cost of the people needed to prepare the car for rental and accept it for return. If you begin your rental on Thursday at noon and return it by the same time Monday, you're usually eligible for weekend rates that are up to 70 percent below weekday rates.

WHERE TO BUY TRAVEL

If you don't take vacations often, you're more likely to be conned by scam operators who pretend to be in the travel industry. These scam artists use many different techniques in their attempts to steal your money, the most common being a prize drawing offering a free vacation to the winner. No one ever wins the trip, but almost anyone who enters will be called and told he or she has won. The catch is that winners are expected to pay a registration fee, an administrative fee, a deposit, or taxes. The fees for this supposedly free trip will be more than it would cost you to buy a vacation on your own.

One of my callers got taken for $398 for a "free" trip that was actually just a promotional offer to sell him a trip. He got a call saying he had won a trip with a hotel stay in Fort Lauderdale, Florida, a cruise to the Bahamas, and then a hotel stay there. He was told his cost was $398. He paid the money, and all he got for it was a coupon good for a couple of nights in Fort Lauderdale, a five-hour ferry crossing to the Bahamas, and a couple of nights in the Bahamas. He certainly didn't get $398 worth of travel. Worse yet, sometimes these coupons are completely worthless and the scammers just vanish with everybody's money.

The legitimate way to buy travel is from a local travel agent. A real travel agent has met financial and managerial standards that qualify him or her for what's known as appointment. It's like licensing but more difficult to obtain. You have to show financial worthiness and that you have staff in the agency with the experience necessary to operate a travel business.

Before you do business with a travel agent, ask if she's a member of the Airline Reporting Corp. (ARC) or the International Air Transport Association Network (IATAN). If the agent doesn't know what you're talking about, you're not dealing with a legitimate travel agency.

When you buy travel, pay for it only with a credit card. Normally I advise people to use a credit card to protect against getting scammed; but with travel, you need to use a credit card because the entire industry is so tumultuous. You could buy a ticket from a perfectly legitimate company that might go out of business before your trip. Airlines, tour operators, and cruise lines go bust regularly. In a single week a few years ago, for example, two large international tour operators went bust. If you pay by check or by cash and an operator folds, you lose your money. If you pay by credit card, you're protected by your chargeback rights.

Don't buy tickets directly from an airline; if you do, you almost certainly will pay more. While seven or eight airlines may offer fares between two cities, an airline will give you only the fares it offers. Worse, many airlines embargo fares. That means the airline instructs its employees not to quote certain fares unless the traveler knows to ask for those fares specifically. Airlines try to sell you the most expensive tickets they can. A travel agent, on the other hand, can check the fares of each airline in a more thorough effort to find the best fare.

As I write this, the airlines have cut the commissions they pay to travel agents twice in 24 months. To make up for the lost revenue, a majority of agents now charge a modest fee for using their services. Although travel agents used to charge customers nothing, it's worth it to pay the fee. Over time you will pay significantly less using an agent than trying to buy directly from the airlines, and the experience will be far more pleasant. Airlines offer lousy customer service and no accountability. If you call an airline and the clerk quotes you a fare, then call back 20 minutes later and say you want it, there's a good chance you'll have a problem. The airline employee you talk to the second time almost certainly will be someone different than the first person you spoke to. He may have no idea what you were quoted and won't care. There's total diffusion of responsibility. That won't happen when you call a travel agent.

Having said that, it's even more important now to judge travel agents by how well they serve you, because agents vary enormously in quality. You should make sure you're getting the kind of attention and professional counseling you expect.

It's not easy to choose a travel agent, because you'll want a very personal relationship with your agent. I put the emphasis on the agent because choosing the individual you work with at an agency is even more important than the agency itself. Ask friends, co-workers, and relatives for the names of travel agents they've used and liked. Then call these agents to talk to them about a trip you're thinking of taking and see who seems on the ball and interested in you. If you're new to an area, call half a dozen agents at random for suggestions on a particular trip. You'll find out quickly who's interested in you and wants your business.

There are so many travel agents, and they have widely varying outlooks and specialties. I was an extremely price-oriented travel agent — no surprise there — and I was not the right person for someone who wanted to stay in the very best hotels and resorts. But I was as good as you could get at finding deals. Some agents are really good at business travel; others specialize in cruises. Some are great at planning Caribbean trips, while others are really good at European vacations. You can't find one agent who does everything well, so choose one who's good at arranging the trips you take most often. Many agents will be up-front about their specialties. If you call an agent who does all your business travel about a trip to the Galapagos Islands, he may refer you to another agent in his office.

If price is your main consideration, it's especially important to choose an agent who is willing to take a few minutes to help you. If you want to find the cheapest way to fly from Dallas to Los Angeles, a thorough agent will ask you questions and give you options. Are you flexible about the day and time you leave, the airport you fly out of or into, and the airline? You want someone who thinks in a third dimension.

Unfortunately, most agents are judged on their productivity — how many dollars' worth of tickets they book per hour and per day — and, as a result, are under intense pressure. The more time an agent spends with you to find you a better deal, the less revenue she generates. The most

TIPS ON WHERE TO BUY TRAVEL

- Don't accept "free" trips for which you have to pay any fee.

- Buy travel from a local travel agent who is a member of the Airline Reporting Corp. (ARC) or International Air Transport Association Network (IATAN).

- Pay for travel only with a credit card. You'll be able to get a refund if the company goes out of business.

- There's a big difference among travel agents in their outlooks and specialties. Choose one who's good at arranging the trips you take most often.

- If price is your main consideration, it's especially important to choose a travel agent who will take a few minutes to help you and offer you different options.

- Never call an airline directly to buy tickets. Many will try to sell you the most expensive ticket you will buy.

- Many travel agents now charge a modest fee for their services, but the fee is worth paying.

- When you buy a cruise, use a travel agent who specializes in cruises.

INTERNET

www.cdc.gov

customer-oriented agents look to build a relationship with you over time, rather than worrying about the transaction time involved in one purchase.

One consequence of the commission cut is that some travel agents are pushing travelers toward products that make them more money. You have to make sure your agent is looking out for you, rather than trying to push you into a higher-commission travel package you might not want.

When you buy a cruise, use a travel agent who specializes in cruises. That could be a cruise specialist within a travel agency or an agency that does cruises exclusively. Don't buy a cruise through an out-of-state 800 number unless you are an extremely experienced cruise passenger and you purchase it by credit card. Otherwise, buy the cruise locally and from someone who does a big volume in cruising. A large-volume agency may be able to offer you special low rates that are not available through other travel agents. If a cruise line has a sailing date that's selling terribly, it won't put out a special to all agents, because it doesn't want to hurt the retail price of all its cruises. So it offers the equivalent of a private sale through a few high-volume booking agencies.

It's important not to buy a cruise just because it's cheap. Cruise ships have their own personalities, and if you take a cruise on a ship that doesn't fit your lifestyle or interests, that's not a bargain at any price. Someone may go on a cruise seeking some peace and quiet to recharge her batteries. If the cruise is host to the senior class of a local high school and the students drink and party all night long, that would ruin a dream vacation. I won a cruise once as a travel agent, when I was in my twenties, and the average age on the ship was 71. A good cruise specialist might tell you, for example, that a particular ship is older, has large cabins, and doesn't have much entertainment but that the service is very personal. Ask the agent if the ship you're considering has what you want.

Cruise lines have done a mediocre job of maintaining food standards and cleanliness. The U.S. Public Health Service publishes ratings on ships, called the "Summary of Sanitation Inspections of International Cruise Ships." It's

available on the Internet at www.cdc.gov. Click on "Travelers Health." If you don't have Internet access, ask a friend, or your travel agent can show you the figures. The *ABC Star Guide* also has a section on cruise ships that you can see at your travel agent's.

PLACES TO GO

Infrequent travelers often lose out on great vacations by choosing the security of a travel package over the spontaneity of less structured vacations. In a package, everything is arranged in advance — air, hotel, and ground travel.

For people who are going to a beach resort, a package will be a better deal in many cases than buying the individual components separately. In fact, for people from the eastern U.S. going to Cancun, Cozumel, or Jamaica, a package that includes airfare, hotel, and some other features usually will be cheaper than buying airfare alone.

But to nonresorts, such as Europe or Asia, a package usually costs more than going on your own. That's because travelers to Europe and Asia often are looking for more guidance, and there's a cost for that.

I hear a lot of complaints about travel packages designed for the budget traveler, particularly packages to Nassau, Jamaica, and Cancun. In fact, I hear more complaints about these three places than everywhere else in the world combined. Sometimes travelers are victims of overbooking. They arrive at the destination and the accommodations they paid for are not available. At other times, it's just a general problem of poor service.

But the thing that leaves a bitter taste in people's mouths is the attitude that often surfaces when there is a problem. Nobody seems to care or does anything to resolve it. Many people who go to these places have a wonderful time and go back year after year without problems. But it's too risky to plan your vacation around the hope that everything will go perfectly.

If you haven't traveled a lot and want to get real value for your dollar, start off with trips to familiar places. If you're looking for a beach, go to a nice one in Florida. As you get more comfortable as a traveler, then maybe consider the Caribbean. There are lots of wonderful islands in the Caribbean. But be careful what you ask for; I hear a lot of people say they want to go someplace where there's absolutely nothing to do, a place of absolute peace and tranquility. When they get there, they're bored — because there's absolutely nothing to do. Many of us require more activity than we'll find in a completely out-of-the-way spot.

Don't rely on brochures if you're thinking of going to the Caribbean, because every glossy brochure presents a picture that's not really accurate. Instead, buy one of the comprehensive guides to the area. My favorite is *The Caribbean Islands Handbook*. These books give you enough information to select the island that fits your lifestyle. One other thing you need to know is that when you fly to the Caribbean, you'll have to change planes at least once, and often twice. By the time you've been through all that, you will have given up one day in travel time in each direction.

Of the Caribbean destinations, Aruba has become increasingly popular because it's pretty affordable and has good air transportation and decent accommodations. Grand Cayman is a great spot, with beautiful beaches and great snorkeling and scuba diving. It has decent air services, although prices tend to be sky high once you get there.

Florida has a handful of places I really like. On the Gulf Coast, I love Marco Island, Naples, Sanibel Island, Sarasota, Destin, and Pass-A-Grille.

TIPS ON PLACES TO GO

- Travel packages offer security at the expense of spontaneity. Budget travel packages, such as those to Nassau, Jamaica, or Cancun, tend to generate a lot of complaints.

- If you're interested in the Caribbean, buy one of the comprehensive guides to the area, such as *The Caribbean Islands Handbook*.

- The big advantage of going to Europe on your own is that you can concentrate on visiting the smaller towns and villages, where prices are lower and people are friendlier.

- If you have frequent-flier miles, try to use them for international travel, rather than domestic. For international travel, Asia is a better deal than Europe.

- Airlines offer lower frequent-flier mileage requirements to Asia, Europe, and Latin America during off-peak periods. So, if possible, try to schedule an international trip during the winter.

On the Atlantic side, I like Ponte Vedra Beach, Melbourne Beach, and Indian River Shores. All have nice stretches of sand and are relatively uncrowded. The main difference between the Gulf Coast and Atlantic beaches is that the water tends to be very calm on the Gulf side, while the waves are moderate to rough on the Atlantic side.

First-time travelers to Europe seem to have an unnatural fear of moving around once they land, so they remain sealed in a tour bus. Tours offer the safety and security of traveling with a group and removes worries about handling money, picking hotels, and communicating with people who don't speak English. But if you lock yourself in a tour bus, you'll miss the essence of Europe. When I go to Europe, I do it with reckless abandon. I book my airline ticket and my car rental in advance, and that's it. I make no hotel reservations, and I usually don't have an itinerary. When I get there, I am completely on my own. I land, get in the car, and drive. One time I was in France and the highway was about to split in two directions. One direction was to Amsterdam and the other was to Paris. I had two kilometers to decide which way to go. At the last second, I decided to go to Amsterdam.

The big advantage of going to Europe on your own is that you can concentrate on visiting the smaller towns and villages, where prices are lower and people are friendlier. You can stay in small hotels and bed and breakfasts, meet local people, and enjoy local flavor. The bigger cities are so international in size and outlook that there isn't much difference between them. It makes little sense to spend three days in London, three in Paris, and three in Rome. Better to fly into Paris and spend the rest of the trip visiting the French countryside.

I realize there are some cities people desperately want to see, and Paris is one. But Frankfurt has no charm or redeeming value, and you should get out of it as quickly as you can. Brussels is another city to avoid. There are some great cities in Belgium, including Bruges and Ghent, but Brussels is a complete waste of time. While northern Europe is generally cleaner and things run like clockwork there, people seem to have a better time in southern Europe.

For those of you who think my unstructured form of travel in Europe is nuts but are willing to take a little more of a chance than with a fully escorted tour, there is a third choice. It's called a hosted itinerary, and it allows you to take local tours when you get to a city. You have a tour representative in each town you can call for help,

and your hotels are prebooked and prepaid. To me this is a good compromise for people who are willing to step out a little bit but who don't want to wing it.

If you have more money and want more planning, there's a fourth option, called an FIT. Under this format, the travel agent customizes the trip for you, planning details even down to dinner reservations at particular restaurants.

If the whole idea of going to Europe scares you because of the language gap, make your first trip to Great Britain.

My favorite continent in the world is South America. In spite of the similarity in language, the differences from country to country are greater than between countries in Europe.

I've been to Latin America five times. I loved Chile, Argentina, and Bolivia, an odd choice because Bolivia is one of the world's poorest countries. Latin America is dramatically different from either Europe or the United States. People are unusually friendly. Lots of people resist going to South America because of fears of political instability or crime, but I've never been afraid anywhere in South America, except in Brazil, and even Brazil knows it has a major crime problem. I particularly enjoyed the rural scenery of South America and the people. But the beaches were a disappointment. Even the most famous beaches of South America don't touch the quality of a Florida beach. The best travel guide to South America is the *South American Handbook*. Nothing else comes close.

If you have frequent-flier miles, try to use them for international travel, rather than domestic. You often can travel abroad for about the same number of frequent-flier miles as you would spend flying to another American city, even though the cost of the tickets in cash would be far higher for the international trip.

For international travel, Asia usually is a better deal than Europe. However, the airfares to Asia are much higher than those to Europe, so if you're thinking of taking two trips, buy your trip to Europe and use your frequent-flier miles to go to Asia for free.

Most airlines offer lower mileage requirements to Asia, Europe, and Latin America during off-peak periods. So, if possible, try to schedule your international trip during the winter.

Using your frequent-flier miles for domestic travel can, however, make sense in the event of an emergency. I know someone who had to travel quickly because of a family crisis and used 60,000 frequent-flier miles for a pair of tickets instead of paying $800 per ticket. That's smart.

HANDLING MONEY

You can save money before you leave town if you follow a few tips on getting cash. Travelers planning foreign trips traditionally buy foreign currency before they go, but that's a terrible decision because banks in the U.S. tend to offer terrible rates of exchange. The difference between these poor rates and your best deal may be as much as 20 percent of the money you're changing. That can make a huge difference in the final cost of your trip.

There are several other options. AAA members can buy American Express traveler's checks, at no commission, in U.S. dollars, British pounds, and certain other major European currencies. The exchange rate on these checks is okay. You can exchange the U.S. dollar traveler's checks at American Express offices in Europe at no commission, or you can exchange foreign currency checks in specific countries.

But technology has provided an even better solution. When I go to Europe, I use credit cards

TIPS ON HANDLING MONEY

- When planning a foreign trip, don't get foreign currency before you leave town.

- To get a great exchange rate on your money overseas, use credit cards as often as possible and get cash from automated teller machines using your bank ATM card.

- If you're exchanging currency, don't just go for the posted rate of exchange at a change booth or bank. Make sure you know if there's a service fee.

as often as I can. When you use a credit card, you get the banker's buying rate of exchange (the wholesale rate) and you are charged a small service fee. That's much better than any rate of exchange you could get.

The other technique, which now works very well worldwide, is to use the automated teller machine card from your bank. If your bank is a member of the Cirrus or Plus network, you can get cash at many foreign ATM machines. Once again, you get the wholesale rate of exchange, minus a small transaction fee.

Here's an important warning. If you're exchanging currency, don't just go for the posted rate of exchange at a change booth or bank. Make sure you know if there's a service fee or minimum transaction charge. London is infamous for change places that advertise great rates of exchange on the dollar. But when you look at the fine print, the service charges are high. They're a huge rip-off.

When I visit a foreign country, I walk into the airport arrival hall without a bit of local currency. I always find a teller machine or a money-change facility somewhere. Even in foreign airports, where the rate of exchange offered is poor, you'll usually get better deals than at American banks.

The worst problem I've had using an ATM was in 1997. My wife and I got to the airport at Oslo, Norway, to find two ATMs — both broken. Travelers were in a daze about what to do, because using ATMs has become the accepted way of getting foreign currency, especially in Europe, where people often travel from country to country. So we got in our rental car and started driving to town. Lo and behold, we came to a toll booth, but it was an automated toll booth and we had no money. I had to drive through without paying, and I still feel guilty. I've never run a toll booth before or since. The first time I saw an ATM in Oslo, I stopped, and the money came right out. They work.

BED AND BREAKFAST INNS

Because Europe doesn't yet have a widespread industry of affordable hotels, bed and breakfasts have served a very useful purpose by providing travelers with affordable lodging. In fact, no country on earth has the kind of high-quality, affordable lodging that we have in the United States. For that reason, bed and breakfasts have taken a completely different tack in the United States. Since they can't compete at the low end, bed and breakfasts have tried to be fantasy-type getaways. That has worked well in resort areas, but not well in other locations.

The bed and breakfast industry has fallen on hard times, in part because the novelty has worn off for travelers. At first they loved the individuality and homey spirit of a bed and breakfast, but they have since decided that they miss the privacy and no-surprises consistency of standard hotels.

TIPS ON BED AND BREAKFAST INNS

• Bed and breakfast inns are designed as budget accommodations in Europe, while travelers in the United States choose them because they're a homey, charming alternative to standard hotels.

• If you want to stay at a bed and breakfast in Europe, you can book in advance through some reservation services, the Internet, or some travel agents. But usually you're better off just getting a room when you get there.

When the bed and breakfast craze was at its height, many well educated, upper-middle-class people decided they would love to run a bed and breakfast inn. Many lost their enthusiasm and left the industry as soon as they realized it wasn't all so charming. Owners still had to change bed linens, clean toilets, deal with sometimes difficult guests, and wake up early to fix breakfasts for visitors. A fatigue factor took over, and lots of people got out of the business. What was a huge fad probably has found a more proper level in the United States.

I stayed at a bed and breakfast in a non-resort area in the U.S. and paid $49 off-season for a room with no bathroom and a heater that barely worked. It was a neat, charming house, but not worth the price for this location.

On the other hand, my co-author and his wife stayed at a wonderful bed and breakfast in a Maryland resort area, on the Chesapeake Bay, and absolutely loved it. Because it was a resort area, there was a reason to go in addition to the chance to stay at the inn.

Bed and breakfasts and small hotels are changing in Europe, partly in response to the experiences European travelers have had in the United States. More rooms have their own bathrooms, rather than a bathroom down the hall.

If you want to stay at a bed and breakfast in Europe, you can book in advance through some reservation services. For many cities in Europe, you'll also find listings for bed and breakfasts and small hotels on the Internet.

In some cases, your travel agent can help you make reservations. But usually you are better off just getting a room when you get there. It's your choice. If that makes you nervous, call and book a room. It may give you a chance to practice your high school French.

Workbook

The Workbook section is what makes this book a true "Survival Kit." In it, you'll find tools to help you in your consumer battles.

Keep the worksheets in the book, or make photocopies and keep them with your important records. Some of the letters, like the "drop-dead" letter, can be copied and mailed. Just fill in the collector's name and your account number and sign it. Others, like the sample complaint letter, can be quickly modified and retyped to fit your situation.

PROBLEM DOCUMENTATION SHEET

To get results, document your efforts to solve problems. Take people's names, and make a note of what they promised to do. Letters are more effective than phone calls.

The problem:_____

_____

_____

ACTION LOG

Date of letter or call

Name of person you contacted

_____   _____

What action was promised or taken:_____

_____

_____

Date of letter or call

Name of person you contacted

_____   _____

What action was promised or taken:_____

_____

_____

ACTION LOG

Date of letter or call   Name of person you contacted

_____   _____

What action was promised or taken:_____

_____

_____

Date of letter or call   Name of person you contacted

_____   _____

What action was promised or taken:_____

_____

_____

Date of letter or call   Name of person you contacted

_____   _____

What action was promised or taken:_____

_____

_____

Date of letter or call   Name of person you contacted

_____   _____

What action was promised or taken:_____

_____

_____

"DROP-DEAD" LETTER TO COLLECTION AGENGIES

Date: _____

To whom it may concern:

I have been contacted by your company about a debt you allege I owe.

I am instructing you not to contact me any further in connection with this debt.

Under the Fair Debt Collection Practices Act, a federal law, you may not contact me further once I have notified you not to do so.

Sincerely,

_____

Account Number _____

Date: _____

To whom it may concern:

I have been contacted by your company about a debt you allege I owe.

I am instructing you not to contact me any further in connection with this debt.

Under the Fair Debt Collection Practices Act, a federal law, you may not contact me further once I have notified you not to do so.

Sincerely,

_____

Account Number _____

RECORD OF "DROP-DEAD" LETTERS SENT TO COLLECTION AGENCIES

Collection agency	Date notified

MODEL LETTER OF COMPLAINT

Date: _____

John Jones
Regional Vice President
ABCD Company
500 Main Street, Suite 1000
Anywhere, USA

Dear Mr. Jones:

I regret having to write to you about an unpleasant experience I've had with your company. I prefer to contact a company only to praise an employee or the company's actions.

Unfortunately, my situation is such that it is necessary for me to forward a complaint to you.

Give the specifics of the complaint. Say who you've spoken with about the problem, what attempts you've made to solve it, and what specific action you would like the company to take.

_____

_____

_____

_____

I look forward to hearing from you. I hope you can respond within 30 days so that we are able to resolve this problem in a speedy fashion.

Sincerely,

_____

GETTING YOUR NAME OFF MAILING LISTS

Date: _____

Mail Preference Service
Direct Marketing Association
P.O. Box 9008
Farmingdale, NY 11735

To whom it may concern:

I am writing to register with your Mail Preference Service.

Please inform your members that I do not want my name sold to any company for the purpose of placing me on a mailing list and sending me advertising mail.

In addition, I would like my name removed from existing lists.

Thank you very much for your help.

Sincerely,

Name: _____

Street: _____

City: _____ State: _____

Zip code: _____

ACCOUNT NUMBERS

CREDIT CARDS

Creditor	Account number	Credit limit	If lost, call this number	Interest rate
____	____	____	____	____
____	____	____	____	____
____	____	____	____	____
____	____	____	____	____
____	____	____	____	____
____	____	____	____	____
____	____	____	____	____

Your maximum liability if a credit card is stolen is $50 per card. You have no liability for charges made after you report the card as lost or stolen.

BANKS

Institution	Type of account	Account number	Balance as of _____
____	____	____	____
____	____	____	____
____	____	____	____
____	____	____	____
____	____	____	____
____	____	____	____
____	____	____	____

INSURANCE

LIFE

Company:_____

Agent:_____

Phone number:_____

Account number:_____

Policy type:_____

Benefit amount:_____

Beneficiary:_____

DISABILITY

Company:_____

Agent:_____

Phone number:_____

Policy number:_____

How long after disability does coverage take effect? _____

How long does the policy remain in effect? _____

What is the benefit amount? _____

HOMEOWNER'S

Company:_____

Agent:_____

Phone number:_____

Policy number:_____

Features:_____

_____

Does the policy include protections against inflation? _____

INSURANCE

AUTO

Company:_____

Agent:_____

Phone number:_____

Policy number:_____

Features

Liability coverage:_____

Collision coverage:_____

Comprehensive coverage:_____

Other features:_____

Is there reimbursement for towing or car rental expenses?_____

REQUEST FOR REPAIRS TO RENTAL PROPERTY

Date: _____

To whom it may concern:

We are distressed that you have not responded to several requests to make repairs on our apartment.

Briefly describe the nature of the problem and what action you would like the landlord to take.

_____

_____

_____

_____

Please take care of this in the next 48 hours, or it will be necessary for us to hire a repairperson ourselves and deduct the cost of his services from our next rent check.

Thank you.

Sincerely,

_____

Apartment no. _____

WHAT TO DO WHEN YOU'RE IN AN AUTO ACCIDENT

1. Wait for a police officer to write a report.

2. Exchange information with the other driver about yourselves and your insurance companies.

3. Get the names and telephone numbers of as many witnesses as you can.

4. While the accident is fresh in your mind and you're waiting for the police, draw a sketch of the accident scene.

5. As soon as possible, report the accident to your insurance company, even if you don't plan to make a claim.

6. Contact the other driver's insurance company.

LONG-DISTANCE CALLING CODES

Keep an eye out for an expensive rip-off when you use any public phone, but particularly those at airports, universities, hotels, and hospitals. Calls made from phones operated by rip-off companies can cost up to 10 times the rates of legitimate long-distance companies. If you don't recognize the name of the company that's posted on the phone, you can bypass it with the following access codes and go to the long-distance provider you wish to use.

AT&T	1-800-CALL-ATT
MCI	1-800-950-1022
Sprint	1-800-877-8000

CAR-BUYING WORKSHEET

	Model #1	Model #2	Model #3
Base cost:	_____	_____	_____
Options:	_____	_____	_____
Automatic transmission	_____	_____	_____
Air conditioning	_____	_____	_____
_____	_____	_____	_____
_____	_____	_____	_____
Transportation:	_____	_____	_____
Total dealer cost:	_____	_____	_____
Cost to insure:	_____	_____	_____

BIDS FROM DEALERS

What is the lowest price at which they will sell the vehicle I want, with the options I want? Take bids by phone, and ask the top three to fax their bids to you. If anyone refuses to bid, don't buy from that dealership.

Name of dealer (and phone #)	Salesperson	Best price
1. _____	_____	_____
2. _____	_____	_____
3. _____	_____	_____
4. _____	_____	_____
5. _____	_____	_____
6. _____	_____	_____
7. _____	_____	_____
8. _____	_____	_____

SAMPLE CREDIT REPORT

Personal Identification Information
Your Name
Your Current Address
City, State, Zip

Social Security Number   123-45-6789
Date of Birth   Day Month Year

Previous Address(es)
Your Previous Address
Last Reported Employment   Your Position and Employer

Public Record Information
Bankruptcy filed on 02/97 in City of Atlanta with case or other ID number 123456789012341
With Liabilities of $5,000, Assets of $60,234, Exempt Amount of $60,000 Type of Personal, Filed Individual, and status Voluntary Ch-7

Lien filed on 02/97 in United States Marshals Service with case or other ID number 123412341234
For the amount of $599, Release on 02/97, and Verified on 02/97

Satisfied Judgment filed on 02/97 in United States Marshals Service with case or other ID number 123412
Filed by plaintiff against defendant for the amount of $500 with status Satisfied as of 02/97 and verified on 02/97

Collection Agency Account Information
United States Marshals Service (404) 331-6833

        Collection reported 02/97 and assigned to United States Marshals Service on 01/97 by Client
        For account number 123412341234 which is an individual account for the amount of $6,000
        with balance $600 as of 01/96, status in Bankruptcy as of 02/97 and last activity on 02/97.

Credit Account Information

Company Name	Account Number	Whose Account	Date Opened	Last Activity	Type of Account and Status	High Credit	Terms	Balance	Past Due	Date Reported
Macy's	12341234	Joint	02/94	01/97	Revolving - 90 Days Past Due	$4235	50	$243	$0	02/97
Citibank Visa	12341234	Joint	02/97	05/97	Revolving - Pays as Agreed	$10000	50	$243	$0	06/97
Rich's-FACS	12341234		02/94	05/97	Lost or Stolen Card					02/97

Additional Information
Foreclosure reported 02/97 by Firm Name verified on 02/94
Checking Account reported 02/97 opened on 04/83 closed for reason: non-sufficient funds with amount $500

Companies that Requested your Credit File

02/15/97	AR Sears	02/13/97	ACIS 71200003	
02/13/97	Richs/Facs	02/11/97	Equifax - Update	
01/16/97	Macy's		01/13/97	Equifax - Disclosure
11/18/96	AM Macy's	10/16/96	PRM - Citibank Visa	

THE FOLLOWING INQUIRIES ARE NOT REPORTED TO BUSINESSES:
PRM - This is a promotional inquiry in which only your name and address were given to a credit grantor so you could be solicited you with an offer such as a credit card. (PRM inquiries remain on file for 12 months.)
AM or AR - These inquiries indicate a periodic review of your credit history by one of your creditors (AM and AR inquiries remain on file for 12 months.)
EQUIFAX, ACIS or UPDATE - These inquiries indicate Equifax's activity in response to your contact with us for either a copy of your credit file or a request for research.
PRM, AM, AR, INQ, EQUIFAX, ACIS and UPDATE inquiries do not show on credit files that businesses receive, only on copies provided to you.

THE PHONE BOOK (INTERNET SITES ARE LISTED IF AVAILABLE)

American Century Investments
(Formerly Twentieth Century Investments)
4500 Main Street
Kansas City, MO 64141
1-800-345-2021

American Homeowners Foundation
(Remodeling contracts)
6776 Little Falls Road
Arlington, VA 22213
703-536-7776

American Institute of Architects
(For a remodeling contract, ask for the standard form of agreement between owner and contractor: A101, A111, or A201)
2 Winter Sports Lane
P.O. Box 60
Williston, VT 05495
1-800-365-2724
www.aia.org

American Institute of CPAs
1211 6th Avenue
New York, NY 10036
1-800-862-4272
www.aicpa.org

American Society of Home Inspectors
85 West Algonquin Road
Suite 360
Arlington Heights, IL 60005
1-800-743-2744
www.ashi.com

American Telecom Network
10211 North 32nd Street
Suite A-5
Phoenix, AZ 85028
1-800-477-9692
www.callatn.com

Bureau of the Public Debt
Division of Customer Services
Washington, DC 20239
(Ask for the phone number of the Federal Reserve closest to your area.)
202-874-4000
www.publicdebt.treas.gov

Center for Auto Safety
(Auto recalls)
2001 S Street NW
Suite 410
Washington, D.C. 20009
202-328-7700
www.essential.org\cas

Child Support Enforcement
370 L'enfant Promenade SW
4th Floor East
Washington, DC 20447
202-401-9373
www.acf.dhhs.gov/programs/cse/

Council of Better Business Bureaus
Autoline
4200 Wilson Boulevard
Suite 800
Arlington, VA 22203
1-800-955-5100
www.bbb.org (Online complaint form)

Equifax Information Service
P.O. Box 740123
Atlanta, GA 30374
770-375-2500 or 800-685-1111
www.equifax.com

Experian
(formerly TRW/credit report)
P.O. Box 2350
Chatsworth, CA 91313
1-800-682-7654

THE PHONE BOOK

Federal Trade Commission
(For a copy of the brochure *Fair Debt Collection Practices Act*)
Publications Division
Washington, DC 20580
202-326-2222
www.ftc.gov

Fidelity Investments
82 Devonshire Street
Boston, MA 02109
1-800-544-6666
www.fidelity.com

Ford Consumer Assistance Center
(Auto arbitration, Ford vehicles)
300 Renaissance Center
P.O. Box 43360
Detroit, MI 48243
18003923673

Funeral and Memorial Societies of America
(For a directory of memorial societies in your area)
6900 Lost Lake Road
Egg Harbor, WI 54209
1-800-765-0107
www.funerals.org/famsa/

Housing & Urban Development
Operations Division
(Questions regarding landlord/tenant disputes)
Washington, DC
202-708-0547
(Ask to speak with the desk officer representing your state)

International Fabricare Institute
Garment Analysis Laboratory
12251 Tech Road
Silver Spring, MD 20904
1-800-638-2627
www.ifi.org

INVESCO Funds Group
7800 East Union Avenue
Suite 800
Denver, CO 80237
1-800-525-8085
www.invesco.com

IRS Problem Resolution
National Office
Taxpayer Ombudsman's Office
1111 Constitution Avenue NW
Room 3017-C:TA
Washington, DC 20224
202-622-6100

Janus Capital
100 Fillmore Street
Suite 300
Denver, CO 80206
1-800-525-3713
www.janus.com

MasterCard International
Public Affairs Department
888 7th Avenue
New York, NY 10106
212-649-5476

Morningstar Inc.
225 West Wacker Drive
Chicago, IL 60606
312-424-4288
www.morningstar.com

THE PHONE BOOK

Mortgage Banker's Association of America
(Mortgages and refinancing)
1125 15th Street
Washington, DC 20005
202-861-6500
www.mbaa.org

National Association of Remodeling Industry
4301 North Fairfax Drive
Suite 310
Arlington, VA 22203-1627
1-800-440-NARI (For a list of professional
contractors in your area)
1-800-966-7601 (Other calls)
www.nari.org

National Association of Securities Dealers
(Investments)
1-800-289-9999 (Disciplinary history)
301-590-6500 (Licensing information — refer
to your state when calling.)
www.nasd.com
(You may request information online.)

National Charities Information Bureau
(Performance ratings on charities)
19 Union Square West
New York, NY 10003
212-929-6300
www.give.org

National Foundation for Consumer
  Credit Counseling
8611 2nd Avenue
Suite 100
Silver Spring, MD 20910
(303) 589-5600
1-800-388-2227
www.nfcc.org

National Highway Traffic Safety
  Administration
DOT Auto Safety Hotline
1-800-424-9393
www.nhtsa.dot.gov

National Pest Control Network
Oregon State University
333 Weniger
Corvallis, OR 97331-6502
1-800-858-7378
http://ace.orst.edu/info/nptn

Postal Inspector
(Mail fraud)
North and northeastern U.S.: 201-621-5500
Central and western U.S.: 312-765-4605
South and southeastern U.S.: 901-747-7765

Ram Research
Card Trak of America Consumer
  Information Line
(For a comprehensive guide to low-interest
credit cards, no-fee credit cards, and secured
credit cards)
460 West Patrick Street
P.O. Box 1700
Frederick, MD 21702
1-800-344-7714
www.cardtrak.com

Remodelors Council of the National
  Association of Home Builders
1201 15th Street NW
Washington, DC 20005
1-800-368-5242, ext. 216
www.nahb.com

THE PHONE BOOK

Charles Schwab Corp.
101 Montgomery Street
San Francisco, CA 94104
1-800-648-5300
www.schwab.com

The Scudder Funds
P.O. Box 2291
Boston, MA 02107
1-800-225-2470
http\\:funds.scudder.com

T. Rowe Price Investor Services
100 East Pratt Street
Baltimore, MD 21202
1-800-638-5660
www.troweprice.com

Trans Union
(Credit report)
P.O. Box 7000
North Olmstead, OH 44070
1-800-916-8800

Twentieth Century Investments
    (*see* American Century Investments)

USAA Life Insurance Company
USAA Building
San Antonio, TX 78288
1-800-531-8000
U.S. Office of Consumer Affairs
(For consumer and insurance questions and to request a free copy of the *Consumer's Resource Handbook*)
202-565-0040

Vanguard Group Client Services
P.O. Box 2600
Valley Forge, PA 19482
1-800-662-2739
www.vanguard.com

VISA International
P.O. Box 8999
San Francisco, CA 94128
1-800-227-6811 (Traveler's checks)
1-800-847-2911 (Lost or stolen credit cards)

CLARK HOWARD'S FAVORITE WEB SITES

(For links and updates, go to www.clarkhoward.com)

BETTER BUSINESS BUREAU
www.bbb.org (Charity reports and standards)

CAR BUYING
www.edmunds.com

COINS AND STAMPS
www.collectorsauction.com

COLLEGE SCHOLARSHIPS
www.fastweb.com

CREDIT CARD RATES
www.cardtrak.com

CREDIT PROBLEMS
www.nfcc.org (Consumer credit counseling)

CREDIT REPORTS
www.equifax.com

CRUISE SHIP CLEANLINESS
www.cdc.gov

FUNERAL AND MEMORIAL SOCIETY OF AMERICA
www.funerals.org/famsa

HOTELS
www.180096hotel.com or call 1-800-96Hotel

INVENTIONS
www.ftc.gov

INVESTMENTS
www.morningstar.net (Mutual fund information)
www.quicken.com (Investments, mortgage calculator)
www.fundalarm.com (Links to dozens of other investment sites)
www.investorama.com (Stocks, general)
www.hoovers.com (Company and investment news)
www.quotesmith.com (Life insurance quotes)
www.bloomberg.com (Business information, mortgage calculator)
www.netstockdirect.com (Buy stocks direct from companies)
www.sdinews.org (Buy stocks direct from companies)

CLARK HOWARD'S FAVORITE WEB SITES

MORTGAGES

www.irwinmortgage.com (Irwin Mortgage: mortgage information and calculator)
www.hsh.com
www.quicken.com/mortgage/ (Quicken mortgage information)
www.countrywide.com (Countrywide Mortgage: online mortgage application)

NATIONAL CHARITIES INFORMATION BUREAU

www.give.org

NATIONAL HIGHWAY TRAFFIC SAFETY ADMINISTRATION

www.nhtsa.dot.gov/

REAL ESTATE RELOCATION

www.homefair.com
(To get information on your new city, including cost of living and schools.
You can also create a checklist of things to do before moving day.)

TRAVEL

www.bestfares.com
www.travelocity.com
www.expedia.com